web
developer's guide to
sound & music

web

developer's guide to

sound & music

Anthony Helmstetter

Ron Simpson

⊘ CORIOLIS GROUP BOOKS

PUBLISHER	**KEITH WEISKAMP**
PROJECT EDITOR	**RON PRONK**
COVER ARTIST	**GARY SMITH**
COVER DESIGN	**ANTHONY STOCK**
INTERIOR DESIGN	**MICHELLE STROUP**
LAYOUT PRODUCTION	**DOROTHY BUNGERT**
COPY EDITOR	**JAMIE ARONSON**
PROOFREADER	**PAT VULAR**

The Coriolis Group, Inc.
7339 E. Acoma Drive, Suite 7
Scottsdale, AZ 85260
Phone: (602) 483-0192
Fax: (602) 483-0193
Web address: http://www.coriolis.com

ISBN 1-883577-95-0 : $39.99
Printed in the United States of America
10 9 8 7 6 5 4 3 2 1

This book is dedicated with deepest love and affection to my children,
Teh-Teh Fauf, Boogs, Rachel-fuss and Shayne-a-roo.
Anthony Helmstetter

I'd like to dedicate this book (or at least my share of it) to my late father
Ronald K. Simpson Sr. Even though it's been a while, I'm still listening.
Ron Simpson

Acknowledgments

Anthony Helmstetter

I've often wondered what kind of people actually read the acknowledgments. Obviously, our friends and relatives will read them to see if their names are mentioned. But for everyone else, seriously, are you expecting to see someone's name you recognize?

I learned long ago to surround myself with competent people and take partial credit for their efforts. This book is yet another example of that very successful formula. To that, I extend my deepest gratitude to Ron Simpson for inviting me to do this. Thanks Ron, and I owe you one.

I and all the readers of this book are especially indebted to numerous unsung heroes behind the scenes of all this technology. Without them, it would not be happening. For their help and direction, thanks to James Lippard at Primenet, Jim Turano at US Robotics, Tom Ringcomp at Cox Communications, and Mark Shander at Formgen. I'd also like to thank my co-workers who encouraged me, gave me feedback, and tolerated my impossible schedule; Steve Weaver, Karl Knelson, Curtiss Prickett, Candace Wade, and all the gang at Hoskyns & Associates. And thanks to Don Hoskyns for not firing me.

And a special thanks goes to Mom and Dad for preparing me for this project, and to my wife and kids for trying to be a little quieter at night and letting me dominate the computer for months. And a life-long "Thank you" to one of the finest minds I've ever had the pleasure of working with, my brother Greg Helmstetter, whose keen insight always makes me think, laugh, or both.

Lastly, without Ron Pronk, every paragraph in this book would be a mess. Thank you for making us look good.

Ron Simpson

I'd like to start by thanking my Mom and all my family and friends for putting up with me all these years. Its been an interesting journey to say the least. I'd also like to thank Scott Jarol, Shannon Bounds Karl, and Keith Weiskamp for the initial interest and for helping me get this idea off the ground.

There were also a number of people and their respective companies that supplied me with a wealth of information and in some cases lent us some of the hardware and software that made much of this book possible. So here goes.

Doedy Hunter and Keri Walker at Apple Computer; Bennett Lincoff at ASCAP; Peter Sabin at Audio Technica; Lisa Bormann of Bormann and Associates for Bose; Chris Rice and Carl Jacobson at Cakewalk; Bill Woods at Digidesign; Scott Whitney at The Hollywood Edge; Candice Denton at InVision Interactive; Keigo Kiyohara and Rachel Schindler at Macromedia; Diane Gershuny at Mackie Designs; Jan Schrieber at NuReality; Paul DeBenedictis at Opcode; John Files at Power Computing; Scott Willing at QSound; Dan Meyer at SESAC; Tyson Heyn at Seagate Technologies; Rimas Buinevicius at Sonic Foundry; Amy Reardon at Syquest Technologies; Robert Jacobson at Supra; Phillip Anast at U.S. Robotic; and Mike Overlin at Yamaha. If theres anyone I've missed, I do apologize.

I'd also like to thank a few of the musicians who waited till the sun was warm (3:30 or 4 in the afternoon) to show up and make a little noise. Joey Trujillo on surf guitar, Steve Millhouse on bass, Fred Robinson on soprano sax, and Tyrone Johnson on alto saxophone. While a good portion of the music on the Incredible Sound Resource CD-ROM was MIDI based it was nice to have a little realtime playing going on as well.

Last but not least I'd like to thank Anthony Helmstetter for showing up and Ron Pronk for guiding the Rookies through the process.

Contents

Chapter 4   Building Some HTML Examples   57

Chapter 5   More About Streamed Audio   87

Part 3   The Tools of the Trade—Hardware, Computers, and Software   115

Chapter 6   Microphones, Mixers, And Speakers   117

Preface

When was the last time you sat down to watch your favorite 30-minute television program, with the volume turned off? Why on earth would you deprive yourself of the actors' dialog, the sound effects, and the mood-setting music? Of course, you wouldn't—assuming you're not deaf.

Try this experiment. If you have others living in the household with you, have them participate. Gather around the television, turn the volume off, and see what happens. Notice how quickly they are distracted. Notice how much more difficult it is to follow the program's story line. In short, television becomes a lot less entertaining, and less effective too.

Clearly, the Web is no substitute for television—*yet* (more on this in Chapter 2). But the mass-communication lessons learned from TV are valid for the Web too. Why would people sit for hours gazing glassy-eyed at a silent Web

Just as our expectations of television have changed, so too have our demands of the Internet. Today, audio is currently the most attainable and powerful enhancement to Web pages.

page? They would if that was all that was available, but their attention span, and the effectiveness of the message, would also be greatly diminished. (Admittedly, the analogy is not perfect. The *interactivity* of the Web creates its own attentiveness.) The point is, *sound is more engaging than silence.*

Sound on the Web is a reality today. If you haven't heard it yet, we'll direct you to some examples right away so you can experience the impact for yourself. Just as silent movies of the 1920s quickly lost out to the "talkies," audio-enhanced Web pages also *outperform* the silent sites. Notice we say *"outperform."* We won't predict when audio-enabled Web pages will *outnumber* silent pages, but we suspect they will eventually. There may always be a use for silent Web sites. Many sites would not be improved by the addition of audio. But if the objective is to convey a message with the greatest possible impact, make it engaging, make it entertaining, or make it memorable, then sound is an inevitable requirement.

There are a host of technology players providing audio tools and capabilities for the Web. They have all seen a clear vision of the future and they like the sound of it. In fact, they're dedicating millions of dollars to make it an *expected* part of the Web experience. There is a lot to learn, but if you take things one step at a time, producing sound on the Web is a snap. Keep in mind that we're not inventing anything new here; we're simply implementing what has already been created for us. This book takes you step-by-step through everything you need to know, most of which you probably didn't even know you needed to know.

One step at a time. It's a journey worth taking and we look forward to traveling with you.

Anthony Helmstetter
Ron Simpson

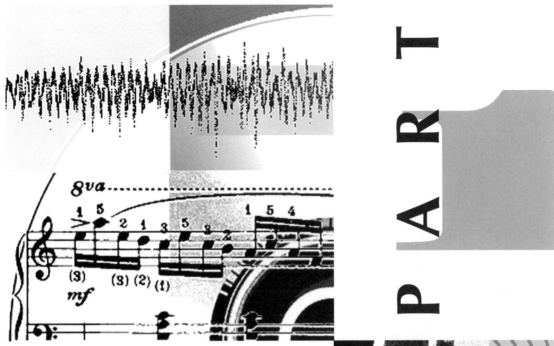

Getting Set Up

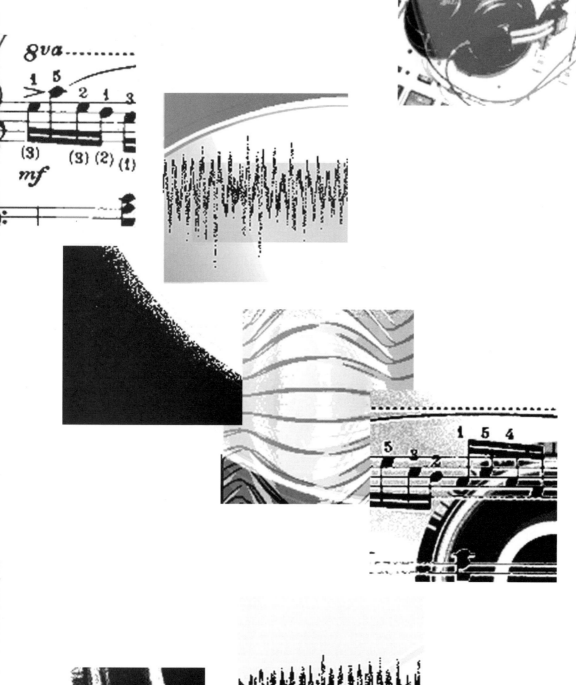

Anthony Helmstetter

Key Topics:

- **How information is organized in this book**

- **The incredible Sound Resource CD-ROM**

- **The Sound Advice Web site**

All About This Book, The CD-ROM, And More

Who Should Read This Book?

C'mon! We're hungry authors. Everyone should read this book! If you're still flipping through pages in the bookstore trying to decide whether to buy it, take our word for it, *buy it!* This book will help you lose weight, improve your love life, increase your I.Q., and squeeze 4 to 5 more miles per gallon of gas out of whatever kind of car you drive.

Now that our retirement funds have been secured, let's get down to specifics. We've designed the book to appeal to four distinct, yet overlapping audiences:

- *The hobbyist*, who has a personal home page, but needs to jazz it up to keep up with increasing expectations of cool Web stuff.

- *The professional Web page developer*, probably working within an advertising or design agency, marketing, or public relations firm, who needs to position client pages as progressive and competitive in production quality.

- *The Web server administrator*, who must now deal with hundreds of client requests for sound integration, technical support, and be able to sub-contract or manage production services.

- *The accomplished musician, sound designer, or recording engineer,* who desires to expand services into interactive media, specifically multimedia and the Web.

As a bonus, a solid 75 percent of the information contained in this book is relevant and applicable to the creation and integration of sound into *multimedia* applications. The technical differences are relatively simple to grasp, so once you've added sound to a Web page, you can add the line "Audio integration for Internet *and* multimedia applications" to your résumé. You will soon know a great deal about how to add sound for either.

If your intent is to put audio into a Web page, we assume that you have already browsed some Web pages and, ideally, authored a Web page or two of your own. A basic understanding of HTML (what other kind of understanding is there?) is helpful (we'll provide specific HTML code in the tutorial sections later in this book). We also provide an introduction to audio options on the Web, including *Shockwave, TrueSpeech, RealAudio, and QTMA* (QuickTime Music Architecture) and to help you understand when and where each may be appropriate.

How This Book Is Organized

Let's put one issue to rest right now. This book is *platform-independent*. We do not favor PCs, Macs, Unix or any other computer platform. You've most likely made up your mind about which is the "best" platform for you, so we'll let it go at that. Every *principle* we convey in this book works without regard

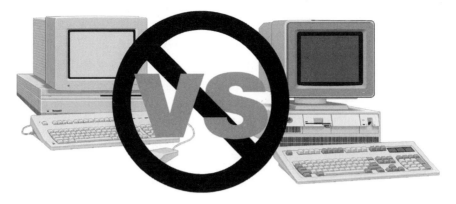

Figure 1.1

No platform wars here; Web development requires you to develop for all platforms.

to platform—in fact, nearly half the information in this book deals with issues *not related* to computers or software.

For the tutorials, we provide both PC and Mac examples. If you're working on a PC, just do the designated PC tutorials and skip over the Mac tutorials; if you're a Mac fanatic, skip the PC stuff. The example screens come from both platforms so regardless of your preferences, much of what you see will look familiar. Just focus on the screen content rather than the interface.

Regarding the specific software applications we use, in every case we've provided some information about our reasons for selecting a particular browser, waveform editor, or nifty utility. We intentionally make reference to *popular* software as well as *better-performing* software. "Better-performing" isn't always popular, easy-to-use, or affordable. But these are factors we have carefully considered in selecting which tools to introduce you to, and rest assured, the losers were cut long ago.

In Chapter 2, we lay some groundwork, get onto the Web, hear some sounds, learn some things about the industry today, do the first tutorial and begin using the *Incredible Sound Resource CD-ROM* that came with this book. Chapter 2 concludes the introductory portion of this book.

Part II is comprised of Chapters 3, 4, and 5. These chapters focus intently on putting sound into Web pages and include comprehensive tutorial sessions.

Using the samples on the CD-ROM, you'll be able to put quality audio, *optimized for the Web,* into your Web pages. (At the risk of sounding obvious, you'll need a set of speakers and a properly installed sound card on your computer to get much out of this part of the book.)

Part III (Chapters 6 through 9) covers the tools of the audio process from capture to delivery. We cover hardware; not just computers, but all hardware from the microphone to the speakers and everything in between. Each step in this process means the potential for loss-of-quality, so we cover all the details. Keep your highlighter handy. We also cover software, file formats, and the basics of each as they pertain to your objectives.

Part IV (Chapters 10 through 12) emphasize audio manipulation (editing, mixing, amplitude, etc.) as well as the different kinds of available audio. For instance, there are distinct differences among audio narration, music, and sound effects. And we've included a fascinating chapter on audio licensing, contracts, and copyrights to help keep you out of jail. In fact, Chapter 12 is a "must read."

Chapter 13 is full of really trick stuff. Some may be of great interest for your Web page projects, but all will make you a big hit at cocktail parties. When you're ready to explore topics like *audio special effects*, *3D sound*, and *music for games on the Web*, you'll surely be on everybody's "A" list. We even tell you some secrets of successful karaoke! Now, *that's* value in a book.

In the back, you'll want to flip through and then dog-ear the glossary for basic audio technical terms and musician's slang. You'll soon understand your bass player when he says, "I have to get a stitch to get some jack for a new ax." (Translation: "I am hoping to obtain gainful employment in the field of music in order to obtain remuneration with which to purchase a new musical instrument.") Check out the hardware and software vendor appendix if you'd like to dig a little deeper into what hardware and software we use and why.

We don't expect you to read this book sequentially, cover-to-cover, unless you find our wit and humor so compelling that you can't put it down. If, however, you find yourself jumping around a bit from chapter to chapter, that's okay. Each of the four sections is almost a book unto itself. And we've designed each chapter to stand on its own.

How To Use The Incredible Sound Resource CD-ROM With This Book

The companion CD-ROM is in both Mac and PC formats. (Sorry, getting Unix on there too was a bit farther than our publisher was willing to go.) Regardless of your platform, you'll find a valuable assortment of demonstration software, utilities, tutorial components, and a nice collection of professional quality audio clips that you may use in your Web page projects. See the "What's on The CD" appendix for a library directory of the audio clips. The audio clips can be used royalty-free (see Chapter 12) provided that you do not re-sell any of the content. If you do not have a CD-ROM drive on your system, the tutorial files can be downloaded from the *Sound Advice Web Page*. The address is:

```
http://www.monsoon.org/sound_advice/tutorial
```

A complete listing of the CD-ROM contents can be found in the "The Incredible Sound Resource CD-ROM" appendix or on the README file stored on the CD-ROM.

The *Sound Advice Web Site*, An Invaluable Resource For Sound Integrators

If you have any experience on the Web, you already know that the rate of technical development and information obsolescence is mind boggling! Everything changes so fast that every developer I know woefully echoes the words, "It's a full-time job just to keep up!" So, you are not alone. And, in fact, it is a real problem. In our attempt to provide you with the most up-to-date information on the tools and techniques of Web audio, it became immediately apparent that a disturbing portion of everything we wrote would be obsolete within months, perhaps even weeks, of publication.

So, we designed a plan to help you, the reader, ride the crest of this unending information wave. Step one was to clearly define what information was relatively timeless, such as sampling audio or WAVEFORM versus MIDI sound. The requisite basics are here and will remain accurate for years. Next, we updated darn near every line of this book during the last few weeks prior to publication. We acknowledge that much of the information will be obsolete, eventually. Where a specific product, version number or capability is likely to change soon, we tell you about it so you can follow up on the latest information. But that alone was not enough.

Get your browser and Internet access ready. As a companion resource to this book, you are entitled, invited, and actually required to visit the *Sound Advice Web Site* at http://www.monsoon.org/sound_advice. This site is updated continually with the latest information regarding the creation and application of audio on the Web.

What This Book Does Not Cover

We do not delve into music theory, we do not teach anyone how to play any musical instrument, nor will we tell you how to make money on the World Wide Web. We do not attempt to provide product comparisons of the latest hardware and software because, if we did, there would be newer and greater stuff on the market by the time you read this. Visit the *Sound Advice Web Site* for information on current product reviews and links to dozens of hardware and software vendors' sites.

We chose not to discuss sound integration within video formats such as QuickTime or AVI. There are numerous books, written specifically on the subject of video, that go to great lengths to explain the compression and interleaving issues associated with the audio-video formats. For our purposes, audio within a movie is first and foremost a movie; audio independent of anything else is the focus of this book.

Finally, as our personal pledge, from this point forward we will never use the expression "cyber" because we're all sick of seeing it concatenated into phrases like *cyber-space, cyber-surfer,* or *cyber-sounds.*

Chapter 2

Anthony Helmstetter

The Sound Impact On The Web— An Overview

You've probably heard and perhaps even bought into all the hype about how "the Web is going to change the world." While it may not solve world hunger, we (both of us) buy into the hype, largely because it has already happened. Society *has* changed, information *is* distributed differently, and commerce *has* found new channels and bypassed existing ones.

It would be foolish to assume that, for change to occur, the old way of doing things has to vanish. The automobile changed the nature of transportation and, consequently, society. But we still have horses. I even ride one occasionally. At some point, however, my great-grandfather thought it time to retire the family horse and buggy, and buy a motor vehicle.

My great-grandfather's objective was to get to his destination faster, more easily, and perhaps without saddle sores. We submit that the Web can, *and does,* bring many destinations *to you* — also without saddle sores.

There are many models of what the 21st century, information superhighway, telecommuting, instant on-line access to anything you can imagine, virtual everything world of tomorrow will look like. Most are probably partly correct and partly incorrect. I have my view (which is in a state of perpetual revision), Bill Gates has his, and you undoubtedly have yours, whether invented on your own or provided to you by the evening news.

Let's proceed under the assumption that any model you can imagine is at least *partly* correct. In your scenario, is audio a likely part of the model? It should be. Gutenberg set us on a course that has trained millions of people throughout history how to communicate and distribute that information as text; as reproducible pigmented ink on paper; later as mechanical keystrokes against a carbon ribbon; and now as clickety-clicks generating excited phosphorus on someone's monitor on the other side of the globe. But with all of history's resources dedicated to written communication (text), it pales compared to how much communication actually occurs as *sound waves.*

Most of us *hear* many times more data in one busy hour than we *read* in an entire day. Logically, since sound is the easiest and most efficient (not necessarily the most comprehensive) way to communicate, why would anyone think a great new global forum like the Internet will remain silent? It has already begun. And you are now at a unique time in history to participate in its maturation. Sound on the Web is going to change your world.

Communications

The Internet and World Wide Web are all about communication. One-way audio, as in Internet *radio applications,* is here. One-way audio is broadcasting its messages to everyone around the globe, something for which the FCC would never grant a license. Unlike conventional radio programming, a Web-based radio station can offer on-demand radio listening. There is no longer a need to listen at a designated time — programs can be available for instant access any time of the day or night. As for radio commercials, I suspect they will migrate nicely to the Web as well.

Beyond broadcasting communications, *personal* audio communications are gaining in popularity and accessibility. You have probably already experienced e-mail. How about voice-email? At least one of the major online services already offers it. You can listen to your audio-e-mail while you eat your Wheaties every morning.

Internet phone applications (Figures 2.1 and 2.2) are becoming increasingly popular. With the entire telecommunications industry in a tail-spin over the changes, nobody knows yet who or what will emerge as the AT&T of the Web. (It may even be AT&T.) A dozen or more two-way Internet audio applications (Internet phones) are currently available. Internet phones utilize existing technology to allow two-way, full-duplex audio conversations over the Web. New audio/visual Internet phone technologies such as scratchpad and image transfer capabilities are here as well. With innovations like these, about the only way to avoid having the Web impact your life is to avoid the Web itself.

Commerce

I recently read a report in a well-respected national publication about the *failure* of commerce on the Web. *Failure?* I'd like to know how this particular bozo defines *failure*. "Failure" probably means someone's expectations were not met, regardless of what those expectations were in the first place.

We'll admit that we haven't become instant millionaires with our commercial Web ventures yet, and we don't personally know anyone who has . . . yet. But then again, we only know a few people who have become millionaires *off* the Web, and it didn't happen overnight.

Commerce exists over the Web, and it is growing. Major financial institutions have committed millions of dollars to ensure that secure transactions occur. Virtual banks and virtual malls selling both information and real stuff have sprung up. Millions of customers are window shopping. Often, they buy.

Figure 2.1

Check out WebPhone from NetSpeak at http://www.netspeak.com/.

Taking decades-old purchasing and lifestyle patterns, and expecting them to be completely replaced overnight is unrealistic. Utilizing the Web to expand into a new market and perhaps compete with the big boys *is* realistic. Successful commerce on the Web is no different than successful commerce anywhere else. It's work. It's creating a competitive advantage. It's being at the right place at the right time with the right message. Sometimes, it's luck.

If I have the opportunity to sell you something, and I can either send you a letter or speak to you in person, I'll opt to speak to you in person every time. I'll sell more that way. If I can't speak to you in person, I'd still rather send a video tape, audio tape, or computer-based presentation to convey my message. Letters don't talk—if I want you to hear my message, audio speaks volumes.

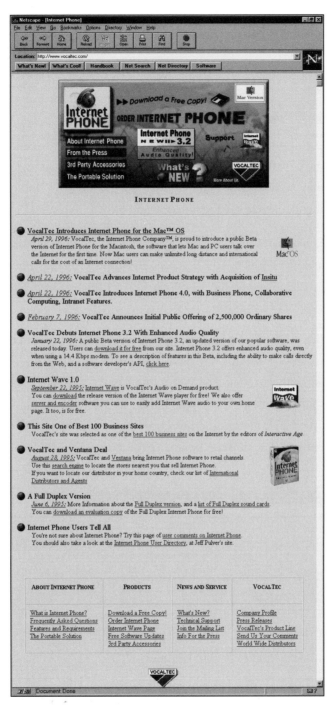

Figure 2.2

Internet Phone at http://www.vocaltec.com/ is one of several Web-based phone applications.

If your goal is to buy or sell something on the Web, the process will be easier with an audio-enhanced Web site. More people will remember your message if they hear it as well as see it. Skeptical? Do a test. You'll see.

Entertainment

We demonstrated with the silent TV experiment in the preface that entertainment without audio is rather un-entertaining. As the shift to Web-based games, movies, music, interactive books, contests, and other forms of entertainment continues, expect that sound will be expected.

If you are unsure of this, track the sales of sound cards and computer speakers over the past five years. You'll see pretty impressive growth. Guess which sub-industry spawned all that growth? That's right — computer games! (See Figure 2.3 for an example.)

We owe the computer gaming industry a huge debt of gratitude. Without its contributions, we would not have the millions of MPC, audio-capable computers out there today. The Web could have all the audio in the world, but without sound cards and speakers, all those browsers would remain silent. Thankfully, this nightmare did not occur, and we have a pool of millions of audio-appetized Web surfers looking for something to listen to.

Education And Information

My 13-year-old son began a computer lab in junior high last month. Within three weeks, he was surfing the Web, downloading GIFs and JPEGs, editing them in Photoshop, and writing his own HTML code with an HTML editor that *he* found. My email was clogged with the HTML code samples his friends were sending him. I was crushed that I hadn't taken him camping this spring; after all, I was on a book deadline. But I also missed the opportunity to male-bond with him over HREF links.

The educational system, formal and informal, has become Internet-aware. "Educational system" refers to all aspects of the education system: all ages, grade school through grad school; public and private schools; tech schools; and a million personal and professional research projects every day. The Internet is the best encyclopedia ever. It is dynamic, it lives, and it almost breathes.

Figure 2.3

AT&T enters the on-line multi-player gaming world with ImaginNation at http://www.inngames.com/.

Microsoft officially announced recently that the Internet is its "platform of choice." Having heard that, we can safely assume that the gurus at the world's largest and most influential software company recognize the accessibility and immense potential of the Internet as an information and computational medium. Do you think the software industry is willing to leave behind all its multimedia, interactivity, audio, video, and animations? Not a chance. We, as consumers, won't let them. We want to be entertained while we learn and work. (How else could *After Dark* have become so popular?)

The State Of Technology Today

There is no way to write this section and maintain accuracy. By the time you read this, something will have changed. That's part of the essence of the industry—unbridled change. Deal with it. The single most important aspect of the technological development path, as it pertains to audio, is *bandwidth*. Bandwidth is analogous to lanes on a superhighway: the greater the number of lanes, the greater the number of cars (data) can travel to a destination within a specified period of time. To me, bandwidth is like RAM or sex—I can't get enough. The Internet was originally designed as a text-only data exchange system for the U.S. Government. Needless to say, it has changed a lot in the past 25 years.

Text files are generally very small (in bytes), and simple graphics are many times larger than text files. So, rampant graphics can begin to clog the bandwidth-constricted lines connecting the Web. Bottlenecks can occur at a number of points in the information exchange system. The speed of your modem, the bandwidth of your phone line or cable connection, the server connection, the number of users, and, of course, the *volume* of data you are retrieving all impact how quickly or slowly your data is retrieved. Audio is BIG; the only thing bigger than audio is video. If bandwidth was a controlled, supply-limited substance, prices would skyrocket. It is very-much in demand. So while bandwidth suppliers are working to produce more available bandwidth (cable modems, residential ISDN lines, fiber optic lines, even satellite data links), content providers are working to *compress* their data into the smallest form deliverable. The results of these combined efforts yield greater possibilities for content over the Web today, and even more tomorrow.

For instance, today, you can instantly play a streamed audio program through the Web into your home PC. You cannot do it at CD-quality levels yet. Today, you can play a 30 frames/per/second, quarter-screen, MPEG-compressed video across a T1 line, or at 3 frames/per/second through a 28.8 Kbps modem. Obviously, the Web hasn't replaced the local video rental store yet. You can call anywhere in the world for free if the other party has the right software installed, but quality may not compare to AT&T. And you can audioconference or group-chat in spoken voice, if the group is small.

If anyone complains about the poor quality of audio over the Web, remind him or her about how the first telephones sounded compared to today's pin-drop quality. Our society tends to innovate and improve things. (Just not as quickly as everyone thinks we should.) We've seen significant achievements just in the last six months of research for this book. Things will continue to improve.

What's Coming Tomorrow, *Literally!*

Perhaps the hottest and most anticipated development in the race to provide more bandwidth (and the ability to charge for those superhighway lanes) is the arrival of residential cable modems. In many metropolitan areas, higher bandwidth ISDN, T1, and T2 phone lines are available, but they are expensive. Even if price is not an issue, they may not be available. Just for fun, check with your local phone service provider to see if and when these lines are available in your area.

Veins of Gold

Look out phone companies, cable companies are here! Most people think of cable companies as those folks from whom we rent a box, put it on top of the TV, and get 200 channels of stupid programming with an occasional run of good movies. Their greatest asset may no longer be the movie of the week. Instead, it is most likely the cable "veins of gold" running from house to house in over 92 percent of the homes in the U.S.

These cable lines are the *broad* bandwidth conduit for a presently unseen volume of on-demand data. This data is not video going to your TV set. Rather, it is high-quality audio, video, and instant interactivity going to your computer at speeds an order of magnitude faster than any phone modem! All you need is a cable modem connected between your computer and coax (TV) cable outlet, and you're set. Well... almost.

There are a few problems. In the cases of 90 percent of the cable service providers, the cables laid to homes and businesses were designed to send video (data) *to the customer* from the cable headend. Nothing was ever expected to come *from the customer* to the headend. The lines are *one-way*, and that means you can receive data, but you cannot *request* data (like a Web address) through these one-way lines. Bummer.

But there's a solution looming on the not-too-distant horizon. Zenith and General Instruments, in conjunction with US Robotics, have pioneered network solutions for data modem communications over one-way cable systems. In simple terms, your existing phone line and phone modem will be used to request data (an http address for example). The request data packet size is very small and moves very quickly through the narrow bandwidth phone lines. The system will return the requested data (say, for example, a 60 minute, full CD-quality musical performance) through the cable headend and cable lines, to your cable modem in your computer.

By using an existing narrow bandwidth phone line with the existing one-way, broad bandwidth cable line, consumers can get unimagined amounts of data instantly, without download times. (A prediction: you will soon be able to request any popular movie to be played *on demand* on your computer through cable Internet service providers.)

A fortunate, forward-thinking 10 percent of the cable service providers have *two-way* cable lines (fiber optics) already installed in some areas. (Check with your cable service provider to see which type of cable service is planned for your area. If it's too far out, consider moving.) These two-way cable systems eliminate the need for any phone modem connection. Don't look for cable modems to be in stores soon; they'll be manufactured and sold in quantity to the cable companies, who will probably *rent them to you!* Just as the box on top of your TV allows you to access *for a fee*, the cable modem will allow you Internet access for a projected $30 to $40 (US) per month.

I'll be one of the first in line to sign-up! Consider the speed of this delivery system. Today's phone modems over standard phone lines can deliver (on a good day) 28.8 Kbps—28,800 bits per second. Cable modems are currently running at 4 *million* bits per second and we've heard that 10 to 20 Mbps cable modems are on the way. New industry protocol standards to be established by late 1996 or early 1997 will again change the face of cable modem access by moving the hardware into a consumer retail marketplace.

If this hasn't painted a picture of the Web as the greatest emerging frontier, pick up any computer or software trade publication and read. The writing is on the wall. Sound is a major part of the information explosion. Developing the skills and foundation to ride this wave can position you ahead of the competition. Take advantage of it.

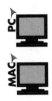

LISTEN AND LEARN

If you have never heard audio over the Web, you are in for a treat. Here are the basics that you will need:

- A computer

- A properly installed and configured sound card

- A modem, 28.8 Kbps suggested

- Multimedia speakers (The best you can afford; they make a big difference!)

- Internet access and a Web browser

To get the most out of this book, you'll also need the ability to record and edit your own audio files. There is a lot to learn about editing software, microphones, and mixer boards. Parts III and IV of this book are devoted to these issues.

Once you have all of the required or suggested equipment ready, it's time to go to work. Your first assignment is to determine which sounds your browser can currently play for you. Your browser probably doesn't play sounds directly. Rather, it relies on plug-ins and helper applications to play sounds. When a specific type of file is encountered, and your browser recognizes it as a specific audio format (there are over a dozen common ones), it will call to the plug-in or helper application to process and play the sound for you. This assumes that your browser has been told *what to do* when it encounters a particular type of sound file.

You need to test your browser. Visit our *Sound Advice* audio Web page (Figure 2.4) at

```
http://www.monsoon.org/sound_advice
```

and click on "On-Line Companion". This will take you to our pages that have a number of different audio files for you to test. By clicking on each one, you will quickly learn if your browser is configured to play audio files such as .WAV, .AIFF, .AU, .MIDI, .VOX, .MPEG, .GSM6.10, .TSP, .DCR, .RA, and more. (You didn't know there were that many, did you?) As you successfully complete each audio format test, check it off and move on to the next one. When you encounter a file that your browser *cannot* play, the real fun begins.

It isn't practical to instruct you how to configure your browser to play each type of audio file. There are too many different browsers, platforms, sound card configurations, audio players, and plug-ins available. That could also be a book in and of itself! Instead, we're going to point you in the right direction and make you go through what everyone else has had to do.

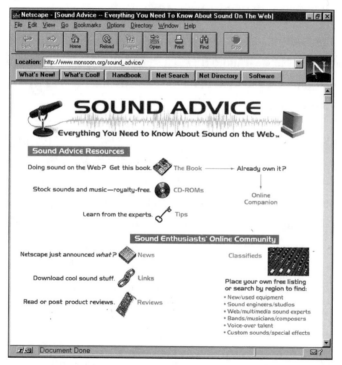

Figure 2.4

From the Sound Advice Web site at www.monsoon.org/sound_advice, click on "On-Line Companion" to test your browser's audio configuration.

When you encounter a sound your browser cannot play, you must determine why you don't hear anything. If a message from your browser is absent, quickly check the obvious things first:

1. Are your speakers turned on? Are all speaker cable connections plugged in? Is the volume turned up? Test run an audio file or system sound to verify that these things are not the problem.

2. Have you ever heard this type of audio file on your system before? For example, if you are attempting to play a .MIDI file for the first time, is your sound card MIDI map set up properly? In this case, you should refer to your system or sound card reference manual.

3. Here's one that many people forget. Your speaker volume may be maxed, but still there is no sound. Remember that computers have software volume controls as well, and they may appear in more than one place. For example, all PC Sound Blaster card installations include a software utility called SB Mixer. This utility controls the relative volume of all audio inputs. If the mixer setting for a .MIDI file is zero, you will never hear it even though you can hear your system sounds and .WAV files perfectly. Thoroughly familiarize yourself with your system's software volume controls.

Assuming the above items are OK, your next hope is that the system is fine, but your browser does not know how to process the selected audio file. This will usually be indicated by some sort of error message (Figure 2.5) within the browser when it attempts to "view" (play) the file.

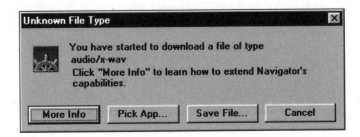

Figure 2.5

Netscape tells you no helper application has been associated with this type of file format.

Your next step is to associate the file format with a specific player. For example, if your Netscape browser has never played a .WAV file before, it may give you the message that you need to associate the file with a helper application or plug-in the first time you attempt to play one. You can then browse your system for any application you have that will play the file. In Windows 95, Sound Recorder is a good choice, but you can use any sound editing program or shareware utility as well.

For convenience, try associating files with smaller, quick-loading utilities rather than with bigger, audio editing programs. They'll play sooner, and you can always save them to disk for editing later. (Note: *Helper applications* are external stand-alone applications spawned by the browser once an association has been made. You may choose which helper application you want for each file type (Figure 2.6). *Plug-ins* are internal software additions which allow the browser to process the file, e.g., *Shockwave* plug-ins are necessary for processing "Shocked" files. Most plug-ins are downloadable from the Web for free and include installation instructions.)

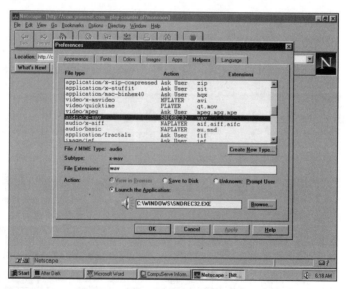

Figure 2.6

Netscape allows you to associate any type of file extension to an external application to view/play the file.

Refer to your browser's documentation for specific steps and options regarding external helper applications and plug-ins. Through the course of this book and your audio explorations on the Web, you will likely set up helper applications and plug-ins for ten or more audio file formats. You could look at this as a lack of standards in the industry, or, more accurately, as the fortunate availability of a bunch of standards in the industry. How many different types of audio you will want to process is up to you, and so is how badly you want to hear a particular selection. The good news is, once you configure for each type of file, you'll probably never have to do it again, unless your Mom needs help with her computer.

Based on the content of this book and the current proliferation of audio formats on the Web, we recommend completing browser testing and setup for the formats mentioned in Table 2.1. You do not have to configure them all in one sitting, but we'd suggest doing so before you really need them. The "Playable?" column is included in case you want to mark off which formats your browser and helper applications can currently play.

Visit Some Sites

Once you've configured your browser to hear various types of audio, there is a whole new audio Web-world out there for you to explore. New sites are appearing almost daily. To test your new-found capability, the following sections present sites that may prove to be fun, informative, or a good waste of bandwidth.

When browsing other Web sites and those you discover on your own, carefully analyze *how* the Web designers utilize audio. Some *emphasize* audio and some *accent* with audio. You can observe a lot about good and poor audio usage based on the things other designers do. Don't be afraid to be critical. Several of the example audio sites we reference throughout this book are not well-designed for *audio*. Learn from their mistakes.

Table 2.1 Popular File Extensions and Format Names

Extension	Name	Playable?
.WAV	Wave or PCM waveform format	_____
.AIFF	Macintosh waveform format	_____
.AU	Unix, NeXT & Sun Sparc audio waveform	_____
.MIDI	Musical Instrument Digital Interface (music)	_____
.MPEG	(Motion Picture Experts Group) Compressed audio and/or video format (Xing Technologies)	_____
.GSM6.10	Compressed audio format, widelyused in Europe	_____
.VOX	ToolVox compression, speech file	_____
.TSP	TrueSpeech compression, optimized for voice but can handle music	_____
.DCR	Macromedia "Shocked" Director Movie, can include audio	_____
.RA	RealAudio, can be compressed for 14.4kbps or 28.8kbps delivery	_____

WAV Files

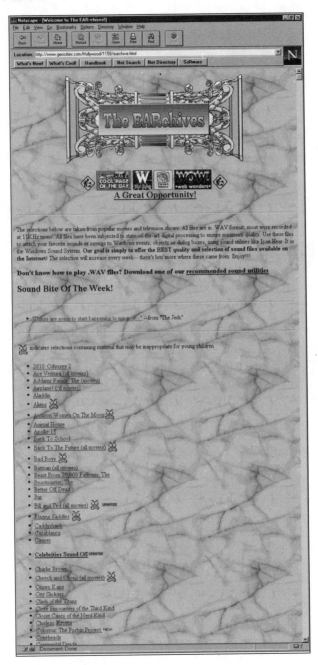

Figure 2.7

Earchives, thousands of TV and movie audio clips at http://
www.geocities.com/Hollywood/1158/earchive.html.

Figure 2.8

You can find hundreds of .WAV files at *Duane's, The Simpson's Picture and Sound Archive* at http://www.hookup.net/~coachkc/souns.html/.

Figure 2.9

. . . or try *The Simpson's Ultimate Sound Site* at http://
www.wam.umd.edo/~mdmoyer/simpson.html.

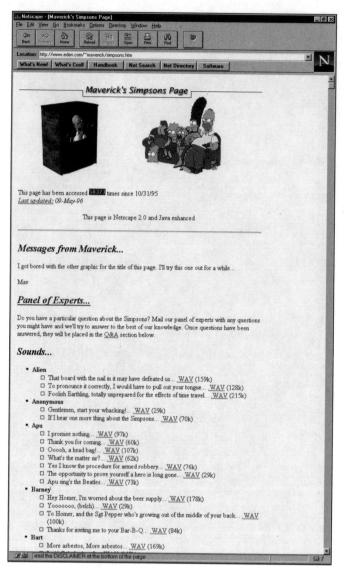

Figure 2.10

. . . or try *Maverick's Simpson's Page* at http://www.eden.com/
~maverick/simpsons.htm.

Figure 2.11

. . . or try an *Unofficial Simpson's Page* at http://www.wantree.com.au/
~richmond/simpsons.htm.

AU Files and MPEG

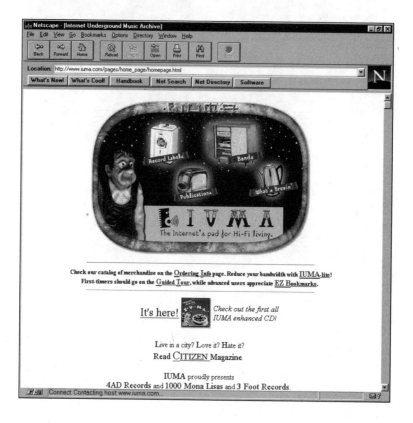

Figure 2.12

A cornerstone of web-audio, IUMA archives the music of over 800 independent bands at http://www.iuma.com/pages/home_page/homepage.html.

MIDI Files

Figure 2.13

Here's a good resource for MIDI information, *The MIDI Farm* at http://
www.midifarm.com/midifarm/free.shtml.

RealAudio

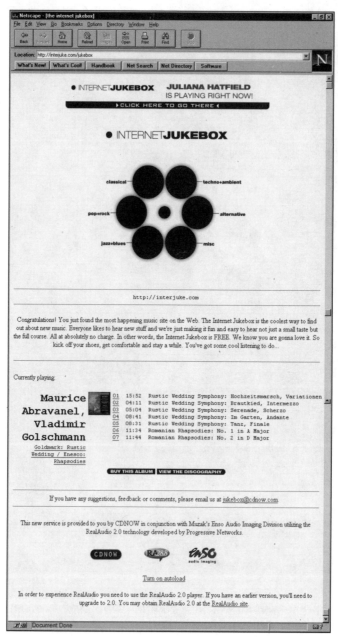

Figure 2.14

After downloading the RealAudio player, visit the *Internet Juke Box* at http://interjuke.com/jukebox.

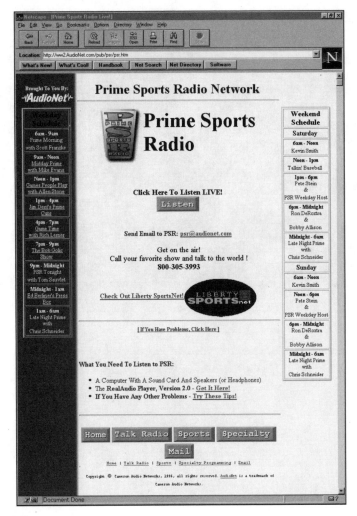

Figure 2.15

If your prefer something other than music, try *Prime Sports Radio* at http:
//ww2.AudioNet.com/pub/psr/psr.htm.

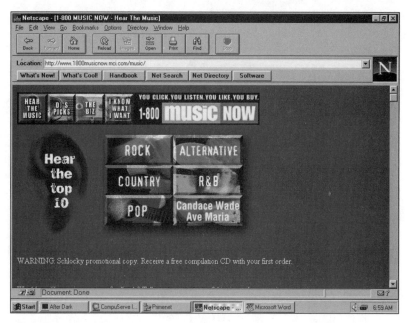

Figure 2.16

And if you want to listen before your buy, check out *Music Now* at http://www.1800musicnow.mci.com/music.

PART 2

Getting

Your Sound

To The Web

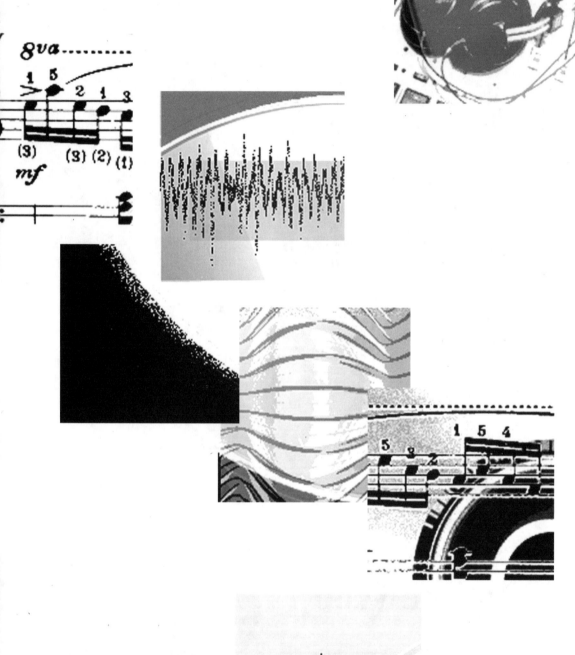

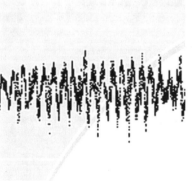

Chapter 3

Anthony Helmstetter

Developing For the Web

The first strategic decision you must make is *how* your audio will be received. You have two options: *downloadable* audio and *streamed* audio.

Downloadable audio is an audio file that the Web visitor selects to be transferred from the Web server to his or her system. This audio file can be played from the visitor's system only after the file is transferred in its entirety. The visitor does not have the option to listen to anything prior to downloading the entire file. Intolerable download times are determined primarily by the length of clip, sample rate (quality), and file format.

Streamed audio refers to a continuous stream of uninterrupted audio, much like a radio station. In fact, many of the current streamed audio Web sites *are* Web-radio stations. There is no download time other than a few brief seconds of initial buffering. Figures 3.1 through 3.5 provide examples of Web-based streamed audio.

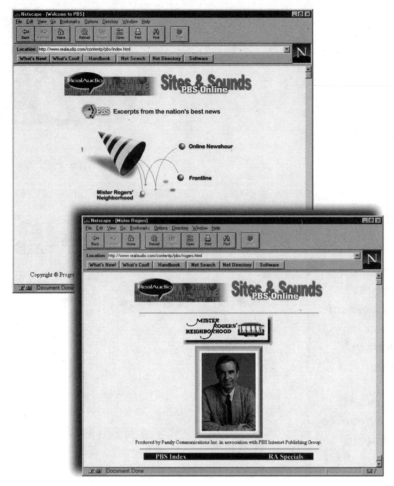

Figure 3.1

PBS offers a broad selection of streamed programming including favorites like *Mister Rogers' Neighborhood*.

The delivery system you need should be determined by your specific objectives of audio inclusion in your Web pages. If you wish to provide samples of your music for visitors to preview before purchasing, you would likely opt for brief, high-quality downloadable clips. If you are offering to replay a 15 minute speech or celebrity interview, you may opt for instantaneous, lower-quality streamed audio.

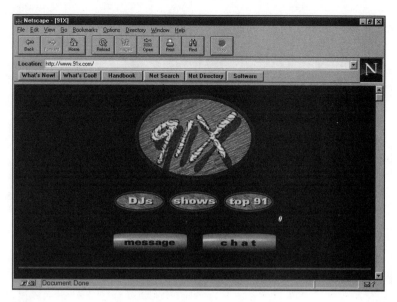

Figure 3.2

In this broadcast from San Diego, you'll hear alternative music, surf reports, and Howard Stern Live (http://www.91x.com).

Figure 3.3

AudioNet (http://www.audionet.com) offers live broadcasts of a dozen talk and music radio stations.

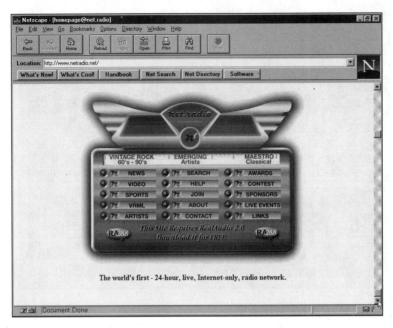

Figure 3.4

Net radio is a full-blown radio network broadcasting live, 24 hours per day, offering multiple formats in a traditional, radio-style delivery. Classic rock and classical music are currently available, with more to come. Check out this station at http://www.netradio.net/.

Downloadable Audio

Downloadable audio lets a visitor choose an audio file from your Web page and download it to his or her personal computer. The visitor will not know what the audio sounds like until after he or she downloads, decompresses and plays the audio. There will be a period of inactivity while the file is downloading, the length of which is determined by your file size, modem speed, and other uncontrollables. Table 3.1 compares several file lengths and their corresponding download times:

After the selected file has been downloaded, the visitor must play the file with a compatible audio player (which may or may not be a part of his or her browser software). Here is the first opportunity for disappointment. Imagine waiting eight minutes for a highly anticipated audio file only to learn that it doesn't play. It is important to clearly label the size and type of audio files so visitors can select files that are compatible with their hardware and software.

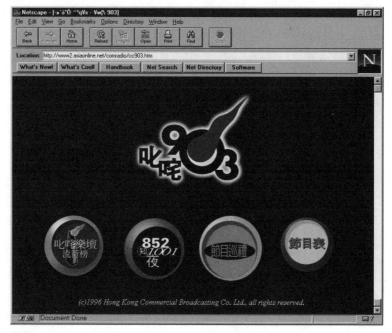

Figure 3.5

Chinese language radio direct from Hong Kong. Listen to streamed, pre-recorded news broadcasts or live radio broadcasts of music, news and other programs at http://www2.asiaonline.net/comradio/cc903.

Table 3.1   Use these figures for comparison only. Your test results will vary widely due to Web server speed, Web traffic line connection, and lunar cycle. Double the file size and download times for stereo files.

Approximate Download Times

15 seconds of audio (WAV or AIFF)

File Size	8-bit Mono			16-bit Mono		
	162 kb	323 kb	6457 kb	323 kb	647 kb	1.29 MB
14,400 baud modem	11 seconds	22 seconds	45 seconds	22 seconds	45 seconds	1 1/2 minutes
28,800 baud modem	5 seconds	11 seconds	22 seconds	11 seconds	22 seconds	45 seconds

But even when you label audio files, visitors may still experience problems you cannot fix. For example, if they download your MIDI file to play as background music while browsing your Web site, but don't have their MIDI sound card driver installed, the MIDI file won't play. In the midst of trying to browse your Web page, they've been distracted by the initial download only to learn they have a technical problem with their systems as well.

This problem is no different than what was experienced with multimedia sound, video, animation, or all other new capabilities that have become popular. Those who are interested in a new capability modify their systems to accommodate it, and those who have no interest don't bother. As more MPC systems are purchased, and as browser software continues to improve, this problem occurs less frequently.

There are many instances in which downloaded audio is preferred over streamed audio. If you want to physically "give" the audio files to your visitors, they need to download the files. You can still restrict who can access your files, license how they are to be used and even sell them, but the audio file is, regardless, transferred.

Streamed Audio

Set aside the issue of whether or not streamed audio is an appropriate use of Web bandwidth. The fact is, it's here. Streamed audio technology has greatly improved in both quality and compression. Provider bandwidth is increasing, and faster access methods like cable modems and affordable residential ISDN lines are just around the corner.

For many Web pages, streamed audio offers unique features that are not practical with downloaded files. Background music for your pages, lengthy audio, and real-time broadcasts can all be achieved with this remarkable technology. On the down side, it is a bit more involved. The Web server will require software and performance capabilities that not all service providers can supply. A number of new options are developing, however, which we'll discuss in chapter 5.

For the streamed audio listener, the only item required is a plug-in module for his or her browser. If you haven't yet experienced streamed audio you should visit the RealAudio Web page at http://www.realaudio.com/ (Figure 3.6) and download the proper plug-in (Figure 3.7) for your browser. Once you install it, I recommend visiting one of RealAudio's listed audio sites. It's pretty slick. By RealAudio's counter, over 5 million people have already downloaded the plug-in. This means there are at least 5 million people who can immediately listen to your audio message if you choose this streamed audio format for your Web site.

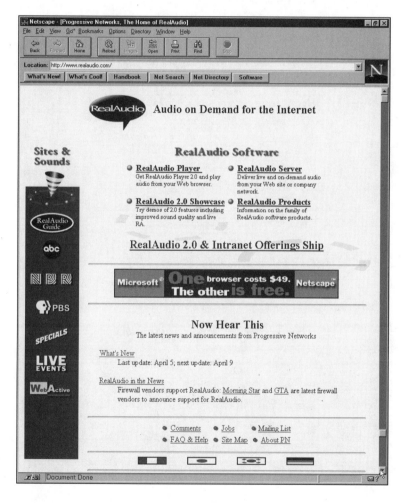

Figure 3.6

The *Real Audio* Home page at http://www.realaudio.com/.

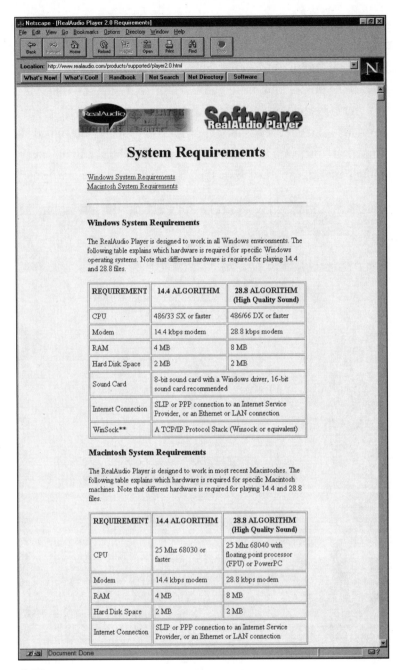

Figure 3.7

The RealAudio player is a plug-in available for Mac and PC Web browsers at no charge. Specific versions exist for 14,400 and 28,800 baud modems as well.

After you've sampled a few streamed audio sites, you can decide whether streamed audio makes sense for your Web project. If so, you should next begin the analysis of the system requirements, software requirements and bandwidth implications as they pertain to your server. Chapter 5 addresses these issues.

The Art Of Using Sound (Why, What, Where And When)

Now that you have a better understanding of the ways to deliver audio through the Web, you must ask yourself, "Should I use audio on my Web page?"

Why

I'm reminded of an industry-wide setback caused by the unrestrained proliferation of desktop publishing fonts in the late 1980s and early 90s. Desktop publishing was the rave, and the ability to use fonts with a laser printer delighted office workers everywhere. Layout, design, and typesetting no longer belonged to skilled professionals—untrained employees assumed the responsibility. Unfortunately, most did not have much artistic sense. The most blatant example of their lack of proficiency was the simultaneous use of every font available on their systems. Why did they do it? Because they could. The more the better, right? Wrong.

It had nothing to do with whether or not all the particular fonts should be used. The wrong decision was made tens of millions of times simply because people *could* use all the new fonts. Lest we repeat the same error, ask yourself, "*Why* should I put sound into my Web project?" If you answer, "Because I can," please consider all those poorly typeset documents floating around, filled with misused fonts.

Sound adds a new dimension to a Web site. It can give your Web site a competitive edge, and can dramatically increase visitor interest, return visits and information retention. Sound can stimulate powerful emotional synaptic responses that cannot be activated through the written word. For example, imagine a Web site that promotes child safety products. The sound begins by fading in a gentle music box tune like the kind found in a baby's nursery. After a few moments, you unexpectedly hear the shrill wail of an infant in pain. It gets louder and louder until it suddenly stops, and a calm, soothing female voice says, "ACME child safety products are designed to prevent injury-causing accidents...." Try accomplishing that effect with a text-based Web page! Sound can achieve results and create responses that you cannot achieve by any other means.

Relatively few Web sites are audio-enhanced. Another advantage to adding sound to your Web pages is that it's still new enough to be very novel. Novelty can draw more people to your site. If your marketing objectives include getting more hits, you should actively promote the audio enhancement. Modify your initial site description paragraph (usually the first 25 words that appear in your home page) to include audio capabilities, then notify or update all pertinent search engines and Web crawlers.

When a Web surfer has a list of 100 sites from which to buy a product, he or she is more likely to visit the site that mentions "audio-enhanced" in the site description paragraph. Contrary to logic, you also increase your chances of visits from surfers who don't even have sound cards in their systems.

What

"What sound should I use?" That's a lot like asking what kind of shoes to wear. It depends upon the situation. You may need spoken voice, background music to set an atmosphere, sound effects or funny noises to add an element of humor to your Web page. (Example: the sound of crickets chirping on the *Camp Wachatka* web page.)Sound design is as much an art as graphic design. You've seen pages with great graphics and pages with poor graphics. Sounds can be appropriate and high-quality, or inappropriate and poor-quality. I remember one of the first audio files I downloaded off CompuServe. It was a poorly recorded woman's voice saying something seductive, but the audio quality and background hiss were so bad that it was incoherent and unusable (I wanted it as my Windows start-up audio message, but I quickly replaced it with Robin Williams' "Gooooooood Morning, Vietnam!").

Make note of the sounds you hear during the day. Close your eyes and listen. (Don't do this while your driving.) Listen to the sounds of kids playing in a school yard, or phones ringing in the background of a busy office. Listen to the heart-pounding thump of a bass guitar during a great rock & roll song. Listen to radio commercials. Radio created masters in the art of integrating sound effects without the benefit of visual reinforcement. Audio techniques that work well on the radio work well on a Web page too.

Your sound design might be limited to interactive responses as a buzzer noise when a wrong answer is selected, or clicks and beeps when a button is pressed. These types of applications can be better implemented as Shockwaves, Java applets or other specialty programs, but they too have their place on the Web.

Where and When

In this context, "Where?" and "When?" mean almost the same thing. You should integrate audio into your Web site anywhere that it will help convey your message and is practical to do so. If your home page has depth to it, instead of a scant menu of selection options, bring the audio in right away. But don't assume that every page must have audio. Use it selectively and appropriately.

Let visitors know that your page is audio-enhanced, and what type of audio you are using. Add a graphic or message near the top announcing the site's audio capabilities. Carefully consider the site's main objective, and ask yourself if an audio icon will distract visitors from your information path.

Here is a list of some very practical example ideas for audio integration into a Web site. Functionally, many of these examples would be jsut fine as downloadable, which is likely to be immediately accessible by a greater percentage of people on the Web today.

- Hear what our customers are saying about our _____. (Download)

- Listen to how quiet our dishwasher is compared to three of the other brands. (Download)

- This type of child's cough requires an expectorant. (Download)

- Listen to the hot new release from (insert musical group name). (Download)

- Hear the difference ACME carburetor cleaner makes in this engine. (Download)

- A message from our president. (Download or stream, depending on length)

- An interview with _____. (Download or stream, depending on length)

- Congressman _____ 's campaign promises that were kept. (Download, because it is very short)

- Click here to play the background theme music for this Web page. (Stream)

- This week's gardening tip for spring planting. (Download or stream)

- Kids, click here to have this page read to you. (Stream)

- Top 10 list of _____. (Download)

You may have trouble shoehorning these specific examples into your Web site. Take a look at your Web site and consider which functional audio clip could be used, and where it should be placed. Remember to apply the acid test: "Does placing audio here support my intended message path or distract from it?"

How To Deliver Sound Through Your Web Page

As you begin the process of integrating sound into your Web pages, you may find it helpful to mentally separate the job into three phases:

- *Acquiring* the sound

- *Preparing* the sound

- *Integrating* the sound into your HTML code

In a simple scenario, you might speak into a microphone connected to your personal computer, sample it down, move it to your Web server, and update your HTML code to link to it. Simple enough? It is, but the specific steps and options you will encounter during the process are numerous.

Acquiring the Sound

Acquiring could mean buying, borrowing, stealing or recording your own sounds. Each method has its own set of rules, obstacles, advantages and hidden land mines. When placing audio on the Web, keep in mind that you are making the audio publicly available. You are broadcasting your audio around the world. Potentially tens of thousands of listeners may be listening to what you have "borrowed." To stay out of jail, read Chapter 12.

Preparing the Sound

Preparing includes manipulating the sound to your liking plus the arduous task of balancing your desire for hi-fidelity CD quality audio with the size limitations of Web delivery. Sample rates (or sound resolution), compression, file formats and platform all come into play. Your job here is to satisfy as many visitors to your Web page as is practical.

Integrating the Sound

Integration refers to the actual HTML code you will need to allow visitors to play your audio. The code itself is easy, as is most code in HTML. The challenge lies in selecting *how* you want to deliver the audio. Your delivery method will determine the technique you use for integration. If you have sound integration experience in multimedia applications, You may have a shorter Web audio learning curve. But the rules are vastly different due to several annoying realities:

1. *You are preparing audio for a variety of hardware platforms.* If you are a PC person, don't think that your downloadable WAV files will suffice for millions of Mac users. If you are Mac-myopic, the PC folks won't understand how a file can have a four-letter extension like .AIFF. Add in Unix systems, and you are preparing audio for three different platforms. You must also consider the wide array of sound cards installed into these computers. Millions of sound cards are 16-bit and millions are only 8-bit. Should you sacrifice 16-bit quality for a few million people? Probably, unless you have a good reason not to.

2. *All browser software is not created equal.* While *Netscape* captured the lion's share of the browser market, it relies on helper applications (Figure 3.8) or plug-ins to enable audio playback. Each individual who visits your Web page may have several, one, or none of the necessary components to play audio on his or her system. You cannot anticipate every possibility, but you can let visitors know what they need to take full advantage of the sound on your Web page.

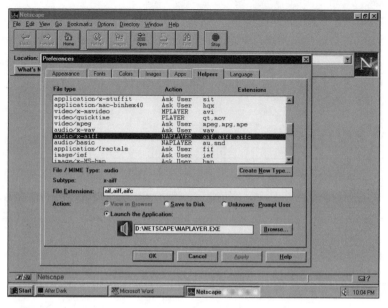

Figure 3.8

The Netscape 2.0 helper applications setup screen can accommodate as many file formats and players as you will ever need.

3. *Bandwidth Limitations.* Bandwidth describes the rate of information flow through various channels of the Web. Sitting at your home or office, you are connected to the Web by a standard phone line, an ISDN line, or, if you are lucky, a T-1 line. Each of these offers a different rate of data throughput, which as you will see, becomes critically important where audio is concerned. As a general rule, which is too often ignored, a typical graphic on a Web page should be limited to about 35 Kb. This file size represents a generally-accepted rate for data throughput, and the resulting amount of time it takes for the graphic to appear on a monitor. Of course, graphic files can be bigger—they just take longer to load. So how long is too long? If the visitor gets bored and leaves your Web page, the it took too long.

4. *Miscellaneous Uncontrollables.* How fast is your Web server? How busy is it normally, and how busy is it during peak times? How fast is the computer that the visitor of your Web page is using? How much RAM does your visitor have? What is the speed of your visitor's modem? Is he or she connected at the maximum speed? Which browser software is he or she using? Is your visitor accessing your page via an on-line service?

These issues are beyond your control, yet they have a huge impact on how your Web page is received. You have to compromise between size, quality and amount of data you want to make available. This fact applies to graphics as well as audio: audio is just bigger.

File Formats

You must convert your audio files into at least one of several standard formats in order for visitors to listen to them. If your sound editing software does not support the format you desire, a number of shareware and conversion utilities are available that will do the trick. The chart below (Table 3.2) gives you a reference point for platform and corresponding audio file formats. You may acquire and prepare your audio using any of these formats, and then convert them to alternate formats for download from your Web site. (Note: From this point on, it is assumed that you will be making your downloadable audio available in several formats. You may choose which formats to make available based on personal preference, available resources and time allotment.)

Table 3.2   Common Platform and File Formats.

	WAVEFORM	MIDI
PC	.WAV	.MID
Mac	.AIFF, .AIF or .AU	.MIDI, SDS
Unix	.AU or .SND	.MIDI, SDS

If your objective is to stream your audio, you must first convert the audio into a format that *can* be streamed. This is accomplished with an encoder provided by the proprietor of the streaming technology you are using. Each streamed format will require its own encoder, player and server setup. The encoder software converts the audio file into the format the player expects to play.

Download Basics

Let's assume that you have your audio file in the format you desire, and its resolution is sampled down to a comfortable compromise between audio quality and file size (which impacts transfer time). Your Web page must give the visitor an <A HREF> link to the download file and some descriptive information about the nature of the file to be downloaded. This can be done by putting a simple line of code into your HTML page. For example, the code

```
<P>A sample <A HREF="a_sample.au">audio</A> file is available in .AU
   format.</P>
```

would look like:

A sample <u>audio</u> file is available in .AU format.

When the visitor clicks on the reference link "audio," the browser will call the corresponding audio file, which in this case is a file named "a_sample.au" located in the same directory or folder as our HTML file (yes, this works just like graphics files). The browser will retrieve the file, and when completed, store the file to the hard disk and/or play the file. The option to store and/or play is determined by preference settings associated with each browser, or by a helper application called by the browser.

Knowing how easy audio inclusion is, why are so few Web sites audio-enhanced? The answer lies (partly) in the inherent limitations of downloadable audio. Small, low resolution files are a snap, but long or high quality files quickly become tiresome. The casual visitor may only wait a minute or two for a file, while someone truly interested may wait a while longer. This is why it is so important to clearly label the content, format and file size of any downloadable file. For example:

The award was received by Dr. Smith. You can listen to his comments in this 30 second <u>audio</u> file available in .AU format. (647 Kb)

This is more than good manners or proper Netiquette. It is functionally necessary to prevent visitors to your Web site from wasting their time with downloads that don't interest them (See Figure 3.9). Clearly labeling your downloadable file keeps them moving smoothly along your information path, and improves their Web experience. They tell their friends, your hit count soars, and you retire to the Bahamas.

Mister Rogers' Neighborhood

Mister Rogers and King Friday

Hear Mister Rogers and King Friday's Welcome Message

(misterr.aiff, misterr.wav)

Figure 3.9

This isn't very neighborly. Multiple formats are available, but no information about the file size or length of the audio message is listed. How are we to know what we are about to download?

Streamed Audio Basics

As on-demand audio-over the Internet nears ubiquity, a variety of technical approaches are gaining popularity. When the developers at Progressive Networks began developing RealAudio in early 1994, they spent a substantial amount of time investigating and prototyping a range of approaches before settling on a generalized client-server system. During the development process, Progressive Networks discovered what works and what doesn't under the real world conditions of the Internet.

The Problem

The Internet is a fantastically scaleable packet-switched network, but it is not designed to handle isochronous (continuous time-based) information. As a result, to get a system such as RealAudio to work reliably and consistently in the real world, engineering design decisions had to be made very carefully.

The Internet can send data reliably, without guaranteed speed (the TCP protocol), or quickly, without guaranteed reliability (the UDP protocol). UDP does not guarantee packet delivery. Instead, it provides a stream of audio packets without significant delay at the cost of occasional lost packets. TCP is more reliable, but at the cost of occasional substantial delays when the protocol "retransmits" information from the server to the client, and waits for its receipt to be acknowledged. Neither method gives the user guaranteed throughput rates or guaranteed minimum latency periods, although UDP is generally superior to TCP in both regards.

Another problem with the Internet is that time-based streams are often very long—a 30-minute news program, for instance. Visitors often only want part of a program, such as the part that is 15 minutes into the program. Information sharing protocols on the Internet, called FTP and HTTP, are designed for one-way continuous transmission. They are not designed for bi-directional communication between the client and server that would allow the client to ask the server for a particular portion of a file.

Possible Solutions

There are a range of solutions to the problem of delivering time-based information (streamed audio, for instance) over the Internet.

Web servers are one possible solution. Web servers are commonplace and use the HTTP protocol, which, in turn, sends information using TCP. Web browsers, particularly commercial-grade browsers such as Netscape, present some of the information to the visitor before it has arrived in its entirety, thereby shortening presentation delays.

Unfortunately, when Web servers are used to send time-based data, such as audio that is rapidly "consumed" by the listener, the TCP "delay" problem can really bog things down. Even a 2 or 3 percent re-transmission rate can bring a low bitrate audio data stream over a standard modem (8 kilobits/second over a 14.4 modem) to a grinding halt. This problem is less commonly observed over high bandwidth communication paths such as T1 lines, but for the content publisher who wants to make audio available to Internet users through standard phone lines and 14.4 or 28.8 modems, it is a killer.

A second problem with Web servers involves the HTTP protocol. The HTTP protocol is designed for one-way continuous transmission. It does not allow for features such as "fast forward," "rewind" and "seek," which would allow visitors to go to a particular part of an audio program. Audio and video users have these features on their VCRs and CD players, and expect these features on the Internet.

One might think that there are advantages to delivering all types of information—including audio and other time-based media—via a Web server that is already in place. Because sending too much audio information is inefficient, especially when dealing with long programs over high bandwidth pipes, the advantages are nonexistent. A Web server typically tries to send the whole file as fast as possible - whether it be a 10 second audio clip or a two-hour program. Since visitors listen to short segments averaging four minutes in length, even when the source material is an hour or longer, sending the whole file as quickly as possible often results in wasted bandwidth and transmission time.

The RealAudio Solution

Progressive Networks conducted field tests in late 1994 and early 1995, and discovered, for the reasons listed above, that Web servers are not an appropriate vehicle for delivery of audio or other time-based media. As a result, it created the RealAudio protocol and the RealAudio client-server architecture. RealAudio's key underlying technology is a new protocol for time-based media that supports bi-directional communication between clients and servers. This new protocol enables RealAudio users to pause, fast forward, rewind and skip to particular tracks or particular sections quickly and reliably.

While the RealAudio system and protocol support TCP and UDP protocols, Progressive Networks learned that the results are much better when audio is delivered via UDP. UDP-delivered audio most often results in a continuous presentation. To circumnavigate the problem of occasional packet loss, Progressive Networks developed a sophisticated loss correction system. This system minimizes the impact of a lost packet and enables the client to "recreate" the missing pieces of the signal. The loss correction system works very well under normal conditions, degrades gracefully when packet loss is in the 2 to 5 percent range and works acceptably when packet loss is as high as 8 to 10 percent.

Visitors typically use a standard Web link to access a RealAudio sound file. The visitor clicks on the Web link, and after a second or two of start-up, the sound file plays without any further hindrances. Since the RealAudio server runs on nearly all the same platforms as popular Web servers, the RealAudio server and a Web server can run as separate processes on the same physical hardware. The RealAudio server is more efficient at sending time-based data than a Web server - it sends only the information the visitor needs plus a little extra for buffering. As a result, this configuration supports a higher level of overall usage than a Web server alone. Also, when it is time to scale up and add hardware, it is easier to scale up by moving the RealAudio server to a different physical machine without having to restructure and split the Web site. This scaleability enables support of hundreds, thousands and soon-to-be hundreds of thousands of simultaneous listeners.

Hundreds of thousands of RealAudio users already enjoy global access to live and on-demand RealAudio content that is deployed in hundreds of server sites around the world.

The implementation of streamed audio (RealAudio or one of the 10 other competitive formats) requires coordination between you and the Web server administrator. Chapter 5 describes the how-tos of this process.

Don't Forget The Sound-Impaired Web Browsers

The term "sound-impaired Web browser" sounds like an overt attempt at political correctness where browser limitations are concerned. We are referring to a person visiting your audio-enhanced Web site who cannot hear audio. Sound impairment can be due to any number of reasons: no sound card, no helper applications, unplugged speakers, ear wax build-up, etc. Regardless of your efforts to make audio available, chances are that someone will not be able to hear it.

Accepting that a percentage of your visitors are sound-impaired, you should not rely on audio alone to convey your message! If your Web page already exists, don't worry; you already use text and graphics to communicate your message. Just don't delete all your text and replace it with audio (Notice the term "audio-*enhanced*," not "audio-*substituted*."). Your greatest impact will be achieved when you coordinate a well-written text message with high-quality, supportive graphics *and* audio.

Chapter 4

Anthony Helmstetter

Anthony Helmstetter

Building Some HTML Examples

Key Topics:

- **Build a Web page with downloadable audio files**

- **The keys to multiple download file formats**

- **Simple streams with ToolVox Audio**

- **Super capabilities with Shockwave audio**

If you've never actually built a Web page with a word processor or an HTML editor, this is the wrong place to start. There are dozens of books that go into great detail about HTML levels 1, 2, and 3, Netscape extensions, form-based CGI scripts, and so on. You should have a couple of these books in your collection.

If, on the other hand, you've put up at least one personal page, you are probably qualified to proceed with our Web audio tutorials. In this chapter, you will either build a few sample pages, or copy pertinent parts of our code into your pages. This chapter emphasizes several types of downloadable audio, while Chapter 5 focuses on streamed audio. All the sample audio files you will need are in the tutorials subdirectory or folder in the Incredible Sound Resource CD-ROM. Feel free to use your own audio samples for the tutorials if you prefer. Just remember to match your file names with the file names in your HTML code.

If you skipped some of the browser tests in Chapter 2, make sure your browser can play the types of files we will use. You can't test your code if your browser (or system) isn't audio-ready. Run a quick check of your sound card, turn your speakers on, and turn your volume up. Let's some breathe life into a Web page.

SIMPLE HTML AND DOWNLOADABLE AUDIO

I've always thought of myself as a stickler for "correct" HTML code. If you've ever done any other type of programming, you know that a minor infraction can mean test, failure, debug, test, failure, debug, go home. I thought *I* was a stickler, until one day I received e-mail from a Web master who analyzed a page of my code. He sent me a couple corrections he felt my code needed in order to be perfect. I thanked him, and learned that there are people more particular about good code format than myself, and people with too much time on their hands as well.

HTML is more forgiving than most programming methods in getting things to work. You can code a surprising number of sloppy tags and most browsers will still display something useful. Let's begin with the basic page format for all HTML pages.

(If you are working on a Mac, skip to page 61 for the Mac version of this tutorial.)

WAV FILE FORMAT:

1. Set up a base page (Figure 4.1).

Set up the following base page code and save it as an ASCII text file named "chapter4.htm":

```
<HTML>
<HEAD>
<TITLE>Your Page Title Here</TITLE>
</HEAD>
<BODY>
<H1>My Audio Page.</H1>
<P> This is where we place the content of the page.</P>
<HR>
<ADDRESS>&#169  Copyright 1996 by Your Name Here.  All rights
  reserved.
</ADDRESS>
</BODY>
</HTML>
```

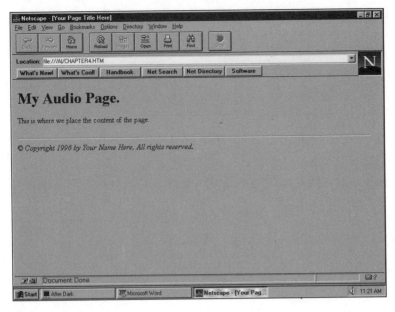

Figure 4.1

The base Web page viewed with Netscape's Windows browser.

If you are confused at this point, you should read one of the HTML books I previously mentioned. Everything we do in the tutorials falls into this simple framework. You will most likely take the examples we develop here and paste them into your existing pages.

2. Take the code listed above, and insert

```
<P><A HREF="a_sample.wav">Audio Sample</A></P>
```

as an <A HREF> tag (Figure 4.2) like this:

```
<HTML>
<HEAD>
<TITLE>Your Page Title Here</TITLE>
</HEAD>
<BODY>
<H1>My Audio Page.</H1>
<P> This is where we place the content of the page.</P>
<P><A HREF="a_sample.wav">Audio Sample</A></P>
<HR>
<ADDRESS>&#169  Copyright 1996 by Your Name Here.  All rights
  reserved.
</ADDRESS>
</BODY>
</HTML>
```

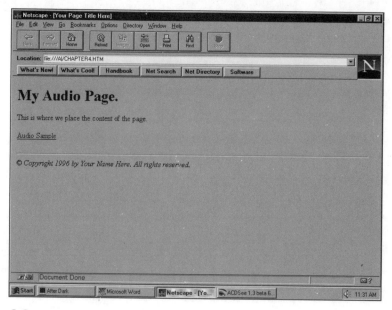

Figure 4.2

The active <A HREF> link will call to the audio file.

3. Put a sample audio file on your computer.

Access the Incredible Sound Resource CD-ROM and locate the tutorial subdirectory or folder. Copy the file named "a_sample.wav" to the same location as your HTML file.

4. Test the link.

Open your Web browser and load the file named "chapter4.htm". Click on the "Audio Sample" link text displayed in your browser. You should see the file being downloaded, then your browser should either play, or launch a helper application, to play the file (Figure 4.3).

If you hear audio, congratulations! You can now do what relatively few Web developers have ever done.

If your browser doesn't play the file, check your code and file names. Make sure your browser is configured to play WAV files (see Chapter 2 or the Sound Advice Web Page to check your browser's audio capabilities).

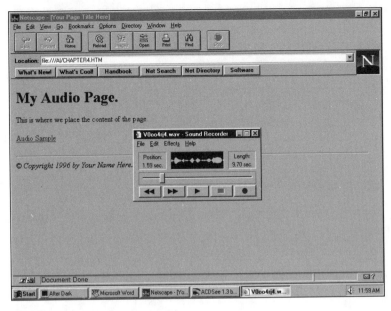

Figure 4.3

The audio file loads, and Netscape launches a helper application, such as Windows Sound Recorder, to play the audio file.

AIFF FILE FORMAT:

1. Set up a base page (Figure 4.4).

Set up the following base page code and save it as an ASCII text file named "chapter4.html":

```
<HTML>
<HEAD>
<TITLE>Your Page Title Here</TITLE>
</HEAD>
<BODY>
<H1>My Audio Page.</H1>
<P> This is where we place the content of the page.</P>
<HR>
<ADDRESS>&#169  Copyright 1996 by Your Name Here.  All rights
  reserved.
</ADDRESS>
</BODY>
</HTML>
```

If you are confused at this point, you should read one of the HTML books I previously mentioned. Everything we do in the tutorials falls

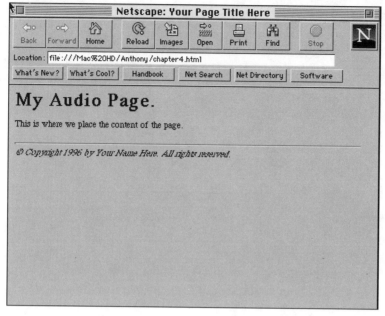

Figure 4.4

The base Web page viewed with Netscape's Macintosh Web browser.

into this framework. You will most likely take the examples we develop and paste them into your existing pages.

2.   Take the code listed above, and insert

```
<P><A HREF="a_sample.aiff">Audio Sample</A></P>
```

an <A HREF> tag (Figure 4.5) into it like this:

```
<HTML>
<HEAD>
<TITLE>Your Page Title Here</TITLE>
</HEAD>
<BODY>
<H1>My Audio Page.</H1>
<P> This is where we place the content of the page.</P>
<P><A HREF="a_sample.aiff">Audio Sample</A></P>
<HR>
<ADDRESS>&#169  Copyright 1996 by Your Name Here.  All rights
  reserved.
</ADDRESS>
</BODY>
</HTML>
```

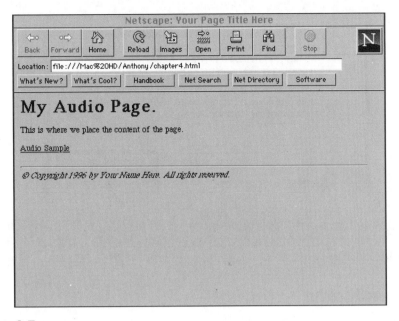

Figure 4.5

The active <A HREF> link will call to the audio file.

3. Put a sample audio file on your computer.

Access the Incredible Sound Resource CD-ROM and locate the tutorial folder. Copy the file named "a_sample.aiff" to the same location as your HTML file.

4. Test the link.

Open your Web browser and load the file named "chapter4.html". Click on the "Audio Sample" text link displayed in your browser. You should see the file being downloaded, then your browser should either play, or launch a helper application to play the file.

If you hear audio, congratulations! You can now do what relatively few Web developers have ever done. If you receive an error message like the one shown in Figure 4.6, you'll need to configure your sound helper application

If your browser doesn't play the file, check your code and file names. Make sure your browser is configured to play WAV files (see Chapter 2 or the Sound Advice Web Page).

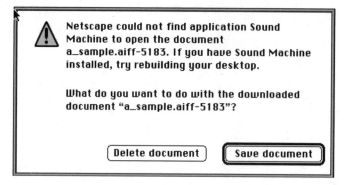

Figure 4.6

The audio file loads, and Netscape launches a helper application, such as Sound Machine, to play the audio file. A properly installed helper application will prevent these types of error messages.

Conclusion

The <A HREF> call to an audio file is no different than one to any other file. The file name extension dictates how the browser should handle the requested file. If a file has a .JPG extension, most browsers will attempt to display an image. If it has a .WAV, .AIFF, or .AU extension, most browsers will recognize it as an audio file and view (play) it accordingly.

MULTIPLE FILE FORMATS AND QUICK CONVERSIONS

We've already discussed the need for multiple file formats for downloadable audio. There are more than a dozen commonly used audio formats, but you'll cover most Web surfers' needs with WAV, AIFF, and AU. With that in mind, let's continue to build your audio page with some file conversions for the convenience of your Web visitors.

(If you are working on a Mac, skip to page 69 for the Mac version of this tutorial.)

1. Modify the code from your base page.

Utilize the code from the previous tutorial and add the following <A HREF> links:

Replace the line

```
<P><A HREF="a_sample.wav">Audio Sample</A></P>
```

with a new line:

```
<P><A HREF="sample42.wav">Download an audio sample in WAV
   format</A></P>
```

Then, add these two additional lines:

```
<P><A HREF="sample42.aif">Download an audio sample in AIFF
   format</A></P>

<P><A HREF="sample42.au">Download an audio sample in AU
   format</A></P>
```

The resulting code should look like this:

```
<HTML>
<HEAD>
<TITLE>Your Page Title Here</TITLE>
</HEAD>
<BODY>
<H1>My Audio Page.</H1>
<P> This is where we place the content of the page.</P>
<P><A HREF="sample42.wav">Download an audio sample in WAV
   format</A></P>
<P><A HREF="sample42.aif">Download an audio sample in AIFF
   format</A></P>
<P><A HREF="sample42.au">Download an audio sample in AU
   format</A></P>
<HR>
<ADDRESS>&#169  Copyright 1996 by Your Name Here.  All rights
   reserved.
</ADDRESS>
</BODY>
</HTML>
```

Save the file and view it with your browser (Figure 4.7).

Of course, the actual files are not yet available for download. If you already have a file conversion tool or WAV editor that can export AIFF or AU formats, you may use it to complete the next step. If you don't have the means to convert the files, we provided some assistance. The Incredible Sound Resource CD-ROM has an evaluation "save-disabled" version of Sound Forge on it. You can install the software to your system and use it to convert the files. Be aware that you can't actually *save* the files. Though this may seem inconvenient, you'll be able to complete the tutorials and test a great software package at the same time. Also, if you

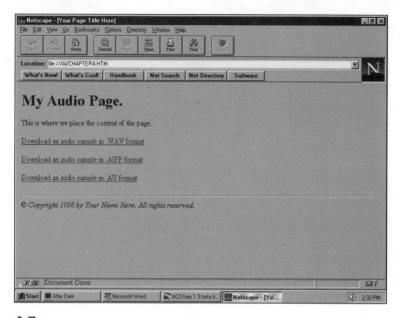

Figure 4.7

Three clearly-labeled file formats available for download.

purchase Sound Forge, you'll already be somewhat familiar with it. We provided *saved* versions of the files on the CD-ROM (and on the Web site) so you can complete the next part of the tutorial.

(Check the Incredible Sound Resource CD-ROM appendix at the back of the book for a list of other sharware conversion utilities included on the CD-ROM.)

2. Retrieve the sample file in WAV, AIFF, and AU formats.

Retrieve the prepared files from the Incredible Sound Resource CD-ROM. From the tutorial subdirectory, copy the files named "sample42.wav", "sample42.aif", and "sample42.au", and place them in the same location as your HTML document.

3. Convert a WAV file to AIFF, and AU formats (Optional).

Use Sound Forge (or a similar editing/conversion program) to open file "sample42.wav". Sound Forge (Figure 4.8) will need to be installed on you system prior to completing this step. Click on "File|Open." Select the file named "sample42.wav" from the tutorial subdirectory of the CD-ROM.

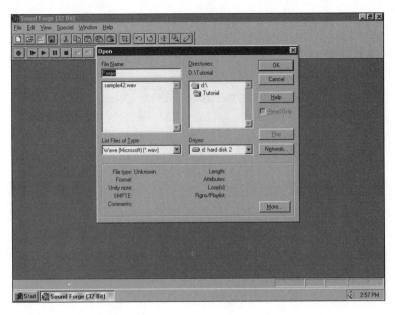

Figure 4.8

The Open File dialog box within Sound Forge. Many other WAV editors have similar capabilities.

Once the "sample42.wav" file is opened, test-play it once (Figure 4.9) to verify that you have the correct file (plus, it's fun to listen to new stuff).

Click on "File|Save As" and select the Macintosh AIFF option (Figure 4.10) under "File Save Type."

Name the new file "sample42.aif" and place it in the same location as your HTML document.

Important Note: The evaluation copy of Sound Forge from the Incredible Sound Resource CD-ROM is "save-disabled." It will not allow you to complete the "save" operation. Use the pre-converted files mentioned in Step 2 of this tutorial.

Repeat the above steps to create the AU version of the file, or, if you think you've got the hang of it, you can utilize the pre-converted "sample42.au" file.

4. Test the links.

Open your Web browser and load the file named "chapter4.htm". Test

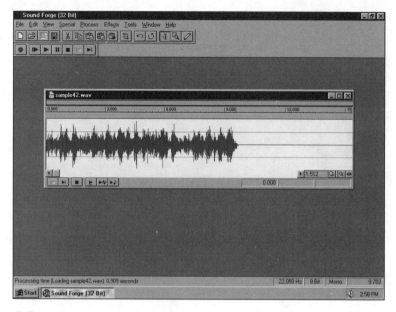

Figure 4.9

A sample audio file in a WAV format. Notice the status bar in the lower right-hand corner showing sample resolution, bit depth, and number of channels.

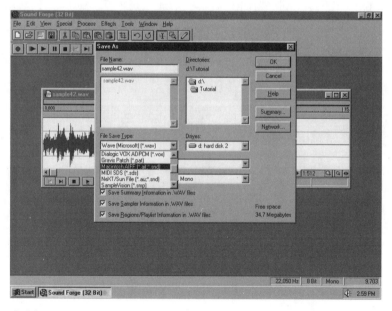

Figure 4.10

Sound Forge makes 15 types of file conversions very easy.

each of the three "Download Audio Sample" text links displayed in your browser. You should see a file being downloaded, then your browser should either play, or launch a helper application to play the file. Depending on how you set up your browser, each file format may be played by a different helper application.

If you hear audio, congratulations!

If your browser doesn't play one of the files, check your code. Make sure that you converted and named the files correctly, and that your browser is configured to play each of the file formats. Another sound helper application is shown in Figure 4.11.

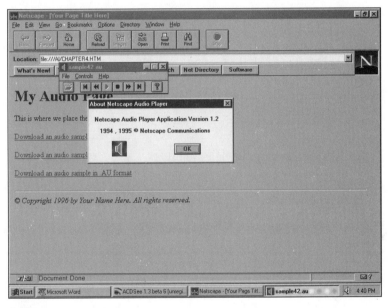

Figure 4.11

Windows Version 1.2 of Netscape's Audio Player supports AIFF and AU files, but not WAV files.

1. Modify the code from your base page.

Utilize the code from the previous tutorial and add the following <A HREF> links:

Replace the line

```
<P><A HREF="a_sample.aiff">Audio Sample</A></P>
```

with a new line:

```
<P><A HREF="sample42.aiff">Download an audio sample in AIFF
 format</A></P>
```

Then, add these two lines:

```
<P><A HREF="sample42.wav">Download an audio sample in WAV
 format</A></P>
<P><A HREF="sample42.au'>Download an audio sample in AU format
 </A></P>
```

The resulting code should look like this:

```
<HTML>
<HEAD>
<TITLE>Your Page Title Here</TITLE>
</HEAD>
<BODY>
<H1>My Audio Page.</H1>
<P> This is where we place the content of the page.</P>
<P><A HREF="sample42.aiff">Download an audio sample in AIFF
 format</A></P>
<P><A HREF="sample42.wav'>Download an audio sample in WAV
 format</A></P>
<P><A HREF="sample42.au">Download an audio sample in AU format
 </A></P>
<HR>
<ADDRESS>&#169  Copyright 1996 by Your Name Here.  All rights
 reserved.
</ADDRESS>
</BODY>
</HTML>
```

Save the file and view it (Figure 4.12) with your browser.

Of course, the actual files are not yet available for download. If you already have a file conversion tool or AIFF editor that can export WAV and AU formats, you may use it to complete the next step. If you don't

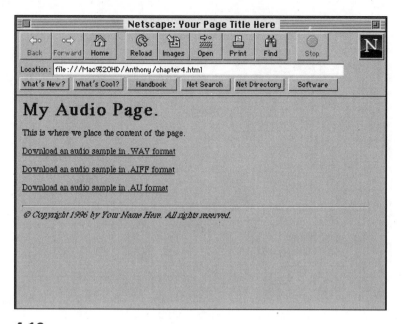

Figure 4.12

Three clearly labeled file formats available for download.

have a means to convert the files, we provided some help for you. The Incredible Sound Resource CD-ROM has an evaluation "save-disabled" version of Sound Edit 16 on it. You can install the software to your system and use it to convert the files. Be aware that you can't actually *save* the files. This may seem inconvenient, but it is a fantastic way to complete the tutorials and test a great software package at the same time. Also, if you purchase Sound Edit 16, you'll already be somewhat familiar with it. We provided *saved* versions of the files on the CD-ROM (and on the Web site) so you can complete the next part of the tutorial.

(Check the Incredible Sound Resource CD-ROM appendix at the back of the book for a list of other shareware conversion utilities included on the CD-ROM.)

2. Retrieve the sample file in AIFF, WAV, and AU formats.

Retrieve the prepared files from the Incredible Sound Resource CD-ROM. From the tutorial folder, copy the files "sample42.aiff", "sample42.wav", and "sample42.au", and place them in the same location as your HTML document.

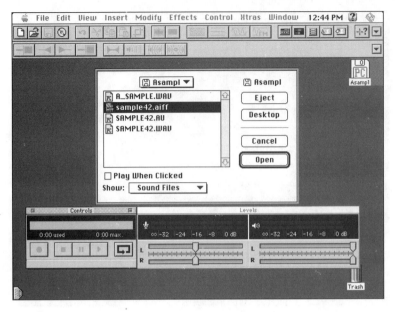

Figure 4.13

The Open File dialog box within Sound Edit 16. Many other AIFF editors have similar capabilities.

3. Convert an AIFF file to WAV and AU formats (Optional).

Use Sound Edit 16 (or similar conversion program) to open the file "sample42.aiff". Sound Edit 16 will need to be installed on you system prior to completing this step. Click on "File|Open" (Figure 4.13). Select the file "sample42.aiff" from the tutorial folder of the CD-ROM.

Once the "sample42.aiff" file is opened, test-play it once (Figure 4.14) to verify that you have the correct file (plus, it's fun to listen to new stuff).

Click on "File|Save As" and select the WAV option under "File Save Type" (Figure 4.15).

Name the new file "sample42.wav" and place it in the same folder as your HTML document.

> **Important Note:** The evaluation copy of Sound Edit 16 from The Incredible Sound Resource CD-ROM is "save-disabled." You will not be able to complete the "save" operation. Use the pre-converted files mentioned in Step 2 of this tutorial.

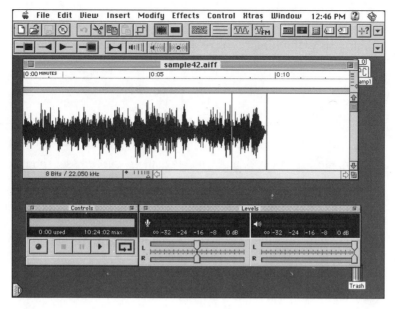

Figure 4.14

A sample audio file in AIFF format. Notice the status bar in the lower left-hand corner showing sample resolution and bit depth.

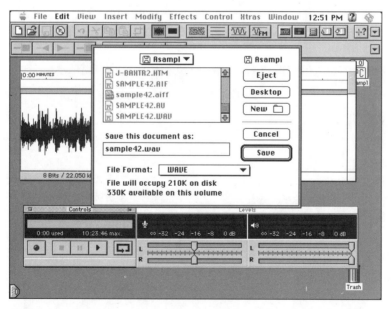

Figure 4.15

In addition to being a full-featured audio editor, Sound Edit 16 makes file conversions very easy.

Repeat the above steps to create the AU version of the file, or, if you think you've got the hang of it, you can utilize the pre-converted "sample42.au" file.

4. Test the links.

Open your Web browser and load the file named "chapter4.html". Test each of the three "Download Audio Sample" text links displayed in your browser. You should see a file being downloaded, then your browser should play, or launch a helper application to play the file. Depending on how you set up your browser, each file format may be played by a different helper application.

If you hear all three types of audio, congratulations! The easy part is over.

If your browser doesn't play one of the files, check your code. Make sure that you named and converted the files correctly, and that your browser is configured to play each of the file formats.

Conclusion

If you want to post the above tutorial page on the Web, I *strongly recommend* adding an additional line of text for each sample. This additional line should

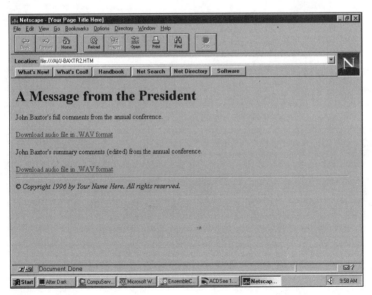

Figure 4.16

Which version of the file would you choose to download? How much time do you have? How long will it take?

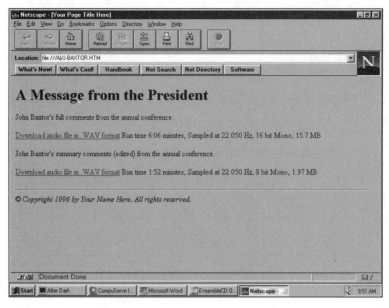

Figure 4.17

Now you can make an informed decision. This type of detail will improve visitor satisfaction with your Web site.

state the file size, run time, and sample resolution. Look at it Figure 4.16) from the perspective of a Web surfer visiting your site.

Compare Figure 4.16 to the screen shown in Figure 4.17.

An Alternative to Downloading

Downloadable audio is relatively quick and easy to add to a Web page, but there are limitations in size and functionality.

Build A ToolVox Page

In this tutorial, we will build a ToolVox-enabled site. ToolVox blurs the line between downloadable and streamed audio. The developers at Voxware (Figure 4.18) advertise it as a streamed audio solution, but how well it streams and the resulting quality depends on several factors, many of which are beyond your control.

The ToolVox Web System is free; there is no charge for the Web Player or the Encoder. Right now, while everyone is trying to establish a defacto standard on the Web, he or she who has the greatest install base wins. (at

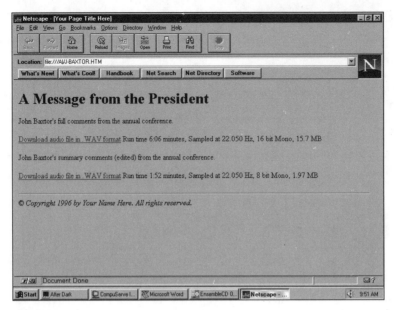

Figure 4.18

The ToolVox Web site at http://www/toolvox.com. Look to ToolVox to play an increasingly visible role in the proliferation of audio capabilities on the Web.

least, that's what they think will happen). The ToolVox Player is installed on a user's system to allow them to play VOX files and the ToolVox Encoder is used to compress audio files into the VOX file format. Before we begin, you will need to download the ToolVox Player and Encoder from the Voxware Web site. The address is:

```
http://www.voxware.com/
```

At press time, Voxware provides players for Windows 3.1, Windows 95/NT (32-bit version), and Macintosh System 7 in both 68xx and PowerPC versions. Compatibility with Netscape's browser, as well as with several others, is assured. Since the players tend to be improved and updated very frequently, we chose not to include them on the CD-ROM. Rather, visit their web site to download the latest version. Follow their installation instructions to configure your browser for VOX audio files.

Voxware developed a "metavoice compression technology" which works very well with audio files that contain spoken-voice, and *do not* contain background noise, or music. The encoder can deliver compression of up to 53:1, which is pretty darn impressive. In our last example of John

Baxtor's spoken comments, we could have delivered far more information in a much shorter period of time with this type of audio format.

No server software is required, but your Web master will have to add a line to the configuration directory of the server before you can play VOX files from your Web site. This procedure varies by server (contact your Web master or check your server's documentation). You should generally add this line to the "MIME.TYPES" file in the configuration directory:

```
audio/voxware vox
```

This entry instructs the server that any file with a .VOX extension is a compressed ToolVox file. The server will then notify the browser, which will call ToolVox to handle the data that is being downloaded.

1. To embed a VOX file in a Web page (Figures 4.19 and 4.20), use the standard <A HREF> tag. Open your "chapter4.html" working file and insert the line

```
<P><A HREF="baxtor1.vox">Listen to John Baxtor's comments</A>
with
<I>ToolVox.</I></P>
```

into the base code as follows:

```
<HTML>
<HEAD>
<TITLE>Your Page Title Here</TITLE>
</HEAD>
<BODY>
<H1>My Audio Page.</H1>
<P> This is where we place the content of the page.</P>
<P><A HREF="baxtor1.vox">Listen to John Baxtor's comments</A>
 with <I>ToolVox.</I></P>
<P><A HREF="sample42.wav">Download an audio sample in WAV
 format</A></P>
<P><A HREF="sample42.aif">Download an audio sample in AIFF
 format</A></P>
<P><A HREF="sample42.au">Download an audio sample in AU format<A>
 </P>
<HR>
<ADDRESS>&#169  Copyright 1996 by Your Name Here.  All rights
 reserved.
</ADDRESS>
</BODY>
</HTML>
```

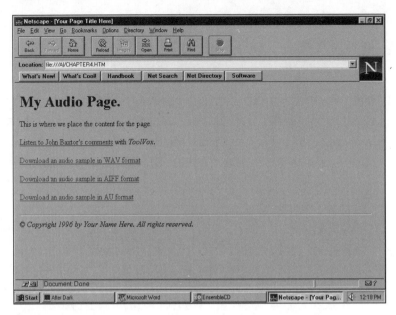

Figure 4.19

The sample page with a VOX file option added, viewed in Netscape on a PC. Just as with other file formats, VOX files require the browser to be configured with a player.

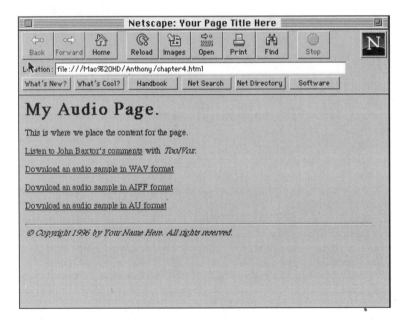

Figure 4.20

The same sample page with a VOX file option added, viewed in Netscape on a Mac.

2. Place the encoded .VOX file.

If you want to take the easy route, or if you don't have the ToolVox Encoder for the Web, we've already prepared a VOX-compressed file for you to use during this step. The file is on the CD-ROM in the tutorials subdirectory/folder, and is named "baxtor1.vox". It is a speech-only file, for which the VOX compression is best suited.

Copy the file "baxtor1.vox" and place it in the same location as your working HTML page.

3. Encode your own VOX file (optional).

If you're interested or ambitious, here's how to encode your own VOX file:

The encoder is designed primarily for speech-only audio capabilities. It uses special algorithms to reproduce only the most important parts of the human voice (singing or speaking). By discarding the less-important data, it can compress the remaining data to between 1/20th and 1/53rd of its original size. This is one of the best audio compression ratios available for the Web. Unfortunately, audio quality is also reduced. Here are some techniques that will help minimize the adverse affects of compression:

- Record with a microphone that has a flat frequency response.

- Use proper microphone positioning when recording to avoid "pops" from consonants like p, b, t, etc. These pops affect your compression results.

- Record in a quiet place with no background noise. Voxware compression focuses on the human voice. Ambient noise degrades your compression results.

- Start with a high quality recording sample. As with any compression technique, it will never get better—it will always get worse.

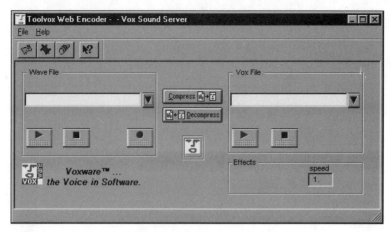

Figure 4.21

The Windows version of the ToolVox Encoder. It's very simple and easy-to-use.

The encoder (Figure 4.21) is a simple utility that allows you to record directly into .VOX format, or import WAV or AIFF for compression. It requires a mono (not stereo) file and automatically samples the file down to 8 kHz.

(If you are working on a Mac, skip the next two paragraphs for the Mac version of this tutorial.)

Once you download and install the ToolVox Encoder for Windows, open the "README.DOC" file for complete encoder instructions and system requirements.

The rest is pretty simple. Record or import a WAV audio file. Click on "compress." You will see a confirmation screen (Figure 4.22) warning you about the effects of down-sampling an audio file (consider this a disclaimer).

Once you download and install the ToolVox Encoder for Macintosh, open the "README.TXT" file for complete encoder instructions and system requirements.

This is pretty simple. Record or import an AIFF audio file. Click on "compress." You will see a confirmation screen warning you about the effects of down-sampling an audio file (consider this a disclaimer).

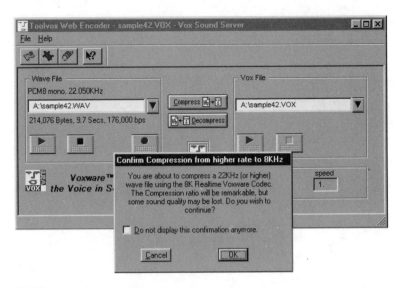

Figure 4.22

You are clearly warned to expect a loss in audio quality.

Conclusion

Once completed, you can use the same control panel to listen to both the original and newly created VOX file side-by-side. This is convenient, but it tends to emphasize the loss of quality. Keep this in perspective. With the bandwidth realities of today, I'll gladly sacrifice some quality if my overall message is enhanced. Now, I know there are many sound designers and engineers out there who'll be appalled at the resulting .VOX file. They'll cry, "It's horrible! My beautiful 44 kHz recording is ruined!"

My response? "Get a life." *You* know what the original file sounds like, but nobody visiting your Web site knows what it sounds like. They'll accept what they hear. This is an issue of *perception threshold*. We've never heard 44 kHz quality over the Web, and I doubt too many other people have either. So compared to what is generally available (which is usually nothing), the VOX quality is a significant improvement over "silence".

For kicks, sample a few small music files. You can't really use the resulting .VOX files, but they are entertaining. For instance, if you don't like your boss very much, copy his or her computer system sounds, VOX them, and replace them back on his or her system. Buy some popcorn and watch the facial expressions. Lots of fun.

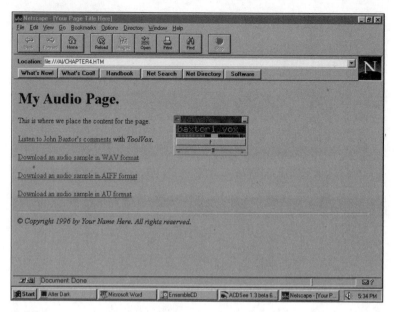

Figure 4.23

Netscape spawns the ToolVox for Windows 95 Player.

1. Test the link.

Open your Web browser and load the file "chapter4.html". Click on John Baxtor's text link, and you should see your browser launch the ToolVox Player (Figure 4.23). If you hear audio, congratulations! You're ready to "stream" in public.

If your browser didn't play the file, check your code. Make sure that you converted, named, and placed the file correctly, and that your browser is configured to play .VOX files.

2. If you incorporate ToolVox audio capabilities into your Web pages, alert your visitors that they need the ToolVox Player to hear the audio. Download the ToolVox logo and create a link to its page at http://www.voxware.com.

ADD SOUND WITH SHOCKWAVE

One of the most exciting developments for the World Wide Web is accessibility of interactive content through Macromedia's Shockwave. (Their Web site is shown in Figure 4.24.) Macromedia is arguably the world leader in interactive authoring tools. Its flagship products, Director

Figure 4.24

Macromedia's Shockwave Web site at http://www.macromedia.com/
Tools/Shockwave/. These plug-ins are a "must" addition to your browsers.

and Authorware, provide professional interactive development
capabilities for a large percent of interactive developers around the world.
Now, with Shockwave, the same interactive capabilities can be delivered
over the Web.

Shockwave currently lets anyone using Netscape's Navigator 2.0 (or above)
view interactive multimedia including animations and sounds. Developers
who use one of Macromedia's authoring tools — Director 4.04, Freehand,

or Authorware 3.5 for Windows or Macintosh — can create a "Shocked" piece for the Web. Simply create the piece (keep in mind inherent bandwidth limitations), compress it using Afterburner (Macromedia's compression utility for Web delivery), link your HTML code, and upload it all to your site.

In this tutorial, we will not teach you how to use Director, Freehand or Authorware, nor will we go through the Afterburner compression process. Complete details on Afterburner and Shockwave can be found by visiting Macromedia's Web page at:

```
http://www.macromedia.com/Tools/Shockwave/Info
```

The process is very simple. Visit its site and download the free Shockwave plug-ins and Afterburner utilities. Once your plug-ins are installed, visit some "Shocked" sites. Macromedia's site includes a directory of very cool "Shocked" sites. Remember, you'll need a separate version of the Shockwave plug-in for each type of "Shocked" application—Director, Freehand, and Authorware. They're all free, so I suggest getting them all.

After you've seen what a "Shocked" site can do, you'll appreciate the vast capabilities opening for the Web. It helps to keep your ambitions small now, but the capabilities are here, and sound can be an integrated part of it all.

1.   Get a Director, Freehand, or Authorware "sample."
If you're already familiar with using one of these tools to program, build, or borrow something small and quick *with sound integrated into it,* save it and compress it with Afterburner. It will now be even smaller and platform independent (Web-ready).

If you do not have access to a home-grown sample, access the Incredible Sound Resource CD-ROM, look in the tutorial folder or subdirectory, retrieve the file named "buttons.dcr", and put it into your working directory. This sample Director file has already been compressed with Afterburner and will work on both PC and Mac systems.

Insert the line

```
<EMBED SRC="buttons.dcr" width=200 height=75>
```

into the base code like this:

```
<HTML>
<HEAD>
<TITLE>Your Page Title Here</TITLE>
</HEAD>
<BODY>
<H1>My Audio Page.</H1>
<P> This is where we place the content of the page.</P>
<EMBED SRC="buttons.dcr" width=200 height=100>
<HR>
<ADDRESS>&#169  Copyright 1996 by Your Name Here.  All rights
 reserved.
</ADDRESS>
</BODY>
</HTML>
```

Save the file and test it with your Netscape 2.0 (or above) browser. Remember, you must have the Director plug-in properly installed for your browser to display a "Shocked" Director movie. ("Movie" is an established term for any application or animation built with Director. As our example demonstrates, a Director "movie" doesn't have to be a movie at all. (See Figure 4.25.))

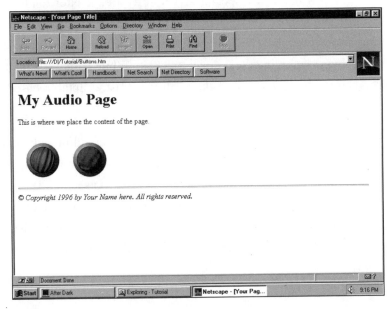

Figure 4.25

This simple Director movie demonstrates interactive audio capabilities via Shockwaves.

2. Test the link.

Open your Netscape browser and load the working HTML file. Click on each of the buttons to hear the corresponding audio. If you hear audio, congratulations! You're ready to "Shock" your Web site.

Sound is easily integrated with these authoring tools for audible interactivity on the Web. If your browser didn't play the file, check your code. Make sure that you "Afterburned," named, and placed the file correctly, and that your browser is configured to play "Shocked" files.

Conclusion

You should now know how to make downloadable audio available through your Web pages. The importance of clearly labeled, multiple formats is obvious given the existence of different platform and playback configurations. Always label the selection's run time, sample rate, and file size, so visitors to your Web site know what they are downloading.

Voxware's ToolVox allows very easy, speech-only streamed audio through your Web site without any special server software. Better quality can be achieved after compression by starting with a clean original recording under studio quality conditions. The ToolVox Encoder only compresses mono-channel samples, always sampling them down to 8 kHz. While compression data loss affects the quality, *you* decide if the quality loss is acceptable based on the nature of your Web page.

Macromedia's Shockwave plug-ins for Netscape browsers allow audio-enhanced interactivity from any Director-, Freehand- or Authorware-developed application. If you don't have experience with, or access to these tools, don't despair. They are used by more interactive developers than all other development tools combined. Visit the Sound Advice Web Site (http://www.monsoon.org/sound_advice) for links to freelance Macromedia content and application developers.

Chapter 5

Anthony Helmstetter

Anthony Helmstetter

Key Topics:

- **Discover streamed audio with TrueSpeech**

- **Use MPEG compressed audio with Streamworks**

- **Create high quality streamed audio with RealAudio**

More About Streamed Audio

In Chapter 4, I explored several options for downloadable audio, and began to explore streamed *speech-only* audio via ToolVox. There are, however, several other options currently available on the Web for spoken voice and musical-streamed audio. In this chapter, I'll compare several of these technologies.

DSP TrueSpeech

TrueSpeech is a family of high-quality, low bit rate speech compression algorithms developed by DSP Group. Several different versions of TrueSpeech are available for licensing at compression rates from 8.5 K'bps through 3.7 Kbps. All offer excellent communications over a 14.4 Kbps or better modem.TrueSpeech has been licensed for a variety of multimedia and communications applications by Microsoft, Intel, NEC, AT&T, Creative Labs, US Robotics, and other heavy hitters.

Internet audio applications are rapidly emerging as a major market for TrueSpeech. TrueSpeech G.723, its highest-quality speech compression technology, operates at 6.3 Kbps and 5.3 Kbps, and is the voice compression standard approved by the *International Telecommunications Union (ITU)*. (Note: The ITU is an international organization chartered by the United Nations to formulate worldwide communications standards.) G.723 is intended to standardize video conferencing/telephony over public telephone networks, and is part of the overall H.324 video conferencing standard.

Intel, Microsoft, and over 100 other companies have supported the ITU H.324 standard for Internet communications. VDOnet, NetSpeak (makers of WebPhone Internet telephone), and Telescape have all licensed TrueSpeech to allow real-time, two-way communications on the Internet. Numerous other Internet video conferencing, chat, voicemail, and on-demand audio companies are in the process of adopting TrueSpeech for their Internet audio applications. Suffice it to say, this company is here for the long haul.

DSP Group also developed TrueSpeech 8.5. With its slightly lower voice quality and compression, TrueSpeech 8.5 requires only about half the MIPS (million instructions per second) and program memory as TrueSpeech G.723. The lower complexity 8.5 speech encoder (15:1 compression) is an integral part of Microsoft Windows 95. This gives automatic player compatibility to a vast number of Windows 95 Web surfers. The player enables TrueSpeech-encoded audio to be played in realtime over the Internet without the need for special server software. This is a real "plus" when compared to the cost and hassle of other server-supported streamed audio applications. Like other streaming solutions, a large audio file can begin to play instantly rather than waiting for a lengthy download.

Currently, TrueSpeech audio files can be created from standard WAV files by using *Sound Recorder* for Windows 95 and Windows NT, and can also be played using the Windows *Media Player*.

A free *TrueSpeech Internet Player* and wave audio encoder can be downloaded from the DSP Group's Web site at http://www.dspg.com or http://

www.truespeech.com (Figure 5.1). Windows 3.xx users will want to download the *TrueSpeech Converter* and also consider the *TrueSpeech DOS Batch Converter* for larger projects. Players are also available for Macintosh and PowerMac. At the time of this writing, the Mac encoder was not yet available. To download the TrueSpeech icon for use on your page, go to http://www.dspg.com/gif/tiny040.gif.

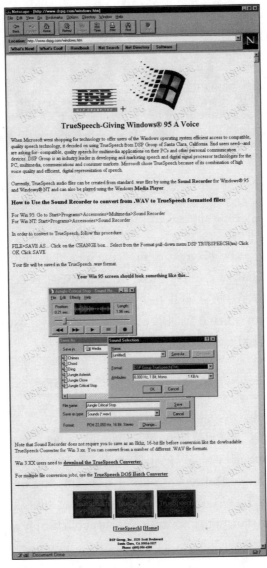

Figure 5.1

DSP TrueSpeech at http://www.truespeech.com.

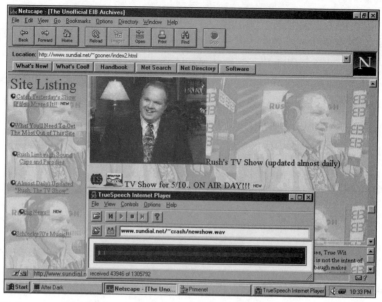

Figure 5.2

Regardless of your political orientation, this unofficial Limbaugh Web page makes good use of speech and music with TrueSpeech. (http://www.sundial.net/~gooner/index2.html)

If you use Netscape Navigator, the TrueSpeech installation program will automatically configure your browser to use the TrueSpeech player. Otherwise, configure your Web browser to "view" files with the extension .TSP by associating them with the TrueSpeech Player (TSPlayer.exe or TSPlay32.exe). The Web page in Figure 5.2 makes good use of sound.

CREATE A TRUESPEECH WEB PAGE

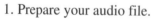

1. Prepare your audio file.

Create a PCM (Pulse Code Modulation)—encoded audio .WAV file at 8 kHz sampling rate and 16-bits resolution. The TrueSpeech compression algorithm has been optimized for this sampling frequency. Recording amplitude should be held to a maximum of 14 bits so that clipping will not occur. (For more information about audio file preparation, see Chapter 10.) It is essential that you record with these settings for highest quality. (Note: Don't let the name fool you. TrueSpeech is optimized for voice delivery, but it can handle music files as well.)

2. Convert your file to a TrueSpeech-encoded .WAV file.

An easy way to convert PCM-encoded .WAV files to TrueSpeech-encoded .WAV files is with the Sound System of Windows 95 or NT, since the encoder is already located there. In Windows 95, the Sound Recorder is located at:

`START>PROGRAMS>ACCESSORIES>MULTIMEDIA>SOUND RECORDER.`

While in the Sound Recorder, simply open the PCM-encoded .WAV file created in Step 1 above; select the TrueSpeech format; use the SAVE AS command to create a new file name with a .WAV extension; change the file type to DSP Group TrueSpeech; and SAVE. The new .WAV file has now been encoded in TrueSpeech audio format, which is compressed by a factor of 15 from the original .WAV file. (For those who are using Windows 3.11, use the PCM to TrueSpeech Conversion utility. This conversion utility will accept PCM .WAV files only if sampled at 8kHz/16-bit PCM format.)

3. Create a pointer text file.

For each audio file, you will need a simple text file (*.TSP) which is associated with the *.WAV file created above. Use a standard text editor such as Notepad, and give this file the *.TSP extension (* is the chosen name of your file). This is done so that the browser will know to launch the TrueSpeech Player when a TrueSpeech-encoded .WAV file is about to be transmitted. The *.TSP file associated with a TrueSpeech-encoded .WAV file should contain the (case sensitive) HTML line:

`TSIP>>URL/*.wav`

The URL above should *not* include the "HTTP://" characters. For example, www.yourpage.com would be appropriate and HTTP://www.yourpage.com would not work. Let's suppose you create a PCM-encoded .WAV file and convert it to a TrueSpeech-encoded .WAV file. Let's give this file the name:

`test_ts.wav.`

Next, suppose that this file is located on your server in the directory www.yourpage.com/audio/testfiles. It is now necessary to create a one-line TSP text file. This ASCII text file should contain the following line:

```
TSIP>>www.yourpage.com/audio/testfiles/test_ts.wav.
```

Now, let's name and save this file as "sample.tsp."

4. Link the *.TSP file into your page.

This .TSP text file should now be referenced on your page. Continuing the example from Step 3, let's assume the sample.tsp file was located in the directory www.yourpage.com/audio/tspfiles. Add one line of HTML code to your Web page to reference this line. This line should look like:

```
<A HREF="www.yourpage.com/audio/tspfiles/sample.tsp">
    SAMPLE.TSP</A>
```

Once a user selects the TrueSpeech audio pointed to in the line above, the sample.tsp file will be sent to the browser. The browser, after initial setup, associates the TrueSpeech Player with the .TSP extension. Upon spawning the player, the TrueSpeech Player reads the location of the TrueSpeech test_ts.wav file from the sample.tsp file. The Player then accesses and plays this test_ts.wav file as it is downloaded. Got it?

5. Set up the server.

If your home page is located on a remote HTTP server, contact your service provider and have your provider configure its server as described below.

Configure the server to accept the .TSP file extension. Because the "TSP" file extension may not be recognized by HTTP servers running on Unix or Windows, it should be mapped in the configuration of the server to MIME type "application/dsptype." To do this on Unix servers, only one line should be added in the HTTP server configuration file MIME.TYPE as follows:

```
application/dsptype tsp
```

On the CERN HTTP Server, the configuration line should read:

```
AddType.tsp      application/dsptype      binary 1.0
```

For Windows-based HTTP servers, registration is performed through the configuration file or control panel. You may need to contact your server system administrator or service provider to have them add it for you. Once this is done, restart the server so that the change will take effect. You have now enabled your page to support the TrueSpeech Plug-in (Figure 5.3).

Streamed Audio (And Video) With *StreamWorks*

StreamWorks, developed by *Xing Technology Corporation*, was the first commercially available, low-cost solution for World Wide Web and local network delivery of live and on-demand video+audio. The National Broadcast Company (NBC) has broadly deployed StreamWorks technology (Figure 5.4 shows their home page) for broadcast delivery of financial news programming to subscribers in the US and Europe. While the company emphasizes its MPEG video compression and delivery capabilities, the same technology is utilized for delivery of high-quality compressed MPEG audio, without video.

The actual characteristics of the streams are different, but they fall into three general definitions:

1. Audio-only streams

2. Video-only streams

3. System (audio+video) streams

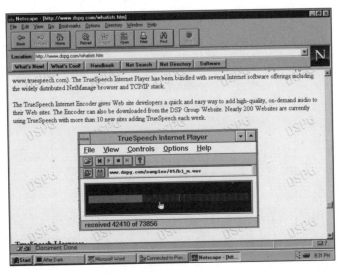

Figure 5.3
The TrueSpeech Internet Player.

For our purposes, we will limit ourselves to the relevant audio-only issues.

StreamWorks was developed as a client-server media distribution architecture that can operate independently or complement existing World Wide Web, HTTP/HTML architectures on local area networks, wide area networks, and the Internet. The system consists of encoder, client, and server software components that collectively combine on-demand (streamed), as well as *live* audio+video.

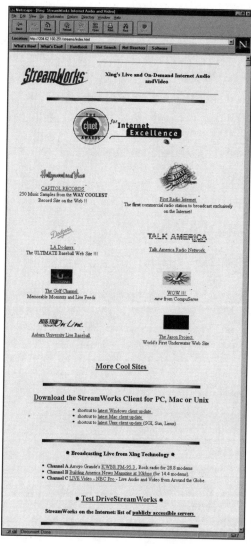

Figure 5.4

The StreamWorks home page at http://www.xingtech com.

Web Developer's Guide to Sound and Music

When you install the StreamWorks client (player) software, it will work in conjunction with your browser as a helper application. In simple terms, when you browse a Web site that has links to a StreamWorks stream, links to an .XDM file will establish a connection between your StreamWorks player and the StreamWorks server, and then the stream begins. You need an Internet connection that supports UDP sockets and transmission of UDP data. Users of Netscape and Mosaic typically have such connections, but users accessing the Web through an on-line service (e.g., AOL), may have to get additional software from their service providers. Any SLIP or PPP account should work. Generally, the faster the modem connection, the better the stream will play.

If all this sounds exciting so far, let me throw a bit of potentially cold water on you. Remarkably, all the other audio delivery techniques we have explored so far have been free. StreamWorks is not. And the bandwidth and server requirements are significantly more demanding than what your local service provider may be willing, or able, to accommodate.

The Cost of Bandwidth— How Much Is Too Much?

This may get a bit technical. Here's an issue we're all concerned about: How much bandwidth will all this data consume? StreamWorks has several common bit rates for streamed audio:

- 8.5 Kbps—referred to as Low Bit Rate (LBR) format, this produces 8 kHz mono audio-only at AM radio quality.

- 24 Kbps—an MPEG audio format that produces 16/22 kHz mono audio. It's better than AM radio quality, but not quite FM quality.

- 56 Kbps—an MPEG audio format that produces 32/44 kHz mono or 16/22 kHz stereo audio only at approximately FM radio quality.

Other bit rates are possible, because the StreamWorks server has the ability to recode pre-recorded streams on-the-fly; e.g., a 112 Kbps audio stream can be reduced to as low as 32 Kbps, a 112 Kbps video stream can be reduced to as low as 40 Kbps, and a 24 Kbps or 56 Kbps stream can be reduced to as low as 16 Kbps. The amount of Internet bandwidth consumed will depend on the sum of the bit rates of all streams concurrently delivered, with two important notes:

- The StreamWorks server has the ability to limit the total consumed bandwidth by setting a maximum amount of simultaneous streams, maximum bit rate per stream, and maximum aggregate bit rate.

- Any StreamWorks server has the ability to feed other StreamWorks servers, which can then take one originating stream and deliver it to many simultaneous users. As a result, actual Internet backbone traffic may be significantly less than the total bit rate delivered to all simultaneous users.

In the worst case (without the benefit of fanout propagation), a T1 connection of 1.544 Mbps can support a maximum of approximately 165 LBR (8.5 Kbps) streams, 60 MBR (24 Kbps) streams, 25 1-B ISDN streams, or 12 2-B ISDN streams. However, with fanout propagation, a StreamWorks server can reach a much larger set of users.

Typically, you will need an Internet Web site with an SGI, Sparc, HP, or Linux Web server (NT was under development, and may be completed by the time you read this). When you purchase the StreamWorks server software, you can provide on-demand audio and video streams. If you add StreamWorks stream generators (encoders), your server will be able to deliver *live* streams as well.

Understand that this is a competitive market and pricing can change overnight. The Windows, XWindows, and Mac/Power Mac Internet Client (player) software is freely distributed, but registration is required for Xing technical support. At the time of this writing, StreamWorks network server software ranged in price from $3,500 to $50,000 depending on total capacity desired. The audio-only stream generator (encoder) costs $2,500. Current pricing can be obtained by contacting Xing Technologies at streams@xingtech.com or http://www.xingtech.com.

At the very least, download the player and visit the StreamWorks links page to explore other StreamWorks sites.

Progressive Networks' *RealAudio* Revolution

Generally deemed one of the oldest and most reliable streamed audio options for the Web, RealAudio required a greater investment in financial, bandwidth, and server resources compared to some of the speech-only streaming techniques. Your decision to implement this type of audio delivery solution will not likely be made by simply reading this book. Rather, you will gain an insight as to the options, the pros and cons, various levels of quality, and associated costs. But if you want to visit a good audio site, a RealAudio site is a good bet.

To complement its existing big-bandwidth, 100+ simultaneous stream solutions, RealAudio recently announced several new products and programs to ease the sting of implementing RealAudio capabilities. As with all information about the Web, it is subject to rampant change and revision. Visit the RealAudio home page at http://www/realaudio.com for the latest information on its Easy Start and Personal Server products.

The RealAudio Easy Start Program

Typically, we would not bother mentioning this type of a "promotional" offering, since availability and price can change at any time. By the time you read this, this offer may no longer exist. But the point is clear; Progressive Networks is working to make RealAudio easier for everyone to implement for the Web. The current offer costs under $500 and includes:

- RealAudio Server 2.0 (with a five-stream license). This product delivers realtime audio and synchronized multimedia over the Internet or your company network without download delays.

- RealAudio Encoder 2.0. This allows you to compress audio for live or on-demand playback.

- A 70 percent discount on upgrades.

- Your Web site listed in *Timecast: The RealAudio Guide.* Timecast, the guide to RealAudio on the Internet, receives thousands of visitors daily.

- A 30-Day money-back guarantee. If you are not completely satisfied, return the software within 30 days for a full refund.

This is a significant improvement in accessibility for the average Joe compared to the options only a few months ago! Read on to learn how the RealAudio system works, then check its current offerings before you decide if it's right for your Web project.

The RealAudio Personal Server

With this recent announcement from Progressive Networks, you don't have to be a large company or have a lot of money, to deliver RealAudio audio to Internet users. Now *individuals* can join the RealAudio broadcasting world! With *the RealAudio Personal Server* (currently available for beta testing), you can do it right from your desktop or personal Web page!

The RealAudio Personal Server supports two external streams and one local stream. This means that both you and two other people can listen to sound clips concurrently, in real-time, without download delays. The Personal Server runs on the Windows 95, Windows NT, and Mac OS 7.5.x platforms, and includes instant access to the RealAudio Encoder for encoding audio files in RealAudio format. A graphical user interface allows you to monitor who's listening and what they're listening to.

The release version of the RealAudio Personal Server will have a suggested retail price of $99. To be part of the RealAudio Personal Server beta test program, you will need:

- A multimedia PC running Windows 95, Windows NT, or Mac OS

- Connectivity to a network that supports TCP/IP (Internet, dialup, LAN)

Overview of the RealAudio System

Users of the RealAudio Player typically gain access to audio content via the World Wide Web. References to RealAudio files are embedded in HTML documents served by a Web server. The method of interaction with the Personal Server is shown in Figure 5.5.

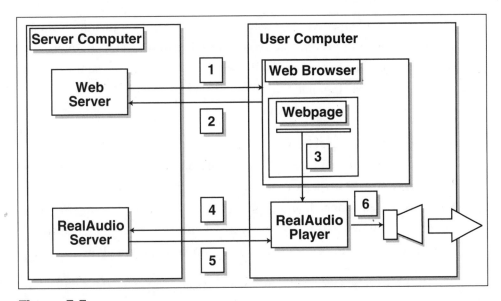

Figure 5.5

Information flow between server and Web browser when activating RealAudio files.

When the user clicks on a RealAudio link, a metafile referenced by the HTML document on your Web page is accessed. The metafile is a document that contains the URL location of the audio file on your Personal Server. The URL information is sent by the Web server (1) to the user's browser (2), and then to the RealAudio Player (3). The RealAudio Player requests the audio file from the Personal Server (4), which streams the audio file to the Player (5), where it is buffered and then played (6).

There is virtually no time delay between the user clicking and the audio starting to play. The RealAudio Personal Server opens the requested audio file and sends it bit by bit in real time to the user's computer, where it is uncompressed and played through the local sound system. The RealAudio Player maintains communication with the Personal Server, allowing the user to control the audio stream like he or she would with a CD.

The RealAudio Personal Server Setup

The RealAudio Personal Server System contains the RealAudio Player, the RealAudio Personal Server, and the RealAudio Encoder.

The RealAudio Player lets you listen to audio streams originating from any RealAudio Personal Server. Once you've installed the Player, you simply click on a RealAudio file to activate the Player and start playing the audio clip. The Player window has familiar control buttons similar to a CD player, allowing users to immediately identify volume, start, stop, and pause controls.

The RealAudio Personal Server is a sophisticated piece of software that runs on Windows 95 and Windows NT platforms, and allows audio streams to be sent over a TCP/IP network to users of the RealAudio Player. The Personal Server is started, stopped, and configured through a user-friendly Windows interface. It allows two remote network clients to connect simultaneously. The Personal Server operates in a manner similar to Internet Web servers.

The RealAudio Encoder enables users and Personal Server operators to capture, edit, and encode standard PC and UNIX audio files into the RealAudio format. RealAudio files containing compressed audio data can be streamed by the Personal Server in real time over low bandwidth connections, such as 14.4 Kbps modem connections.

The RealAudio Personal Server and its accompanying encoding tools enable you to create and deliver RealAudio content. The number of simultaneous users who can listen to content sent from your Personal Server at any given time is called the "number of streams." Personal Servers can deliver two streams to clients connected through a network or over the Internet (each audio stream requires 10 Kbits per second of network bandwidth).

System and Bandwidth Requirements

The RealAudio Personal Server is currently available for use on personal computers with a Pentium processor running the Windows 95 or Windows NT operating system.

The RealAudio Player only requires approximately 10 Kbps, a need easily met by a 14.4 Kbps modem [Kbps means kilobits per second, not to be confused with kilo*bytes* per second, which is 10 times as much (8 bits = byte + start + stop bits)]. The Personal Server requires at least that bandwidth to the Internet backbone for each client connected. Therefore, a 56 Kbps leased line or a T1 line could easily accommodate simultaneous connections.

Web Server Compatibility

Users will normally access RealAudio files via links embedded in your World Wide Web pages. Your Web service must have PPP/SLIP connection capabilities. The server will also need to be configured to recognize the RealAudio MIME types. In general, the Personal Server can be configured to work with any Web server which supports configurable MIME types.

The RealAudio Personal Server is best suited to operate in conjunction with a Web server on the same system. However, it may also be used with a Web server that is accessed through a dialup connection, or it can send audio files across a Local Area Net work (LAN). Each of these situations requires a different setup for the Personal Server.

Creating RealAudio Files

The RealAudio Encoder puts sound files through advanced compression while preparing them for use with the RealAudio Personal Server, resulting in a loss of some sound information. To compensate for this, you must start with a high-quality recording. Satellite signals, Digital Audio Tapes (DATs), or compact discs (CDs), for example, will result in much higher quality RealAudio files. The input file should be 16 bit (rather than 8 bit), and *must use the full range of available amplitude.*

Pre-processing the sound file before encoding also contributes to higher quality sound. For an in-depth explanation about pre-processing audio, see Chapter 10. Or, see the RealAudio Personal Server Technical Notes in Section 3, available from the RealAudio Web site.

If the full amplitude range is not used, the RealAudio files will sound rough. To adjust for this, use your audio editor's "Increase Amplitude" or "Increase Volume" command to adjust the range before encoding the file. Better sound editors have a "Normalize" function that will maximize levels automatically.

Keep in mind that audio files take up a lot of disk space before they are encoded. You can use Table 5.1 to calculate how much space you will need for your recording. Once the files are encoded into the RealAudio format, they will use 60 k/minute (3.6 MB/ hour) of disk space—a significant savings over other audio formats.

Table 5.1   Audio Files Reference Table

File Type	Extension	Disk Space Required Per Minute of Audio Play Time
All Windows .WAV files,	.WAV	662 K @11 kHz, 1.32 MB @ 22 kHz
Sun 8-kilohertz .AU files (u-law)	.AU,	480 K
Sun 11-kilohertz .AU files (u-law),	.A11	660 K
Sun 22-kilohertz .AU files (u-law),	.A22	1.32 MB
Sun 44-kilohertz .AU files (u-law),	.A44	64 MB
PCM (raw 16-bit) 8-kilohertz data	.PCM	960 K
PCM (raw 16-bit) 11-kilohertz data	.P11	1.32 MB
PCM (raw 16-bit) 22-kilohertz data	.P22	2.64 MB
PCM (raw 16-bit) 44-kilohertz data	.P44	5.28 MB

Before converting a sound file to the RealAudio format, the Encoder needs information about the sampling rate used to digitize the audio into a file. Since the file itself does not contain this information, it must be attached to the file via the file extension. You may need to rename the file, using the appropriate file extension, to help the Encoder identify your file. You can also refer to Table 5.1 for file extension information.

To launch the RealAudio Encoder (Figure 5.6), pull down Tools from the menu bar of the RealAudio Personal Server and select RealAudio Encoder. The following window will appear as in Figure 5.6.

Menus used for encoding are found at the top of the Encoder window. The middle of the window is where filenames are displayed while they are encoding. The bar at the bottom of the window shows the number of files that have been encoded during the current session, and the number of files that have failed to be encoded. This bottom bar is useful when you are encoding multiple files.

Before encoding your audio file, move it to the "Audio" subdirectory below the Personal Server directory. When the file is encoded, it will then be saved

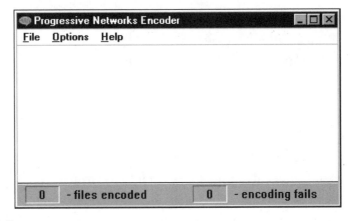

Figure 5.6

RealAudio Encoder Window.

to this same directory. RealAudio files must be located in a directory below the Personal Server in order for the Personal Server to able to locate them.

Go to the pull-down File menu and select the Encode command. The Encode window will open so you may select the audio file you wish to have converted to a RealAudio file. After you have selected the audio file and clicked on OK, the Description Window (Figure 5.7) will open so you can identify the title, author, and copyright information of the recording.

Enter the descriptive information and click on OK.

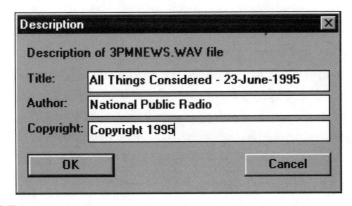

Figure 5.7

RealAudio Description Window.

Encoding time will depend upon the size of the file and the system you are using. A Pentium 90 MHz system with a 32-bit encoder can encode an audio file in 80 to 100 percent of real-time recording. A 16-bit encoder on the same system will take twice the length of the recording to encode the file. For example, a recording that plays in 30 minutes would take an hour to encode.

Once encoded, the RA files will appear in the same directory where the original files were stored. In order to access these files, you must ensure that they are stored in a folder or subdirectory beneath the base path directory, which was designated when you installed the Personal Server. The "Audio" subdirectory was set up for the purpose of storing your RealAudio encoded files, however, you can set up other folders as necessary to accommodate your audio files. These subdirectories can also use any name you choose. It is important to remember that you must either save the original audio file to this directory before encoding, thus ensuring that the encoded file is saved to this directory, or move the RealAudio file to the subdirectory after it is encoded.

Compressed audio files will require approximately 1 K (1,024 bytes) of disk space per second of audio, yielding 3.6 megabytes per hour of compressed audio.

The RealAudio files are now ready to be referenced by a metafile.

Encoding Multiple Files

You can encode multiple files simultaneously by opening the Encoder window, selecting Open from the File menu, and when the file window opens, depressing the shift key and selecting individual files with the mouse. Another way to encode multiple files is to open the Windows Explorer for Win95, select the files, and drag and drop them onto the Encoder window. This will initiate the encoding process. For multiple selections, it would save time if you have defaults set up on your Description Window to include the source and copyright information, since these items will probably be the same for all of the files selected. To set up defaults, select Defaults from the Options pull-down menu and add the appropriate information.

As the files encode, the Description Window will pop up for each file, so you can fill in the title of the file. You can still change any default information that comes up in the display by typing in the new information. This information will then be displayed in the RealAudio Player Window when the sound file is played.

The bar at the bottom of the Encoder Window will display the number of files successfully encoded, and failed encoding attempts. If a file fails the encoding procedure, a message will display on the Encoder Window saying "File filename.ra was not created." Click on OK and the encoder will continue with the next file.

Integrating RealAudio Files into Web Pages

From the HTML documents you created in the past, you know that links to other Web pages are shown in the HTML document as the URL address of the document you wish to access. Since RealAudio files are resident to the RealAudio Personal Server and can only be retrieved by the RealAudio Player, a few extra steps must be taken to complete the network path that links to the audio file.

It may be helpful if you imagine the Web page as a sheet of paper with directions to someone's house written on it. For most Web documents, you would follow the directions and arrive at the house for which you are looking. For RealAudio files, the Web page is like a sheet of paper that gives you directions to a house, and once you arrive at the house, there is another piece of paper attached to the door with a set of directions to another house, which is your actual destination. The first sheet of paper represents a metafile, represented by a .RAM extension, and the second sheet of paper on the door represents the RealAudio file, represented by an .RA extension. Instead of pointing to the audio file, your HTML document will point to this metafile. Unlike the usual HTML link, the metafile does not display information through the browser. Rather, it provides the audio file's location on the RealAudio Personal Server to the RealAudio Player. The Player uses this information to locate the file on the RealAudio Personal Server. Remember that RealAudio files cannot be referenced directly by the Web page because this will cause them to be downloaded *in their entirety* before playback. In order for the audio files to be played in real time, they must be played through a RealAudio Player, and served by a RealAudio Server.

Creating Metafiles for HTML

Metafiles are text files, with the extension .RAM, which contain lines of the form:

```
pnm://hostname/path
```

For example, the text

```
pnm://www.realaudio.com/hello1.ra
```

might be the contents of the metafile:

```
hello1.ram
```

Inserting Metafiles into Your HTML Document

To insert a reference to this .RAM file in your HTML, simply reference the metafile within a hyperlink. For example, create

```
<A HREF="http://www.realaudio.com/hello1.ram">Hello!</A>
```

and then make sure your World Wide Web server is properly configured to understand that the extension .RAM refers to the MIME type x-pn-realaudio. (Detailed instructions for a variety of Web server software are available in the RealAudio Personal Server Technical Notes, Section 5, "Configuring Web Servers for Use with RealAudio.")

You can create a metafile that contains several URLs on separate lines (with no blank lines); the Player will play those documents in sequence. In addition, a beginning point in time other than the start of the document may be specified by appending the time to the URL. For example:

```
pnm://www.realaudio.com/hello1.ra$0:30
```

This URL specifies the same audio document as before, but beginning from the 30-second mark. The dollar sign signifies that the remainder of the URL specifies a position in time. Tenths of seconds, seconds, minutes, hours, and days may be specified (tenths of seconds are separated from seconds by a decimal point; the other values are always separated by colons). The standard form is:

```
$dd:hh:mm:ss.ss
```

The time will be interpreted from right to left, so it is not necessary to put a zero into every blank field, unless you are missing an increment between two other increments. For example, if you wished to show hours and seconds, but not minutes, you would need to put a zero into the minutes space so the time is interpreted correctly.

Once your Web page is written with links to your metafiles, it will need to be placed on the Web server. You will then need to configure the Web server to recognize the RealAudio MIME type.

Configuring Web Servers For Use With RealAudio

Before the Web server will handle RealAudio metafiles properly, it must be configured to recognize files with a .RAM extension as the following MIME type:

```
audio/x-pn-realaudio
```

This MIME type is communicated in the HTML header sent to the user's Web browser. It tells the Web browser to activate the RealAudio Player on his or her computer. If you do not configure the MIME type correctly, the user's Web browser will try to *download* the RealAudio file rather than activating the RealAudio Player. To ensure proper download of audio files, you will need to provide the following information to your Web service provider.

The procedure for creating this association varies from one Web server to another. The following list gives information on MIME type additions for some of the most common Web servers in use today. If you are in doubt, or if your Web server is not on our list, please consult your Web server documentation to learn how to add MIME types.

Netscape Netsite Server

To the "MIME.types" file, add the following line:

```
type=audio/x-pn-realaudio exts=ra,ram
```

To the server's main configuration file (called "magnus.conf" in the examples given in the Netsite documentation), add the following line

```
Init fn=load-types mime-types=mime.types
```

and reinitialize the Web server.

Windows NT (EMWAC HTTPS 0.96)

In the HTTP server applet in the Control Panel, click on the button along the right hand side of the window marked "New mapping." A dialog box will be displayed which shows existing MIME type mappings, along with a "Filename extension" text entry box along the top. Type the filename extension .RAM into the extension field, and then enter the full MIME type

```
audio/x-pn-realaudio
```

into the text entry field just below the words "MIME type," and above the scrollable list of existing MIME types. Finally, select OK to add the new MIME type to the main list. You will then need to reinitialize the Web server for the changes to take effect.

NCSA HTTPD (v. 1.3 and 1.4)

For NCSA, two approaches are possible. (1) Edit the file "MIME.types" in the SERVER_ROOT/conf subdirectory. Add the following line

```
audio/x-pn-realaudio ram
```

or, (2) edit the file "srm.conf" in the SERVER_ROOT/conf subdirectory. Add the following line:

```
AddType audio/x-pn-realaudio ram
```

Either approach will work, but the "MIME.types" file on many installations is often left as distributed by NCSA, with local configuration done by adding the AddType directive to the "srm.conf" file. Once the MIME type is added using either approach (but not both), reinitialize the Web server.

CERN HTTPD (v.3.0)

To the "httpd.conf" file under the server's root directory, simply add the following line

```
AddType RAM audio/x-pn-realaudio binary
```

and then reinitialize the Web server.

O'Reilly Website NT

To change the MIME type on the O'Reilly NT Web Server on the mapping page, use the Admin tool to change the content type by giving the following command:

```
RAM audio/x-pn-realaudio
```

Adding Links for the RealAudio Player

One final suggestion: Once the Web server is configured, you should add a link on your Web page pointing to

```
http://www.realaudio.com/
```

so that visitors to your site can obtain the RealAudio Player.

Using The RealAudio Personal Server

The RealAudio Personal Server System is controlled through a user-friendly RealAudio Personal Server Control Panel (Figure 5.8). When the Control Panel is opened, it automatically starts the Personal Server. When closed, it deactivates the Server. The Control Panel also allows you to monitor connections to the Server. The RealAudio Player and RealAudio Encoder can also be opened using the pull-down Tools menu on the Control Panel.

To start the Server (assuming you've downloaded the software), double-click on the PersServ.exe icon. This will open the Personal Server Control Panel and automatically start the Personal Server. By minimizing the RealAudio

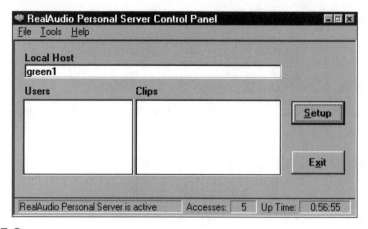

Figure 5.8

RA Personal Server Control Panel.

Personal Server Control Panel, you can allow the Personal Server to continue its operation while you use your computer. The Control Panel must remain activated, and the computer must be left running to allow clients access to your RealAudio files.

To stop the RealAudio Personal Server, select Exit. The Personal Server will close, and audio files will not be served until the Personal Server is restarted.

After the RealAudio Personal Server has been started, RealAudio files have been placed in the correct directory, .RAM files have been linked to your Web page, and the MIME types have been configured, you should test the Personal Server by connecting to it through the network using the RealAudio Player.

Start the RealAudio Player (Figure 5.9) by selecting it from the pull-down Tools menu on the Control Panel. Test your Personal Server and links by connecting to your RealAudio files through your Web pages.

You can also bypass your Web server and test the Personal Server directly. To do this, use the Open Location dialog on the File menu to enter the URL of the test file sound1.ra. For example, if the IP address of your RealAudio Personal Server machine is my.pnserver, then you would enter what's shown in Figure 5.10.

The file sound1.ra should play correctly. If the file does not play correctly, you will see the message box shown in Figure 5.11.

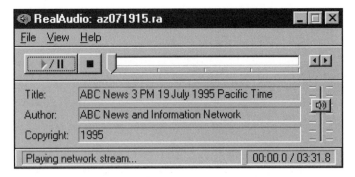

Figure 5.9

The RealAudio Player.

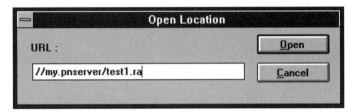

Figure 5.10

Open Location Dialog Box.

Figure 5.11

URL Error Message Box.

If the Personal Server IP address is wrong or non-existent, you will also see the Player error message shown in Figure 5.12.

Correct the IP address and try again.

Figure 5.12

Error Opening Document Message Box.

Figure 5.13

Error Message Box.

If the Player IP address is valid, but the filename portion of the URL is invalid, then you will get an error message similar to the one shown in Figure 5.13. Check the filename and try again.

Serving RealAudio Files From A Dialup Web Site

If you do not maintain your own Web site, and want to allow people to access your RealAudio files through the Internet, you will need to take a different approach to .RAM files and configuration of MIME types in the Web server.

As you may recall, the RealAudio system method of operation is that RealAudio files are accessed when the Player reads its URL from .RAM files that are linked to Web pages on the Internet. While some Web pages are maintained by people who operate their own Web site, others are put on a Web space leased from a Web service provider. If you wish to put RealAudio files on a Web page maintained by a Web service, then you will not be able to make a typical URL connection between the files on your RealAudio Personal Server and the RealAudio links on your Web page, because each time you make a dialup connection to the Web service, you will be given a new IP number. This is the dialup equivalent of a URL address, known as a non-fixed IP Connection.

Since your RealAudio Personal Server will have a different address every time you connect to the Internet, the URL in the .RAM files would need to be changed each time the IP Connection is renewed.

One way to handle this might be to call or e-mail people when you've connected to the Internet, and provide them with the pnm location of the file they want to hear. That way, you bypass the problem of the .RAM file by allowing them to connect directly to the RealAudio Personal Server. They would use the Open Location option from the File menu on the RealAudio Player to enter the pnm address. Of course, you will need to maintain your Internet connection while this is being done. This would still allow the audio to be streamed in real time.

If that muddles things up too much, the complete RealAudio Personal Server technical notes can be found at:

```
http://brinkley.prognet.com/help/persserver/winmanual1.0
```

Conclusion

Even with today's bandwidth constrictions, there are still a number of vastly different options available for audio distribution through the Web. If you have made the decision to provide streamed audio delivery, then the selection of a technology based on spoken word, and/or music, quality requirements, and total bandwidth accessibility all factor into your selection. Oh, yeah . . . how much money do you have?

We have attempted to demonstrate that there is an option for just about every budget and requirement. The competition is fierce as everyone vies for the ubiquitous title of "defacto standard." Bandwidth is increasing, and audio will explode! Whoever gets there first has the chance to carve out a lion's share of the pie. (I didn't even think lions ate pie!)

Now is a good time to investigate, and even implement, a streamed audio-enhanced site. The capabilities are there. It works. It is affordable. And people will listen.

Imagine a small voice whispering in your ear, "If you play it, they will come."

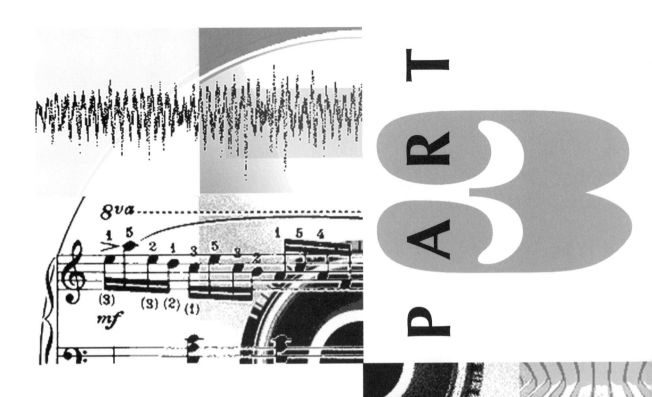

The Tools

of the Trade—

Hardware,

Computers,

and Software

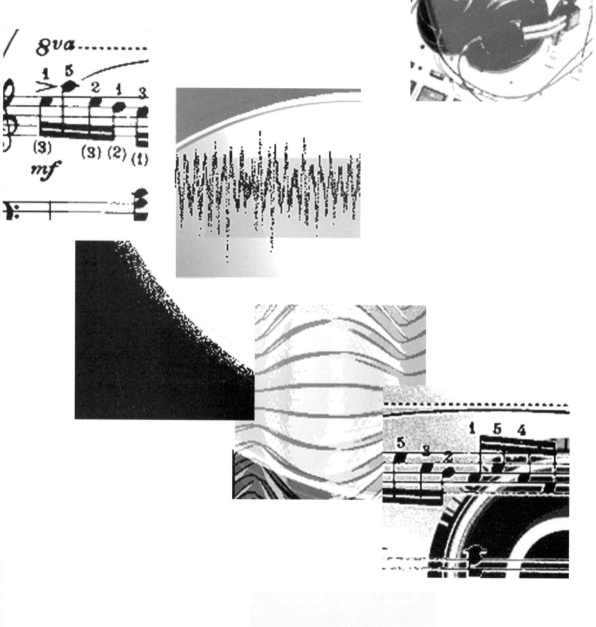
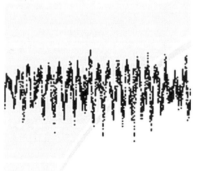

Chapter **6**

Ron Simpson

Microphones, Mixers, And Speakers

The Microphone

When recording voice, sound effects, or music, the quality of the microphone is the first important link in the chain. It's irrelevant whether you have the capability to record CD-quality audio in your computer system if you're not using a proper high-quality microphone, you will just be swimming against the sonic tide. For instance, you have probably noticed the nasty crackling noise that often accompanies low-resolution audio files in most multimedia CD-ROMs. Chances are that a low-quality microphone was used and is adding to the degradation in sound.

In this section, I will try to touch on a happy medium between the cheesy mic that is almost always included (at no extra charge!) with your top-of-the-line multimedia computer system and the ultra expensive (and very sweet sounding) Neumann U89. In the next few sections, I've listed a few microphones, all of which are reasonably priced and are excellent for the entry to mid-level recording scenario. For the purposes of this book, I will assume that the main use of the microphone will be for recording narration.

A Shure-Fire Mic

The Shure SM58 has been one of the standards of the professional music industry for many years. This is pretty much the Sherman Tank of microphones and, although it is used generally as a live performance vocal microphone, its consistency in sound quality makes it a great entry-level microphone for recording voice narration. I used the same SM58 for eight years of live music performance and, although it had been dropped, drooled on by various bar patrons, and abused in ways that are probably illegal in the Bible Belt (not to mention Utah), it still sounds the same as the day I purchased it. If you look around, you can easily find a used SM58 for under $100. Even if it looks a little beat up, it will more than likely sound fine.

The Audio Advantage

Moving on up to the $200 price range, we come to a new favorite of mine— the Audio Technica ATM63HE (Figure 6.1).

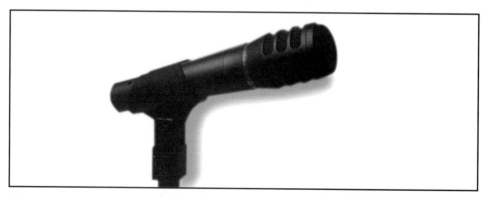

Figure 6.1

The Audio Technica ATM63HE.

Singing through this microphone is a wonderful experience. Not only is it clean and warm sounding, but the overall presence is great. I have been using the 63HE for a variety of different applications including voiceover. For the price, this one is hard to beat. In fact, we liked this mic so much, we used it to record some voiceover segments for the tutorials on the Incredible Sound Resource CD-ROM. With the combination of quality and price, this mic definitely falls into the "best buy" category.

In Stereo

Moving on to specialty microphones and their applications, we come to the Stereo Microphone. This mic is often mounted on a video camera and is also used for recording sound effects. With a good stereo microphone, you can capture some of the feeling of direction that would be otherwise lost. Placing a stereo microphone is also much easier than trying to place two mics in a quick setup situation.

In the preparation of this book and CD-ROM, we used the Audio Technica AT822 Stereo Microphone (Figure 6.2) in some of our own field tests. We experimented with a number of different application—including recording wildlife, industrial sounds, and even a live musical performance—all going direct to DAT. The consistent high quality we were able to achieve with the AT822 has made it an essential addition to my field recording setup.

Figure 6.2
Audio Technica AT822 Stereo Microphone.

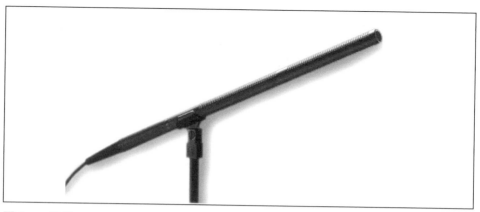

Figure 6.3

The Audio-Technica ATM815.

Riding Shotgun

The Shotgun microphone is an essential tool for recording sound effects in the field. I recently had the urge to add to my library of sounds a close-up recording of a white Bengal tiger roaring and growling. As common sense would dictate, one really doesn't want to be anywhere near a big cat in a bad mood. That's where my shotgun mic came in. I was able to zero in on the locality to which the sounds of feline displeasure were emanating without being all that close to a bad attitude with sharp teeth.

My first field experience with a Shotgun mic was in September of 1995, in Yellowstone National Park, using what is now my trusty Audio-Technica ATM815 (Figure 6.3). I was doing my pre-production for a CD-ROM on Yellowstone and was bound and determined to capture all the sounds of nature that were available in this vast national park. In a period of four days, with a portable DAT deck and the 815, I was able to record all types of geothermal phenomena as well as a few animals and birds. Since it's not really a good idea to get all that close to a geyser spouting boiling water or a loudly bugleing bull elk feeling his oats in the peak of rutting season, the Shotgun mic was extremely handy.

By using a microphone as sensitive as the Shotgun mic, I ran into background chatter in seven different languages while trying to get a clean recording of Old Faithful. I guess that's the price you pay for working in a national park.

Using the ATM815, I was able to get a good start on this particular project and, while as a general rule the animals were not as forthcoming in sounding as natural as I would have liked, the flexibility of this inexpensive Shotgun mic made the experience a positive one.

The Mixing Board

The next important link in the recording chain is the mixer. A number of factors separate the wheat from the chaff when it comes to a mixing board: Sound quality is obviously the major factor, in addition to price and features. In this section, I feature three mixers that are all ground breakers in their own right.

Mackie's Back in Town

The Mackie 1202-VLZ (Figure 6.4) is the second incarnation of the highly successful 1202 micro series. I was one of the first in line waiting to buy the original 1202, and it is still in use and working flawlessly. When a multimedia client insisted on recording and mixing voiceover narration in his office (instead of the recording studio), we just popped a 1202 on his desk, plugged it into the computer's audio input, hooked up a microphone, and went to town.

Figure 6.4
The MicroSeries 1202-VLZ from Mackie Designs.

Figure 6.5

The Pro Mix 01 from Yamaha.

"So what makes the 1202 VLZ so cool and why can't I live without one?" you ask. First, each channel has three bands of EQ, muting, soloing, and stereo panning. Most compact mixers have the infamous wall wart external power supply, but with the 1202, the power supply is internal.

You will find the 1202 in many recording and television studios, as well as in radio stations and, of course, on my desk. The bottom line here: This mixer sounds great, has a clean warm sound, and with a retail price of $439, literally blows away the majority of the competition in the micro mixer catagory. This is another piece of gear I would highly recommend at almost any price.

In the Mix

Now we move into a place you should be familiar with—*the digital domain.* Until recently, buying an automatable digital mixer for around $2,000 was

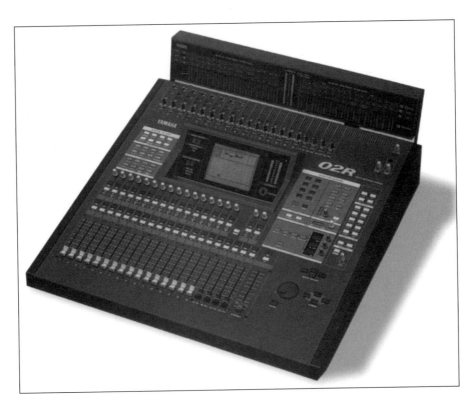

Figure 6.6

The 02R Digital Recording Console from Yamaha.

merely a dream for those of us inhabiting the real world. In developing the Pro Mix 01 (Figure 6.5), the engineers at Yamaha must have been reading my mind. Features like automated mixdown (through a MIDI sequencer) and 19 flying faders are by themselves enough to make it worth the price. It doesn't hurt that there are also two internal effects processors, three stereo compressor gates and 18 three-band parametric EQs. With the digital outputs on the 01, you can mix music and sound digitally to DAT, or even better, straight to the digital inputs of your DAW or computer.

Touring the 02R

The Yamaha 02R (Figure 6.6) might be on the high end of the recording food chain for our purposes, but it would be a crime not to take you on a short tour all the same. Previously, to get a digital mixing console with this quality of sound and features, you had to spend in the neighborhood of $300,000 for a basic setup. The O2R has a list price of under $9,000 and is a fully automated digital recording console with 40 input channels (24 analog and 16 digital) and 8 output buses. With the optional digital interface cards, the O2R is compatible with Pro Tools, ADAT, and the Tascam DA-88 formats.

Thanks to the price and performance breakthrough with the 02R, it is now economically feasible for the interactive developer to set up a high-end digital recording environment in-house. I recently sat through a 2-1/2 hour demonstration of the 02R and was so impressed that I'm thinking of selling a kidney to fund the purchase of one. If it is possible to actually fall in love with a piece of hardware, I think I have.

Sound Processing Hardware

This section covers 3D enhancement hardware for your computer's sound system. Sound processing hardware is traditionally considered to be external audio effects processors, such as reverbs, digital delays, and compressors. In this book, we are covering the recording of sound in a computer environment. So, we have chosen to delegate the responsibility of these tasks to the effects plug-ins (see Chapter 8) available for the various sound editing and recording packages. In this chapter, I'll cover 3D enhancement hardware for your computer's sound system. We will cover 3D sound and its various incarnations and configurations (including encoding hardware and software) in more depth in Chapter 13.

Its a NuReality

We had the opportunity to do a hands-on evaluation of the NuReality Vivid 3D Pro ex (Figure 6.7). This standalone unit can enhance a stereo or mono signal and put you into the realm of 3D sound with two speakers. Based on the patented SRS 3-D sound technology, the Vivid 3D Pro can also enhance encoded 3D sound such as QSound and Dolby Pro Logic. The normally dry sound of many of today's multimedia CD ROMs literally comes to life and seems to jump out at you when using any of the Vivid 3D products. Using the Vivid 3D Pro ex, we experimented with games, narration, sound effects, and music. In short, it's easy to use, sounds good, and is reasonably priced. What more can you ask for?

Figure 6.7

The Vivid 3D Pro ex from NuReality.

Interspacial Sound

Spatializer 3-D Stereo is another technology you will be hearing a lot about in the future. Many companies—including Compaq Computers—have incorporated Spatializer technology into their hardware. This type of 3D sound enhancement can be played back through an encoding process that requires no hardware or through an external device such as the Spatializer HTMS 2510 (Figure 6.8).

Playback is compatible on systems equipped with Dolby Surround Sound, Dolby Pro Logic and many of the other 3D sound technologies currently available.

Figure 6.8

The Spatializer HTMS 2510 from Spatializer Audio Laboratories.

The Pro Spatializer Audio Processor has been used in recording CDs by such artists as Bonnie Raitt, and has also been incorporated in recording the music scores for many films, including *The Lion King* from Walt Disney Pictures.

The Speakers

Your sound is only as good as the speakers that are playing it back. So why not use the speakers that came with your 400 Mhz thermonuclear multimedia computer system? Chances are they are about as sonically useful as the parsley sprigs that garnish your plate in a nuveau cuisine restaurant are nutritious. So why not use the speakers in your home stereo—they've worked great for years? Well, since they probably aren't shielded, your computer monitor will cause them to hum like a UFO coming in for a landing. When listening to, recording, and or editing sound, excess background noise is a bad thing. Finding computer speakers that can reproduce sound accurately is sometimes a difficult but not impossible task.

Bose Is Boss

We were fortunate enough to be able to use both the Acoustimass (Figure 6.9) and Media Mate Multimedia speaker systems from Bose in the preparation of the sound for this book and CD-ROM. Generally, computer speakers are not known for having high-quality sound, but it seems that Bose has set out to

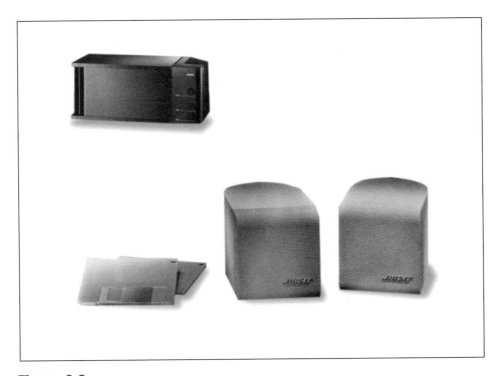

Figure 6.9

The Bose Acoustimass Multimedia System.

remedy this situation. Many other companies will be taking their cue from Bose, and you can bet in the near future that the sound system hooked up to your computer will rival that of your stereo or home theater system—mine already does.

The Acoutimass Multimedia Speaker System is a three-way system with two cube stereo speakers and a subwoofer that also houses the power amplifier and tone controls. The sound in this system runs true from the lowest lows up through the mid range to the high end. If you need a compact speaker system that is huge in sound and presence, there is no way we can say enough good things about the Acoustimass system. We have used it both for listening and mixing sound, and if there is a better compact computer speaker system, I'll buy it—although I haven't found one yet. Multimedia presenters should consider the Acoustimass as both an installed system or for use in off-site presentations. We recorded and edited sound (and music) files, played games, and listened to CDs using the Acoutimass. In all honesty, it will remain as a permanent fixture in my studio.

The Bose Media Mate is the little brother of the Acoustimass Speaker System. If you're looking for that big warm sound that Bose is known for, but you're on a budget, then the search is over. While we're trying to keep as neutral of an opinion as possible, when the sound is this good, it's hard not to shout about it. This system consists of two powered speakers and is good for not only listening but for mixing sound for multimedia and Web playback.

In the Year CS2000

Although the CS2000 Powered Surround Sound System with Dolby Surround Pro Logic from Audio Technica was originally designated as a home theater system, this self-powered, five-speaker setup also works well with your computer. Playing a computer game or listening to music encoded with Dolby Surround Sound is an awe-inspiring experience, to say the least. This particular system consists of a subwoofer, a wireless rear speaker, and left, right, and center forward speakers. As we spend more and more time working and playing on our computers, home theater systems such as this one from Audio Technica are going to find their way into our setups.

Speaking of Yamaha

The Yamaha YST-15 Powered Multimedia Speakers are the latest in a series of speakers for computer consumers and professionals alike. This speaker system is an inexpensive alternative if you want to upgrade your computer's sound. In addition to having 10 watts per channel, these self-powered speakers are also magnetically shielded. Available as a stereo pair, The YST-15 package also allows you to add an optional subwoofer to improve bass response.

Chapter 7

Ron Simpson

Computers, AV Drives, And Storage

In this chapter, we'll describe some of the computer hardware that's useful, or even required, for effective sound recording and playback. We're not going to provide an exhaustive list of products available for this purpose. Instead, we'll feature just a few that we think are the best of the best in each category.

Our criteria include performance *and* price. Some systems provide good sound performance, but are bargains when compared to the top-of-the-line hardware. So, if you don't have an unlimited cash reserve, we'll help out by introducing you to some systems and hardware add-ons that won't break your bank account. Of course, if you want only the best and cost is no object, we'll steer you toward these options too.

Removable Storage

Back in 1985, with my first music computer booted and ready for business (the Yamaha CX5M with a whopping 32 K of RAM), I remember looking at *all* the many options available for storing my MIDI files. Unfortunately, the only technology available at the time for my computer was a data cassette. After about 90 seconds, I was able to load a 10 K MIDI file and with any luck it would actually play back. It kind of makes you wonder: In another 10 years, will we feel the same way about the AV and Removable Drives of today as I still feel about that verdant data cassette?

Fortunately, today there is an amazingly wide variety of options in price and performance for storing and transporting music and sound files. But there is no one standardized format for removable drives. I guess the Iomega versus Syquest debate could be compared to Mac versus Windows. But I'm not going to open that can of worms.

We've had the opportunity to use some of the different drives featured in this section for the Chapter 11 tutorials on hard disk recording. We'll let you know how they work (or don't) in conjunction with the different computer and software configurations available, as well as with the least expensive setup you can put together to do quality hard disk recording.

The Incredible Removable EZ 135

The EZ 135 from Syquest (Figure 7.1) is currently at the top of our list in the removable storage department. Not only is this compact unit a good deal, but it's also fast enough to record direct to disk using most of the software programs that we feature in the tutorial part of the book. While the seek time of 13.5 ms is a little slower than the recommended 12 ms, we were not able to detect any noticeable errors or degradation in quality during stereo recording and playback. Sound for the Web usually involves relatively small file sizes, so the 13 minutes of 16-bit 44 kHz stereo record time available using the EZ 135 cartridges should support most of your needs.

Putting Some Zip in Your Drive

Another equally cool and even more affordable option is the Iomega Zip Drive (Figure 7.2). Because its seek time is slower than Syquest's EZ 135, recording

Figure 7.1

The EZ 135 from Syquest.

Figure 7.2

The Zip Drive from Iomega.

audio from most hard disk recording software programs is not recommended with the Zip. However, you can certainly archive the sound files from your AV drive to the Zip Drive.

The 100 MB Zip disks cost about $15 apiece, and you can store about 10 minutes of CD quality stereo sound on one cartridge. Most corporate clients in the music industry, will have either an EZ 135 or a Zip drive connected to their systems. Both of these drives are inexpensive, so if you do a lot of sound development, it's a good idea to have a pair of these drives on hand.

The next battle for top gun in the 1 GB (gigabyte) range of removable storage is currently between the Iomega Jaz Drive (Figure 7.3) and the Syquest SyJet. The market for hard disk recording has been waiting years for something in the price and performance range of these two units. The big question when examining them side by side: Does one have the edge over the other? Well, the SyJet cartridge has .3 GB more storage and a faster average seek time of 1ms over the Jaz. Both units are available for Mac and PC and can be used externally or installed as an internal drive.

Because both drives have almost identical performance specifications, determining which one is best is a tough call. At this writing, neither unit was available for evaluation. So, to be fair, I have to say I would be more than happy to have either or both of these units installed in my studio. By the time this book is in print, we might have had a chance to road test both the Jaz and the SyJet. If so, we'll let you know via our Web site (http://www.monsoon.org/sound_advice) how things fly.

Figure 7.3

The 1 GB Jaz Drive from Iomega.

Audio Visual (A/V) Drives

Now it's time to take a run with the big dogs—the A/V hard drives. For hard disk recording, you need speed, stability, and a large amount of storage space. In a nutshell, the A/V drive is the answer. An A/V drive rating on a hard drive means you have consistant data throughput and access time when recording audio or video. This prevents the annoying little hiccups caused by dead spots in the data stream. In other words, no more wobbly video or, even worse (for our purposes anyway), wobblier sound.

Quantum Leaps

In the entry to mid-level category, Quantum is planning to release the Viking A/V drives in the fourth quarter of 1996. With performance specifications equal to the more expensive A/V drives, and an estimated street price of $475.00 for the 2 GB ($675.00 for the 4 GB version), it should be well worth the wait. While I've seen the 1 GB Quantum Fireball advertised in several catalogs as an A/V drive, according to Quantum, there are no plans for an A/V version of the Fireball. So don't believe everything you read (except in this book, of course).

Seagate Sets the Standard

When it comes to high-end A/V drives, Seagate is, without a doubt, one of the dominant players in the industry. In fact, for hard disk audio recording, the Seagate Barracuda (Figure 7.4) currently sets the standard for performance and features in a high-end A/V drive. The 8 ms seek time, 7,200 RPM spindle speed, and high reliability are just some of the factors we considered in our evaluation. It doesn't hurt to run one of these drives through its paces in a professional recording studio environment, either. When I used Deck II, Pro Tools, and Sound Edit 16, the Barracuda performed flawlessly in multi-track recording and playback. The fact that the 4.3 GB Barracuda 4 costs about the same as the 1 GB unit of a few years ago is another bonus.

The Micropolis Option

After talking with a number of recording industry professionals, I felt the general consensus was that Micropolis (see Figure 7.5) and Seagate were the two stand-out companies for A/V Drives used in recording. Although we didn't

Figure 7.4

The Barracuda A/V Drive from Seagate.

have the opportunity to evaluate any of the Micropolis drives, their specifications are pretty much neck and neck with the comparable Seagate drives.

The Computer

The heart of any hard drive recording system is the computer. Having said that, we need to apologize in advance to Windows users. Here's why: We wrote letters, placed lengthy and expensive phone calls, and in some cases, even begged for information on the various Windows machines. While we won't mention any companies by name (Big Blue), there was obviously not enough interest in the Web or a book about sound on the Web to even get a press kit released to us. One PR person even claimed they had already

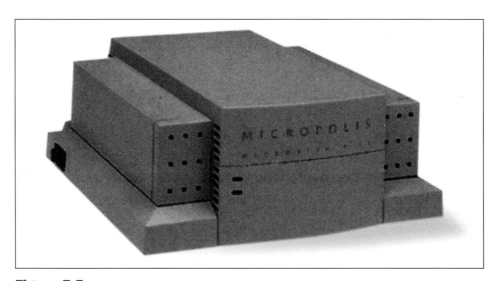

Figure 7.5

The Micropolis AV LT.

exhausted their advertising budget for that quarter, and their company couldn't afford to send one.

Oh well.

Apple, on the other hand, was quite helpful, so when we discuss computers that run on the Mac OS, we'll be more specific about the capabilities of various makes and models than with the Windows machines. And with that behind us....

Processor speed is always at the top of our list when dealing with DSP (Digital Signal Processing) functions. It only makes sense that neither a 386 33 Mhz Windows machine, nor a Mac IIci would be the optimum choice for hard disk recording and editing. Even with the 300 mHz Pentiums and Power PCs that we all know are on the way, you will probably have time to go out for lunch or take a nap while the machine is compressing or normalizing a large sound file. So take our word for it: Be aggressive and go for the speed.

The Mac Attack

It was a tough call in trying to determine which of the new PCI Power Macintoshs offer the best deal, in terms of price versus performance, for sound recording. We went with the middle ground and selected the Power Macintosh

Figure 7.6

The Apple Power Macintosh 8500.

8500-120 (Figure 7.6). One of the features that attracted us to the 8500 was the higher than normal sound quality of the built-in audio interface. Most, if not all, computers being sold today are capable of recording and playing back 16-bit 44 kHz stereo sound, but sound quality when using the built-in mini plug (used with many sound cards), and A/D (audio to digital) converters, is closer to that of a standard audiocassette.

The Power Mac 8500-120 has built-in stereo RCA inputs/outputs and, although you won't get the sound quality of a professional digital audio interface (see Chapter 8), it is certainly an improvement over using a mini plug. Although it has a powerful 120 Mhz PowerPC 604 microprocessor under the hood, the 8500 is also easily upgradeable. We'll road test the 8500 in Chapter 10 when we use it for a number of the tutorial examples on hard disk recording.

Riding the PowerWave

In the past, if you wanted to use the Mac OS, you bought a Macintosh and you had to be happy with that. With the licensing of the Mac OS to other vendors, Apple has made it possible for a number of companies to manufacture Macintosh clones with a wider variety of options than were previously available from Apple.

Figure 7.7

The Power Computing Power Wave 604.

The current stand-out in the crowd is the Austin, Texas-based Power Computing Corporation, which makes the Power Wave 604/150 (Figure 7.7), among other high-end Mac OS systems. While the 604/150 is similar in its performance and its features to the Apple Power Macintosh 8500 and 9500, the Power Wave 604/150 has a few options that even Apple doesn't offer—namely, the Stargate Riser Card. This feature is great for those who already have a large investment in NuBus add-in cards. The Stargate Riser Card gives you two PCI and two NuBus expansion slots (versus three PCI slots for most Power Macs), proving that backward compatiblity can be a beautiful thing.

The downside of the Power Wave line lies in the absence of the superior audio/video input and output found in comparable Apple machines. But Power Computing guarantees 100-percent compatability with all Macintosh software and a slightly better price/performance ratio.

The Audiomedia Advantage

If you want to do serious hard disk recording with a Power Wave machine, we recommend installing Digidesign's Audiomedia II (NuBus) or Audiomedia III (PCI) card. Another plus for Power Computing is the fact that you can have your system shipped with a custom configuration to fit your needs. Check out Power Computing's do-it-yourself configuration engine at their Web site (www.powercc.com). You can use this online configurator to design the system options that you want, and even view the price you'll pay.

Windows System Options

Now let's move on to Windows machines. Fortunately, the lack of information available for specific models should not be too much of a handicap, thanks to the modular nature of this versatile platform. Most PCs are capable of recording and playing back CD-quality audio and, as is true with the Macintosh, it's a good idea to buy a high-quality sound card to accomplish this task. The improved performance of the PCI based-Pentium machines using an Audiomedia III card (Digidesign) is one of the best entry- to mid-level options you will find for hard disk recording.

In Chapter 8, we'll give you a look at a few other low-priced but high-quality options that give the PC a bit of an edge over the Macintosh in the area of entry-level digital sound. Again, we can't stress how important processor speed and RAM is to glitch-free hard disk recording. (If you also plan to do full multimedia development with a high-end video and animation package, such as Macromedia Director or 3D Studio Max, 32 MB of RAM and at least a 100 Mhz Pentium are required. (So run out and buy that 166 Mhz Pentium with 32 megabytes of RAM!)

In Chapter, 11 we'll be using a 486 machine in conjuction with Sound Forge for our basic tutorial on hard disk recording.

Modems

As we've been touting in the pages of this book, the silent Web page will soon be largely a thing of the past. ISDN, T1, and even the personal satellite dish, already give us the blazing speed we need for high-quality realtime audio from the Web. The performance of your modem will dictate the quality and content of what you're able to download and listen to.

It wasn't all that long ago when I was logging onto America Online at 2,400 Bps, being totally amazed at the world that had opened before me. For now and in the near future, most of us will be using regular phone lines, and hopefully, a modem with a connect speed of at least 28,800 Kbps. In the preparation of this book, we were fortunate enough to have at our disposal, modems from Supra (Diamond Multimedia) and US Robotics.

Going SupraSonic

The SupraSonic 288V+ (Figure 7.8) from Diamond Multimedia is a 28.8 external modem, and is available for both Mac and PC. My first experience on the Web at 28.8 was with this little screamer and it has now replaced my trusty-but-sluggish-by-comparison 14.4 modem forever. The 288V+ has both caller ID and advanced voice mail capabilities, as well as Flash ROM so that you can get instant upgrades over the phone. After giving this baby a test run downloading sound files and listening to streaming audio from a number of Web sites, I was ready to sign on the dotted line.

The Speed of Robotics

So you like the feel of the wind in your hair, and you're not afraid of a little speed? If you really want to push the outside of the sonic envelope when

Figure 7.8
The SupraSonic 288V+ from Diamond Multimedia.

Figure 7.9

The Courier V.Everything from US Robotics.

listening to streaming audio, then the Courier V.Everything high speed modems from US Robotics are your ticket to the fast lane. These screamingly fast modems connect at speeds as high as 33,600 Kbps and are available in desktop, internal, or PCMCIA versions.

While we were only able to get our hands on a loaner PC version of the Courier (Figure 7.9), it has definetely been added to our Christmas wish list. In addition to superior speed and reliability, the Courier V.Everything has a lengthy list of impressive features, many of which are found only on modems from US Robotics.

A Glimpse Into The Future

As the new ISDN and cable modems become more readily available to consumers in the latter part of 1996, we will be sure to let you know what impact they are having on sound on the Web. Make regular visits to our Web page (http://www.monsoon.org/sound_advice) for updates.

Chapter 8

Ron Simpson

Ron Simpson

The Software And Hardware

Half the fun of making music and doing sound design is getting to play with all the toys. (Maybe Section 3 should be called Toys of the Trade!) In this chapter, I've tried to touch equally on the Mac and PC, but due to the nature of hardware architecture and the direction of software development (historically, at least), each platform will always have some advantage over the other. In the 11 years that I have been involved in music and computers, the Macintosh has pretty much been the platform of choice for most of my friends and business acquaintances; however, this distinction is changing at a rapid rate, and the line is beginning to blur. While I would never give up either of my Macs, I have lately found myself coveting that screamingly fast Pentium Tower with all its accoutrements.

Until recently, the super cool and ultra expensive hardware/software packages designed for MIDI and sound performance have been almost exclusively Mac territory, while PC developers concentrated on the inexpensive entry to mid-level market. After talking with many developers and engineers in the preparation of this book, I'm happy to report that the race is on to close this performance gap. Fortunately for consumers, the scramble to develop more innovative products should bring prices down and add many new features. If after reading this section, your interest in MIDI hardware runs deeper than a general overview, I suggest you take a look at an issue or two of *Keyboard* magazine.

MIDI Modules And Synthesizers

The multi-timbral MIDI module and synthesizer has changed the way music is composed and performed. With the universal acceptance of General MIDI (GM), manufacturers have finally agreed upon a standard for their hardware (see Chapter 9 for an in-depth look at GM). Two standouts, at the higher end of the external General MIDI sound modules, are Roland's SC-88 Super Sound Canvas (GS), and Yamaha's MU80 Tone Generator (XG). See Figure 8.1.

Both of these units have more than twice the polyphony needed to conform to the General MIDI standard, and both include a built-in computer interface (for Macs and PCs). However, according to Roland, if you run the current version of Windows 95, the interface does not work. Microsoft is aware of the problem, and with any luck, a fix is on the way. While both of these units have similar features, the MU80 has two advantages over the SC88: the ability to mix an external audio signal through its internal effects, and a third effects processor. In addition to the stand-alone MIDI module, many manufacturers offer a keyboard version of their synthesizers.

MIDI Workstations

These all-in-one units provide a keyboard, sequencer, synthesizer, and drum machine. Many composers and musicians use MIDI workstations, both as a scratch pad, and in some cases, for recording a finished piece of music. Some MIDI workstations, such as the Kurzweil K2500 (Figure 8.2), are available with a sampling option as well. These keyboards are also great for live

Figure 8.1

The Yamaha MU80 Tone Generator.

performance and studio situations where dragging along your PC is not a viable option for sequence playback.

PC Sound Cards And Daughterboards

If you're a Macintosh user, run away (just for a moment). All true multimedia PCs have a CD ROM player and, of course, a sound card. The installed base of Creative Labs Sound Blaster 16-bit cards is possibly greater than the number of registered voters in the free world. Even so, a variety of options are available today that provide a definite improvement over these FM-based sound cards. At the start of this chapter, I introduced two extended forms of General MIDI—Roland's GM GS and Yamaha's GM XG (both of which I'll discuss in greater

Figure 8.2

The K2500 from Kurweil.

Figure 8.3

The Yamaha WaveForce SW50XG.

depth in Chapter 9). Both companies have available high-end sound cards that transform the normally annoying MIDI-based music you so often hear eminating from your computer into a pleasureable experience. While any sound card will play back a MIDI or WAVE file, the newer extended-level 16-bit stereo cards are a vast improvement over the grungy sound of the 8-bit mono base level sound cards of the past.

Okay, you know that a great-sounding new card would do wonders toward improving your life sonically, but you already have a SoundBlaster-compatible card in your system, and you really don't want to throw away your investment. Enter the sound daughterboard. Yamaha (See Figure 8.3) and Roland (See Figure 8.4) both offer great-sounding, full-featured sound daughterboards that plug into most of the older, less sonically pristeen SoundBlaster-compatible cards.

A number of companies, including Creative Labs, sell sound daughterboard updates. But unlike the GS and XG stereo cards, none of these updates include the ability for separate Reverb and Chorus (and, in the case of the Yamaha XG units, a third effect) on each MIDI channel. Roland also sells the SCP-55 (Figure 8.5), which is a full-featured Sound Canvas synthesizer, on a PCMCIA card.

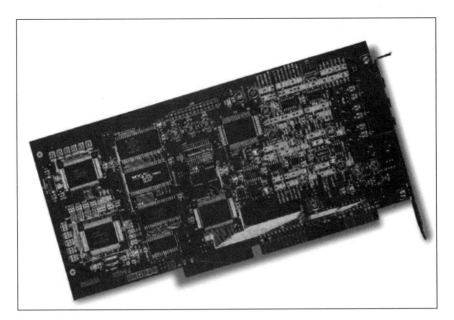

Figure 8.4

The Sound Canvas DB daughterboard from Roland.

Figure 8.5

The SCP-55 Sound Canvas PCMCIA Card from Roland.

Macintosh MIDI Interface Units

If you're a Macintosh user and you want to play (or record) MIDI-based music from an external sound module, you're going to need a MIDI interface. (An exception to this rule is the Yamaha MU50 or MU80, which has a built in Macintosh interface.)

The basic Macintosh MIDI interface has one MIDI input and three MIDI outputs. These interface units are generally inexpensive (around $50) and, in most cases, are idiot proof. Opcode offers a number of MIDI interfaces for the Macintosh from the Translator Pro (Figure 8.6), which provides two inputs, six outputs, and 32 MIDI channels, all the way up to the Studio 5LX (Figure 8.7), which supports 240 separate MIDI channels and 15 inputs. Many industry professionals consider the Studio 4 and 5LX to be the best full-featured MIDI interfaces available.

PC MIDI Interface Units

For the PC, Roland makes the MPU 401, which is now available as the new and improved MPU 401AT (Figure 8.8). This interface is 100-percent compatible with the MPU 401. But with the new AT version, you can plug a Roland GM or GS daughterboard into your MIDI interface.

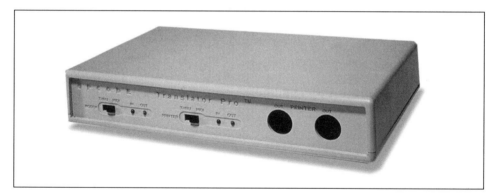

Figure 8.6

The Translator Pro from Opcode.

Figure 8.7

The Studio 5LX from Opcode.

Figure 8.8

The industry standard MPU-401AT PC MIDI interface from Roland.

In July of 1995, Opcode acquired Music Quest and now offers a full line of MIDI interfaces for PC compatibles. This full-featured line includes everything from a basic MPU-401 compatible interface (the PC MIDI Card), to the MIDIEngine 8Port/SE (8 MIDI ports and 128 MIDI channels). Opcode also offers the MIDI Translator PC (Figure 8.9), an expandable 2 input, 2 output, 32 channel parallel MIDI interface.

Figure 8.9

The MIDI Translator PC from Opcode.

Digital Audio Software/Hardware

If you just can't control that urge to record, compress, or dither an occasional sound file, this section of the book is for you. (Dithering a sound file in Arkansas is illegal unless it is done in the presence and with the blessing of a blood relative). In Chapter 9, I'll touch on the basic techniques and tricks of hard disk recording. In this chapter, though, you'll get a look at a few of the tools available for computer-based recording. We also have included demo versions of several hard disk recording software packages on the Incredible Sound Resource CD ROM for use in conjunction with the tutorials. No matter which configuration you use, the basic concept is the same. However, the features, ease of use, and hardware options can cover the entire sound-quality spectrum. I hope that, after reading this section, you'll be able to decide which combination is right for your specific recording needs. At press time, new versions of several products featured in this section were due to be released. Check out the equipment appendix or our Web page (http://www.monsoon.org/sound_advice) for updates.

The Digidesign Approach

One of the more basic recording and editing programs for the Macintosh is Sound Designer II, by Digidesign. Sound Designer II is a powerful program mainly used in conjunction with Pro Tools (also from Digidesign). For example, compressing or normalizing a sound file would be done in Sound Designer II, and then loaded back into Pro Tools for editing. You can also use such Plug-ins as DINR (Digital Intellegent Noise Reduction) in Sound Designer II. DINR is used to get rid of the sonic garbage that may occasionally show up in a sound file.

My first experience with this really cool plug-in occured when I was trying to isolate and extract the song of a specific bird from a field recording. In the background, you could hear the Colorado River, oars hitting the side of the boat, and people talking — in addition to the call of the Canyon Wren. Using DINR, I was able to mask all of these sounds — with the exception of the wren. The results were surprisingly good for a first try, and I was hooked on DINR.

Macromedia Steps In

Although the professional audio world may consider it an entry level Macintosh program, SoundEdit 16 Version 2 from Macromedia (Figure 8.10) is a very useful and powerful tool. I was more than a little surprised at all the cool

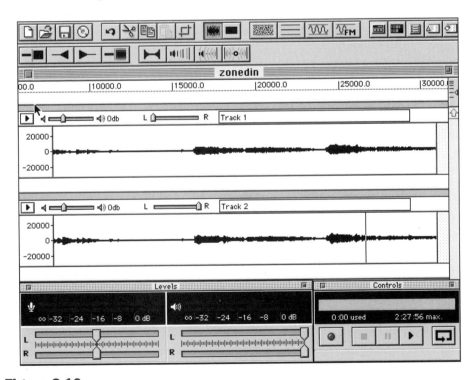

Figure 8.10
SoundEdit 16 Version 2 from Macromedia.

functions geared for the interactive developer. The ability to import or export 10 different file formats (including WAV), and to digitally capture music and sound directly from Red Book Audio CD's, make this little piece of software worth its weight in gold.

Although it probably makes more sense to use Pro Tools or Deck 2 to record large multi-track files, SoundEdit16 is still more than capable of accomplishing this task. Another set of features that I really like is the effects plug-ins. Although some basic plug-ins are included with SoundEdit 16, check out the section on plug-ins to see what is currently available from third party developers.

Forging Sound

If you're a PC user, don't fret. I haven't forgotten about you. So without any further ado, lets head to the PC world. Sound Forge 3.0 from Sonic Foundry (Figure 8.11) is a mid-level sound recording and editing program. Several powerful editing tools and features make this program one of the most usable and comprehensive available for PC compatibles today.

Standard features in Sound Forge — such as a noise gate and the ability to compress or normalize a file — are must-haves for work in multimedia and Web sound development. Another great feature is the compatibility with the NT platforms. It's almost a shame Sound Forge won't be ported for the Mac. Also, a growing number of very cool plug-ins are available for Sound Forge, some of which are listed in the next section of this chapter.

There's no test like the real world, so in the final production phase of the CD ROM "Explore The Grand Canyon," I used Sound Forge 3.0 to edit over three hours of narration and sound effects. This was my first experience editing sound on a PC (versus a Mac), and I found Sound Forge to be intuitive and easy to use. Don't just take my word for it. Check out the Incredible Sound Resource CD ROM, included in the demo version of this program. We also use Sound Forge in conjunction with the PC tutorials in Chapter 10.

If you have an entry-level budget, Sound Forge XP is available for a retail price of $149.00. Most of the features of the more robust version of Sound Forge are retained in XP, although the plug-ins and MIDI support are not.

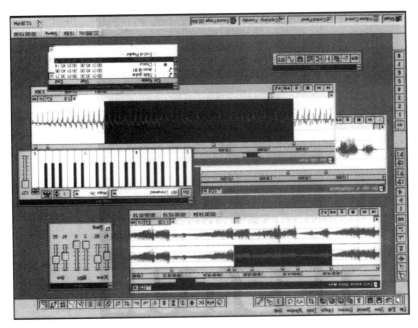

Figure 8.11
Sound Forge 3.0 from Sonic Foundry.

Sonic Foundry has also announced the Sound Forge Interactive CD-ROM. If your brain suffers from vapor lock when using Sound Forge, the tutorials on this CD should set you free.

More Sounds from Digidesign

Session Software (Figure 8.12) from Digidesign is available for both the Mac and PC environments. Although Session has an entry-level price tag, it performs many functions available with considerably more expensive hard disk recording systems, and is usable for all levels of professional recording. Session can be used with no additional hardware, or in conjunction with Digidesign's Audiomedia cards (Audiomedia II NuBus for the Macintosh, and Audiomedia III PCI for the PC compatible and Power Macintosh). Session Software for the PC is available in a bundle with the Audiomedia III card.

Next on Deck...

With the recent absorbtion of OSC into Macromedia the popular Deck II Digital Audio Workstation (Figure 8.13) software for the Macintosh has found a new

Figure 8.12

Session Software from Digidesign.

home. Depending on the processor speed and RAM in your CPU, you can play back up to 32 tracks at one time. With its wide variety of editing, mixing, recording, and signal processing features, Deck II is another program that gives you a lot of bang for your buck.

Although SoundEdit 16 version 2 would normally be used for dealing with smaller sound files, Deck II is better suited for dealing with more complex multitrack recordings. SoundEdit 16 version 2 and Deck II make for a very powerful and reasonably priced combination. We've used both of these programs for a number of real-world applications, and have been amazed at how easy to use and powerful they are. Demo versions of both programs are provided on the Incredible Sound Resource CD ROM, and we will be using them with the tutorials in Chapter 10.

A Tool for the Pros

You've probably heard about Pro Tools. Like many hardworking-hoping-to-get-a-life-in-the-near-future audio engineers, I've lusted after this package, but the sticker shock has always scared me away. Well (long pause for effect), the easily affordable Pro Tools software with DAE Power Mix (Figure 8.14) has finally arrived. Using a Power Macintosh, you can record and play back up to 16 tracks with no external hardware. If, at a later date, your budget

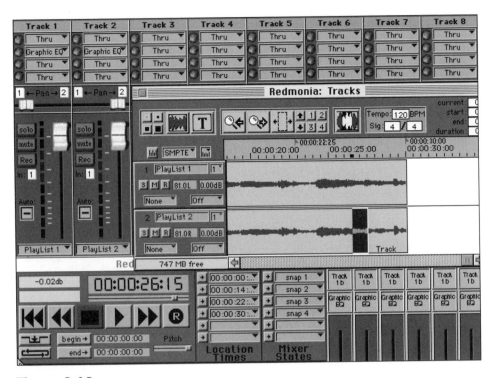

Figure 8.13

Deck II from Macromedia.

allows, you can add Digidesign hardware and upgrade as far as Pro Tools III. Sessions from this software package are compatible with the entire Pro Tools product line. Other features include non-destructive editing, digital EQ with pan, and volume automation.

Digidesign, along with their parent company Avid, currently has the largest installed base (80 percent) of professional digital audio systems in the world. Thanks to third-party developer support, Digidesign will probably retain the lead in Mac-based DAW's, regardless of the quality of the competition.

Pro Tools for Those on a Budget

It might seem as though things are a little slanted in favor of the Mac in the field of digital editing for sound, but this can't be helped. Digidesign entered the race way ahead of the pack back in 1989 with Sound Tools for the Macintosh and, while the gap is rapidly closing, the PC hardware/software combinations still have a little catching up to do. Fortunately, they will.

Figure 8.14

Pro Tools Software from Digidesign.

Pro Tools Project (also for the Mac) might be considered a mid-priced alternative to its higher-priced Mac-based DAW counterpart. All of the features of Pro Tools software are also found in this package, and by using either the 882 or 888 Audio Interfaces, you'll have up to 8 tracks of simultaneous recording and playback at 16-bit 44.1 kHz or 48.0 kHz sampling rates. Pro Tools Project is also compatible with Sound Designer II and Sample Cell II.

For the Uncompromising Pro Tools User...

Standing at the top of the Mac-based DAW mountain is Pro Tools III (Figure 8.15) with TDM (Time Division Multiplexing). This system is the most comprehensive and flexible version of Pro Tools ever.

Some of the features include 16 to 48 tracks of record/playback, and 8 to 64 channels of I/O, as well as an integrated digital mixing and DSP plug-in environment. Pro Tools III runs on a Macintosh computer, and can use one or more SCSI A/V drives. The package has four integrated components. These are:

1. The Pro Tools software

2. The Digidesign TDM Bus

3. The Digidesign Audio Engine (DAE)

4. The Pro Tools III hardware

Pro Tools III is now available for both NuBus and PCI systems. Rumor is there is an increase in performance from the PCI hardware.

I've used Pro Tools on a number of recording projects and have found it to be fast and easy to learn. The powerful new features in Pro Tools III, such as the

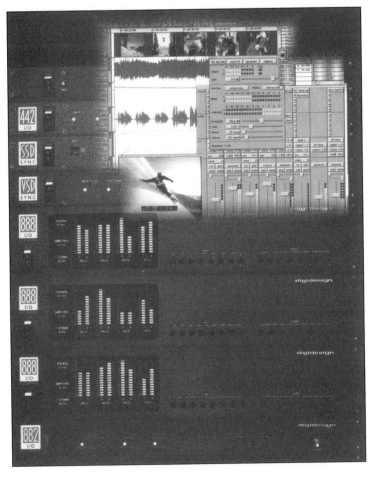

Figure 8.15
Pro Tools III from Digidesign.

TDM bus, have turned this already useful pro system into a virtual digital mixing and effects processing environment.

So, what exactly is TDM?

I sat through a great demonstration of Pro Tools III a few months ago and asked that very question. The answer: TDM is a 256-channel, 24-bit time division multiplexing bus used to route digital audio in the Pro Tools III environment. This dynamic mixing system is expandable by adding software plug-in modules available from the more than 100 third-party developers, as well as additional hardware available from Digidesign. Pro Tools III is used in dialog editing for film, radio and television production, sound design, CD-ROM development, and, of course, recording music. I'm looking forward to the release of Pro Tools IV.

Effects Plug-ins

Any computer-based hard disk recording system that doesn't offer some sort of plug-in support had better get with the program (and soon). These software-based DSP add-ons are the icing on the cake when it comes to sound processing in a virtual environment. Although effects plug-ins were initially expensive, the release of InVision Interactives Cybersound FX for the Macintosh (Figure 8.16) has brought affordable sonic manipulation to the masses. This powerful

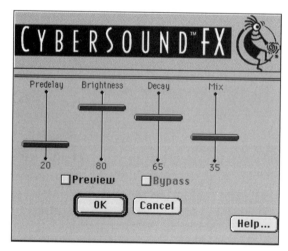

Figure 8.16

Cybersound FX software DSP plug-in from Invision Interactive.

DSP plug-in for SoundEdit 16 and Deck 2 is organized into 17 different effects groups, including Reverb, Chorus, and Parametric EQ. Each effects group has a number of different templates set up to give the user a good starting point for creating their own effects configurations. I did a test run using Cybersound FX, and found it to be a great improvement over the basic plug-ins that come with SoundEdit 16. Cybersound FX is also PowerPC native and, with a retail price of $129, it's hard to go wrong with this package.

Sound Forge Plug-Ins

Sonic Foundry also has a number of plug-ins (Figure 8.17) available for Sound Forge 3.0. I was able to get a first-hand look at the Batch Converter, Noise Reduction, and Spectrum Analysis plug-ins. I found these plug-ins easy to use and an important addition to my sonic tool kit. A notable new release is the Waves L1 Ultramaximizer plug-in (also for Sound Forge 3.0). Based on Increased Digital Resolution (IDR), this plug-in combines an advanced peak limiter, a level maximizer, and a performance re-quantizer. QSound also has a new set of three plug-ins I can hardly wait to get my hands on. To find out more about the 3D technology that is used by QSound, take a look in Chapter 13.

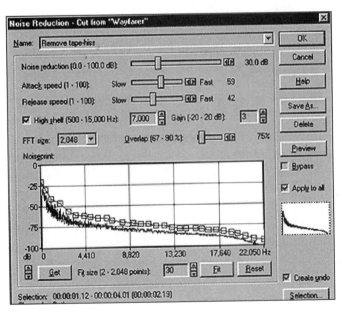

Figure 8.17

Noise Reduction plug-in for Sound Forge from Sonic Foundry.

TDM Plug-Ins for Pro Tools III

You already know what plug-ins are, but what makes the TDM plug-ins for Pro Tools III so special? These software-based DSP processing modules take advantage of the power of Digidesign's DSP Farm. So, wait a minute. What exactly is a DSP Farm?

The Digidesign DSP Farm is the (Nubus or PCI) hardware that powers the Pro Tools III mixing and DSP software plug-ins. So, the more DSP Farms you have in your system, the more processing power will be available to you (even my drummer could figure that one out). Some of the plug-ins available from third party developers, include NuVerb from Lexicon, QSYS/TDM from QSound Labs, and Focusrite d2 EQ (Figure 8.18).

Digital Audio Interfaces

Although hard disk recording software for the Mac is quite plentiful, Digidesign seems to have cornered the market on high-end digital audio hardware. The

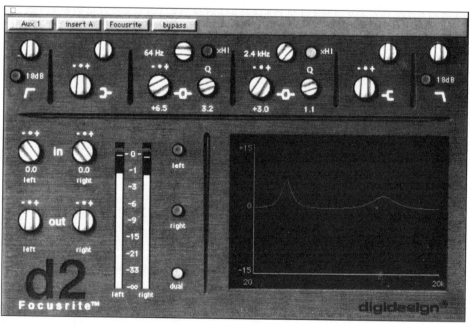

Figure 8.18

The Focusrite d2 TDM plug-in for Pro Tools III. Modeled on the highly-acclaimed Red Range 2 Dual EQ designed by Rupert Neve, the d2 is a 24-bit software-based multi-band equalizer.

Audiomedia II (Nubus) card is currently the most economical option for those who need stereo analog and digital I/O (S/PDIF) in conjunction with the Pro Tools Software. The recently released PCI-based Audiomedia III for both the Mac and PC also runs in the same price range.

Moving up the digital food chain, you have your choice of either the 882 I/O or the 888 I/O I Audio Interfaces (also from Digidesign), either of which can be used with Pro Tools Project or Pro Tools III. The 888 also has a meter bridge in the front panel. I'm wondering out loud that, when PCI versions of these 8 I/O Digidesign Interfaces are released, will they be compatible with Windows machines? Let's hope so.

On the PC-only side of the realm, is the highly recommended Multi!Wav Digital PRO (Figure 8.19) from AdB International. This card has Optical and Coaxial S/PDIF Digital I/O (as well as AES/EBU), and is compatible with most of the professional sound editing software packages for Windows. We were not able to get an evaluation unit before going to press, but in talking with a number of engineers and developers, I was told repeatedly that this sound card is a best buy. Again, we do apologize for not being able to write about more digital

Figure 8.19
Multi!Wav Digital PRO from AdB International.

interfaces for the PC, but there was just not enough information made available to us from the manufacturers involved.

The DAW (Digital Audio Workstation)

The stand-alone Digital Audio Workstation is an incredibly useful tool for the interactive developer interested in recording music and sound. The newly released VS 880 from Roland is a great example of a high quality, reasonably priced DAW. This innovative unit will probably cause as much impact on the project studio market as the Alesis ADAT did with its release in 1991. With 64 tracks of digital hard disk recording, a 14 channel fully digital mixer, and a sticker price of under $3,000, the VS 880 is sure to be a best seller. Additional features include an optional internal multi effects unit and storage from an internal 540 megabyte hard drive, or an optional 1 gigabyte Jaz drive.

Ron Simpson

MIDI

Key Topics:

- **Learn about the evolution of MIDI software patches and improvements**

- **Find out how to use sequencing software for both the PC and Mac**

- **Many MIDI-related terms explained**

MIDI (Musical Instrument Digital Interface) is one the most abused, misunderstood, loved, and maligned technological advances to come out of the early 1980s. Musicians finally had a standardized way for their synthesizers, samplers, drum machines, sequencers, and computers to talk. For the first time in the history of electronic-based music, there was true communication! This has had a profound impact on how music is composed, produced, and recorded. Many good (and some bad) innovations came out of this wonderful new standard. Suddenly, anyone with a computer, some sequencing software, and a few MIDI modules could become an instant composer. Talent was no longer a prerequisite. While this alone could fuel a lengthy and heated debate on the good, the bad, and the ugly of music technology, for the time being, I'll take a hands-off attitude. Even though MIDI has caused many musicians (and non-musicians alike) to stomp, scream, and pull out their hair, I, for one, can't imagine life without it.

If you have absolutely no idea what MIDI is, and why it's in a book like this, you'll probably find this chapter useful and instructive.

As many (and hopefully all) people know, a CD-quality stereo AIFF or WAVE file can eat up a huge amount of disk space, and take forever to load. Since the lack of disk space is one of your biggest enemies, finding an alternative way to play back music for your games, multimedia presentations, and CD-ROMs without taking up too much space is a must. The most common solution has been to use grungy-sounding, 8-bit 11 kHz mono sound files. DVD technology, while looming just around the corner, won't be a mass market reality for sometime, so the logical solution is playback through MIDI. Because MIDI is just musical note on/off (and controller) information, the files are, by comparison, very small. This is a good thing.

Before you read any further, there is one thing you always need to remember: *MIDI data is not audio.* Once, during my brief days in music retail sales, I sold a MIDI sound module to a customer so he could enhance the sounds of his current MIDI keyboard. After explaining how the module worked and how to hook it up, I sent him on his way. The next day, he showed up bent out of shape and frothing at the mouth because he hooked up his MIDI and it did not work.

I calmed him down and had him show me how he connected the module to his keyboard. Sure enough, the MIDI cable was correctly in place. My next question was, "Are you going to hook up the audio cables so you can hear it?"

"I don't need audio. This thing has MIDI!" he exclaimed loudly.

I explained that MIDI is just data, and he put his tail between his legs and left (never to be seen again). One more time — *MIDI information is not sound.*

Okay. Now that we've got that out of the way, let me briefly explain the Standard MIDI File (SMF). An SMF will play back on most, if not all, of the commercially available sequencing packages for both Mac and Windows platforms. Each sequencing program has its own unique file format, and most have the ability to load and save (or import and export) an SMF. We've included a number of Standard MIDI Files on the Incredible Sound Resource CD-ROM and a MIDI sequencer with which to play them back. Later in this chapter, I'll show you how to load and play back an SMF.

General MIDI

Before General Midi (which I'll explain in a moment), there was a little compatibility problem. For example, playing back a MIDI file created with a Roland Synthesizer would sound nothing like the original when played back on a comparable Yamaha Synthesizer. What might be a snare drum on the Roland would be a cymbal crash on the Yamaha. With a considerable amount of editing, you could come up with something that sounded reasonably close, but for most musicians, it was almost faster to start from scratch.

Finally, in 1991, General MIDI System Level 1 was adopted by the American MIDI Manufacturers Association (MMA) and the Japanese MIDI Standards Committee (JMSC). This meant a standardization of program numbers (patch mapping), rhythm sounds, and controller information. Whether your GM hardware was from Creative Labs, Roland, or Yamaha, it would play back the same GM files with more or less the same results.

To conform to the GM Level 1 Standard, a synthesizer or sound card must be capable of playing back 16 MIDI channels, and must have a minimum of 24 notes polyphony. In the GM format, MIDI Channel 10 is assigned to drums and percussion. Table 9.1 shows the program numbers and their corresponding instrument sounds for the complete General MIDI sound set.

Table 9.1 General MIDI Sound Set

#	Instrument Name	#	Instrument Name
Piano			
1	Acoustic Grand Piano	5	Electric Piano 1
2	Bright Acoustic Piano	6	Electric Piano 2
3	Electric Grand Piano	7	Harpsichord
4	Honky-tonk Piano	8	Clavi
Chromatic Percussion			
9	Celesta	12	Vibraphone
10	Glockenspiel	13	Marimba
11	Music Box	14	Xylophone

(continued)

Table 9.1 General MIDI Sound Set (continued)

#	Instrument Name	#	Instrument Name
Chromatic Percussion			
15	Tubular Bells	16	Dulcimer
Organ			
17	Drawbar Organ	21	Reed Organ
18	Percussive Organ	22	Accordion
19	Rock Organ	23	Harmonica
20	Church Organ	24	Tango Accordion
Guitar			
25	Acoustic Guitar (nylon)	29	Electric Guitar (muted)
26	Acoustic Guitar (steel)	30	Overdriven Guitar
27	Electric Guitar (Jazz)	31	Distortion Guitar
28	Electric Guitar (clean)	32	Guitar Harmonics
Bass			
33	Acoustic Bass	37	Slap Bass 1
34	Electric Bass (finger)	38	Slap Bass 2
35	Electric Bass (pick)	39	Synth Bass 1
36	Fretless Bass	40	Synth Bass 2
Strings and Orchestral Instruments			
41	Violin	45	Tremolo Strings
42	Viola	46	Pizzicato Strings
43	Cello	47	Orchestral Harp
44	Contrabass	48	Timpani
Ensemble			
49	String Ensemble 1	53	Choir Aahs
50	String Ensemble 2	54	Voice Oohs
51	SynthStrings 1	55	Synth Vox
52	SynthStrings 2	56	Orchestra Hit

continued

Table 9.1   General MIDI Sound Set (continued)

#	Instrument Name	#	Instrument Name
Brass			
57	Trumpet	61	French Horn
58	Trombone	62	Brass Section
59	Tuba	63	Synth Brass 1
60	Muted Trumpet	64	Synth Brass 2
Reed			
65	Soprano Sax	69	Oboe
66	Alto Sax	70	English Horn
67	Tenor Sax	71	Bassoon
68	Baritone Sax	72	Clarinet
Pipe			
73	Piccolo	77	Blown Bottle
74	Flute	78	Shakuhachi
75	Recorder	79	Whistle
76	Pan Flute	80	Ocarina
Synth Lead			
81	Lead 1 (square)	82	Lead 2 (sawtooth)
Synth Lead			
83	Lead 3 (calliope)	86	Lead 6 (voice)
84	Lead 4 (chiff)	87	Lead 7 (fifths)
85	Lead 5 (charang)	88	Lead 8 (bass+lead)
Synth Pad			
89	Pad 1 (new age)	93	Pad 5 (bowed)
90	Pad 2 (warm)	94	Pad 6 (metallic)
91	Pad 3 (polysynth)	95	Pad 7 (halo)
92	Pad 4 (choir)	96	Pad 8 (sweep)

continued

Table 9.1   General MIDI Sound Set (continued)

#	Instrument Name	#	Instrument Name
	Synth SFX		
97	FX 1 (rain)	101	FX 5 (brightness)
98	FX 2 (soundtrack)	102	FX 6 (goblins)
99	FX 3 (crystal)	103	FX 7 (echoes)
100	FX 4 (atmosphere)	104	FX 8 (sci-fi)
	Ethnic misc.		
105	Sitar	109	Kalimba
106	Banjo	110	Bag pipe
107	Shamisen	111	Fiddle
108	Koto	112	Shanai
	Percussive		
113	Tinkle Bell	117	Taiko
114	Agogo	118	Melodic Tom
115	Steel Drums	119	Synth Drum
116	Woodblock	120	Reverse Cymbal
	SFX		
121	Guitar Fret Noise	125	Telephone Ring
122	Breath Noise	126	Helicopter
123	Seashore	127	Applause
124	Bird Tweet	128	Gunshot

General MIDI Patches

Unfortunately, even though the GM standard works, not all hardware is of the same quality. With automobiles, there's the Yugo and there's the Vette. The same is true of sound hardware. The piano on one sound card might be very realistic and warm sounding, while on another sound card, though residing at the same location (program #), the piano would sound flat and muffled. For those of us who crave superior sound, where do we go?

The Roland Corporation was the first company to introduce an extended GM format, called the GS format. Great, you say. MIDI, SMF, GM, and now GS. We're moving forward. But what does it all mean? Well, the GS format is a set of specifications for sound sources that defines how multi-timbral, sound-generating units will respond to MIDI messages, while still staying true to the General MIDI format.

With the GS format, Roland has taken a good thing and made it a great one. Its proprietary system makes it possible to include separate chorus and reverb for each MIDI channel, and gives you the ability to edit the original GM tones and have them play back on any GS unit, just like the composer or performer wanted you to hear it. Put simply, GS Synthesizers sound great.

 Roland was not the only company to come up with an extended GM format. Yamaha jumped in with XG. Why another format? Although remaining true to the General MIDI level 1 Standard, XG gives you the ability to access thousands of standardized voices with up to 32 MIDI channels (on the MU80). It is also possible to have up to three onboard effects per MIDI channel. With most XG Synthesizers and sound cards, you can route an external audio source through the effects section of the XG unit, and mix it through the audio output.

One example would be to play an electric guitar through the external audio inputs of an XG tone generator. You could mix the guitar through the onboard effects processors, and then mix it with the internal sounds to the audio output.

XG units have a wide variety of MIDI controls, and with three effects processors per MIDI channel, it is possible to customize sounds to a greater degree than with any previous GM-capable instrument. In addition to the advantages offered by GS and XG, the overall sound quality of the samples on these units is clearly superior to that of most other GM-compatible synthesizers and sound cards.

Software-Based GM Synthesizers

Right now, you're probably thinking how great it would be if you could record and play back high-quality, MIDI-based music on your computer without any additional hardware.

Thanks to InVision Interactive's Cybersound VS, you now can. Though currently only available for the 68040 and Power Macintosh computers, Cybersound VS comes with over 500 quality sounds, built-in digital effects, and a 16-track sequencer. Compared sonically to the base-level sound cards on Windows machines, Cybersound VS is a hands-down winner. With 50 megabytes of 16-bit sounds, and the use of physical modeling, as well as other synthesizer technologies, Cybersound VS is the wave of the future. You will see many similar products emerging on both major platforms.

The consistent sound quality of the software-based GM synthesizer will enhance and add an aural flexibility to every type of presentation. For the kiosk developer, no longer do your clients have to listen to a low-resolution, 30-second piece of music repeat itself over and over. With the same amount of disk space, you could easily have a dozen .MIDI files, and over an hour's worth of great-sounding music.

Using the Web as a delivery system for education is one of the realities of the very near future. With a software-based GM Synthesizer installed in your computer, all the tools of sound and music used in film and television can easily be integrated into this emerging market. Normally, silent teaching tools will come alive and become more interactive than ever. Imagine making learning fun and interesting. What a concept.

QuickTime Music Architecture

Apple has also jumped into the business of supporting software-based MIDI Synthesizers with the introduction of QTMA (QuickTime Music Architecture).

 Apple licensed a number of Sound Canvas musical instruments from Roland, and is paving the way for music and synthesizer developers with QTMA. The enhancements available in QuickTime 2.2 make it possible for developers to create custom software synthesizers and sound libraries, and easily play them back through QuickTime. Next time a client says, "It would be nice to have music on this project but we just don't have the disk space," you can say, "QTMA dude!" The client will have absolutely no idea what you are talking about and may even call security. Not to worry. Once you explain the potential of this new tool, the hand cuffs will be off in no time.

As delivery systems on the Web define themselves, QTMA is going to have a major impact on everything from education to commercial advertising. With the integration of OMS from Opcode into QuickTime 2.2, the normally confusing routing and assigning of MIDI information will be greatly simplified. Information on licensing QuickTime for developers is included in the equipment appendix. While quite a few developers are working at integrating their products with QuickTime 2.2, currently everyone is keeping silent about the specifics. Its almost as if old J. Edgar was looking over their shoulders.

At the time of our deadline, there were no PC-compatible, software-based GM synthesizers commercially available to us. Not to worry: InVision Interactive and Yamaha both have them in development.

What Is OMS?

In 1991, Opcode introduced OMS (Open Music System) as a new way to organize MIDI data on the Macintosh. OMS (Fgure 9.1) is a system extension that lets the user configure and save their entire MIDI setup. Using any OMS compatible application (such as sequencing software), you can store and route MIDI information in a very efficient and uncomplicated manner. Needless to say, this is a great improvement over Apple's MIDI manager. OMS 2.0 is now shipping with all new Opcode products, as well as with Cybersound VS. You can expect to see OMS integrated into QuickTime 2.0. and in Microsoft's Windows 95 in the very near future.

The integration of OMS into the majority of all professional Mac-based software packages for music and sound is an idea long overdue. With OMS also being integrated into Windows 95 as well, and hopefully showing up in professional music software for the PC compatibles, true plug and play multimedia will finally become a reality. OMS is making it easier for developers to design cross-platform products that function with an ease the end user has never before known.

I recently installed OMS 2.0 in my Power Macintosh 8500 to oversee the use of hard disk recording software, MIDI sequencing software, Cybersound VS, and an editor librarian. Thanks to OMS, all my software and external MIDI hardware (and there's a lot of hardware here) now work together with seamless perfection.

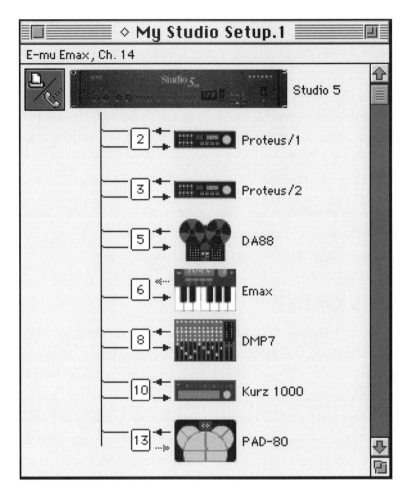

Figure 9.1

The OMS Studio Setup Document.

Sequencing Software

In this section, I'll run through a few different software based sequencers — from entry level to the best of the best. Because I realize you might not be a musician, I won't deal with the actual recording of MIDI files. Instead, I'll touch on loading or importing an SMF, and I'll provide you with a look at a few features common to most sequencing software. Included with the Incredible Sound Resource CD-ROM, are some Standard MIDI Files and a demo sequencer for playback.

What's Out There?

So what do you look for in a basic sequencer? Graphic editing and the ability to cut and paste, as well as edit individual notes, can come in handy. We have included demo versions of Opcode's Musicshop (Mac) and Cakewalk Express (PC) on the Incredible Sound Resource CD-ROM. Other than being "save-disabled," they are both fully functional and will be an excellent way for you learn the basics of loading, editing, and playing back .MIDI files. In the equipment appendix, we list as many downloadable sequencing software demos as we could find so you can try them all out. The Musicshop startup screen is shown in Figure 9.2.

Opcode's Vision

Vision 3.0 from Opcode (Mac, shown in Figure 9.3) is, without a doubt, one of the best full-featured sequencers available today. I have used Vision in its various incarnations since 1.44, and this latest version has become indispensable in my work. Not only is it easy to use, it has such depth that after three years of working with Vision on an almost daily basis, I'm still discovering new features. One of the best new features of Vision 3.0 is the ability to record and edit 16-bit digital audio without any additional hardware (and this in the same window as the MIDI sequences).

Probably to avoid being accused of being Mac myopic, Opcode has released Vision 2.0 for Windows. It looks, tastes, and smells just like the Mac version of Vision, and I for one am glad to see its release. All musicians work best with their favorite sequencer, and being able to use Vision on either platform is a bonus. I hope that other developers head in this direction of cross-platform compatibility.

This One's a Cakewalk

With the release of Cakewalk Pro Audio, what many consider to be the world's leading MIDI sequencer for Windows has jumped into the realm of digital audio as well (Figure 9.4). Using a properly installed sound card or a professional audio interface, you can record, edit, and playback 16-bit, 44 kHz, CD-quality audio much in the same fashion as with Vision 3.0.

Figure 9.2

The Musicshop startup screen.

Even though at heart I'm a Mac guy, I've put in over 300 hours recording and editing with Cakewalk Pro, and I begrudgingly admit it sort of grows on you. Cakewalk Pro Audio has over 50 new features and, like all of the latest professional sequencing packages, it will print your music in professional notation form. There are a lot of features in Cakewalk Pro Audio — such as multiple undo — that can really save your butt. If you're a Mac user who needs or wants to move to the Windows platform, once you get used to the basics of operating a Windows machine, you'll enjoy working with Cakewalk.

Studio Vision Pro Sets the Standard

At the very top of the mountain is Opcode's Studio Vision Pro 3.0 for the Mac (Figure 9.5). The integration with Pro Tools, and the Audio-to-MIDI™ and MIDI-to-Audio™ feature, sets this high-end package apart from the rest of the pack. Imagine being able to take a great, but slightly out of tune vocal performance, convert it to a MIDI file, straighten out the pitch, and covert it back to an (in tune) audio file.

You gotta love technology.

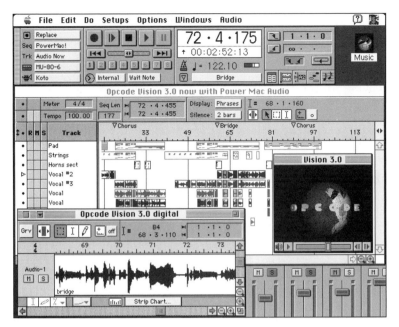

Figure 9.3

Vision 3.0 from Opcode.

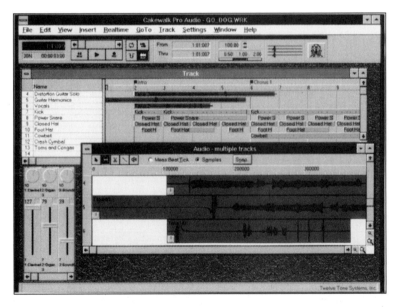

Figure 9.4

Cakewalk Pro Audio.

As is true with Vision 3.0, you can record and edit CD-quality audio in the same window as your MIDI files. With Studio Vision Pro, you can also use any of Digidesign's professional audio interfaces. Included with all Vision sequencing software is the Galaxy Librarian (Figure 9.6) and OMS 2.0.

Band In A Box

We also shouldn't bypass the auto pilot sequencing programs. If you remember the Teen Tango Waltz button on your Grandmother's old Wurlitzer Console Organ, then Band In A Box (Mac and PC) should tweak your interest. Pick a style, type in the chord changes and melody, and away you go. What would you get if you loaded one of these programs into a HAL 9000? *Tangerine Dream* perhaps?

Sequencer Basics

In this section, I'll show you how to load (or import) an SMF, and take a look at a few basic editing features. While this is more of an overview, you should be able to easily pick up on the terminology and basic concepts of sequencing.

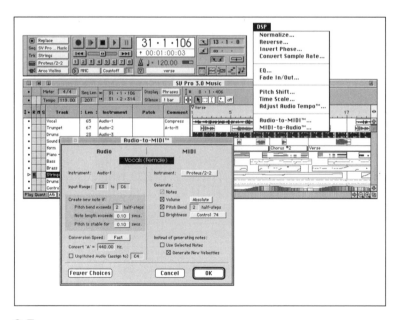

Figure 9.5

Studio Vision Pro 3.0 from Opcode.

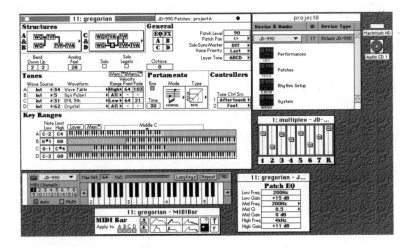

Figure 9.6

Galaxy Plus Editor/Librarian from Opcode.

With any luck, after you have read this chapter, MIDI will be a lot less confusing. We've included a number of Standard MIDI files on the Incredible Sound Resource CD-ROM, as well as tutorial examples, for you to work with.

A Few Things You Need to Know Before Starting

What's the difference between a MIDI channel and a track? Actually, the MIDI channel and track go hand in hand. The MIDI channel is used to send data between MIDI devices while the track is used to store a recording of MIDI data. Every track *must* have a MIDI channel assigned to it (Figure 9.7) To keep it simple, we will assign MIDI channel 1 to track 1, and so forth.

Some MIDI and Sequencing Terminology

Here's a brief glossary of MIDI terms to help you understand MIDI concepts and techniques a little better.

All Notes Off: On occasion a note will get stuck and ring out sometimes indefinitely. Using this command will give relief by shutting off all notes.

Dynamic Allocation: In multitimbral synthesizers, this feature allows a shifting of notes to where they are needed as each unit can only play a specified number of notes at one time.

Local Control (on/off): When using a MIDI keyboard with a synthesizer on board for sequence recording, you should turn your local control off. At this point, the internal synthesizer and MIDI keyboard will act like separate units, and be controlled through the sequencing software in your computer. When you want to return to normal playback, turn the local control back on.

Marker: Used to mark a location in a sequence.

MIDI: Musical Instrument Digital Interface.

MIDI channel: This is used to send data to 16 different MIDI devices over one MIDI cable. For our purposes, we will be sending note information to one multi-timbral synthesizer or sound card capable of playback on all 16 MIDI channels simultaneously.

MIDI controller: The MIDI controller (usually a keyboard) is used to play or enter note and controller information to your computer or synthesizer/sound card. MIDI drum pads are also one of the alternate controllers used to record and play MIDI information.

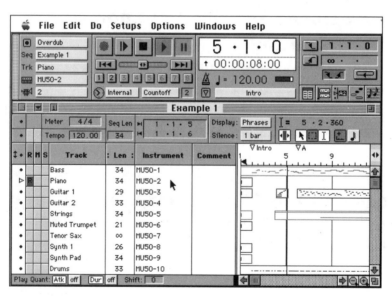

Figure 9.7

Using Vision 2.0 as an example, notice how each track has been given a name (Track1=Bass, Track2=Piano, etc.). Under Instrument, notice the MIDI device and channel assignment (MU50-1 translates to the Yamaha MU-50 receiving on MIDI channel 1).

multitimbral: This describes a MIDI device that is capable of receiving and playing back multiple MIDI channels simultaneously using a different sound for each channel.

Omni Mode: In the Omni Mode, the receiving synthesizer reacts to all MIDI channels sent its way. Someone once told me this was called the idiot mode and to turn it off. It was good advice.

Polyphony: The actual number of notes your sound card or synthesizer can playback at any one time.

Example: Conforming to the GM level 1 standard, you will have a minimum of 24 notes (of polyphony) available for playback.

program or patch#: This is the instrument assignment. You must assign an instrument to each MIDI channel for playback. (See Table 9.1)

quantize: This feature is for MIDI error correction, and is used to move notes recorded into your sequencer to the nearest definable beat (such as an eighth or sixteenth note). Sort of an auto correct for sloppy MIDI input.

Sys Ex (System Exclusive): Sys Ex data can be used for storing patch and parameter setups for specific synthesizers. Each manufacturer has their own Sys Ex Identification that works only with their equipment.

HARDWARE AND SOFTWARE SETUP

1. *The MIDI interface.* When installing your MIDI interface, read the directions that come with your hardware. What a concept.

For Mac users: A standard Macintosh MIDI interface usually has one MIDI input and three MIDI outputs, and is capable of playing back 16 separate MIDI channels. It is normally connected to the modem port. With any luck, you have already purchased Cybersound VS, and can import and play back an SMF without any additional hardware.

For PC users: I'll assume you already have a properly installed sound card and will be able to load and play back an SMF. If you don't have a sound card, get one! If you are feeling brave and think you might want to use external MIDI devices for recording and playback, go back to Chapter 8 to review some of the options for a PC MIDI interface.

2. *The MIDI keyboard controller.* Follow this step if you're experienced enough with music to record your own sequences. Again, read the directions that come with your keyboard to ensure proper setup. If your MIDI keyboard is also your sound source, turn the local control off before attempting to record and play back a sequence.

3. *The external sound module.* To make sure you have made the proper audio and MIDI connections to your MIDI interface, read the directions that come with your module. We're not trying to pass the buck here, it's just impossible to for us to know what exact hardware configuration you'll be using.

LOADING AND PLAYING BACK AN SMF WITH THE MACINTOSH

1. Following the instructions that come with your MIDI interface, connect it to the modem port. Now take a MIDI cable, and connect the MIDI output to the MIDI input of your synthesizer or sound module.

2. Go to the Incredible Sound Resource CD-ROM, and load the demo of Opcode's Musicshop (Figure 9.8). Under the Setups pull-down menu, click on MIDI setup or press Command+U (Figure 9.9). Now enable the correct port (modem in this case), and refer to the instructions for your MIDI interface to set the correct communication speed. The standard communication speed required by most MIDI software is 1Mhz. Also, make sure you disable Apple's MIDI manager if it is on. Due to the nature of this basic MIDI sequencer, it is best to use only one GM-compatible device at a time.

3. Now for the easy part. Under the File pull-down menu, go to Import (or opt O), and import the Standard MIDI File **exam1.mid**.

4. Go to the control bar at the top left hand corner of your screen and press play. Assuming you followed instructions 1 through 3, you are

now listening to music. If you are still listening to silence, move to step 5 for some possible solutions.

5. Make sure your audio cables are properly connected.

6. Now check the volume controls on your speakers and GM device.

7. Check your MIDI cables and the connection between the MIDI interface and the modem port of your Mac.

Figure 9.8

When you open Musicshop, this is what you should see.

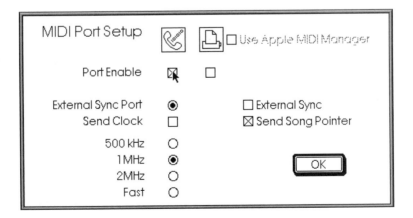

Figure 9.9

Musicshop's MIDI Port Setup window.

8. Now repeat steps 1 through 4.

Since this is a demo version of Musicshop, you can't really hurt anything by experimentation, so try opening all the different windows, do a little editing and see what happens (the Mixer controls are shown in Figure 9.10).

Here are a few hints on how to get around in Musicshop. The transport controls in the control bar operate Music Shop just like a tape deck. In the edit window of Music Shop, you have the choice of viewing a track using the notation or piano roll window. And help is only a button click away (Figure 9.11).

Loading and Playing Back an SMF with the PC

1. Playing back a SMF from your PC should be a breeze if you already have a properly installed soundcard. Although you may already have a utility for MIDI file playback, I'm going to send you to the Incredible Sound Resource CD-ROM and ask you to install the Cakewalk Express demo to your hard drive. While this program is basically a light version of Cakewalk Professional, it has recording and editing features that rival many of the more expensive professional sequencers.

2. After properly installing Cakewalk Express, go to your MIDI devices

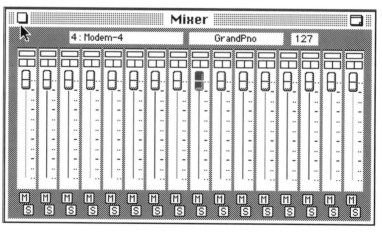

Figure 9.10

Use the Mixer to adjust the individual instrument levels in Musicshop (option M) during playback.

Musicshop On-Line Help

Most boldface words and numbers in Musicshop may be changed by clicking on them.

Command-Option-Shift-click on any field for pop-up help.

Command-Option-Shift-choose any menu item for a help window.

Figure 9.11

Confused? This should help.

window (under the Settings pull-down menu), and make sure the MIDI output is set to play back through your installed sound card (see Figure 9.12). If you plan to trigger an external MIDI device, set your MIDI output to the MPU-401 interface. If you have a MIDI controller and plan to record your own sequences, make sure to set the MIDI input port as well.

3. Now we're ready to load an SMF. Cakewalk Express comes with a number of demo MIDI files, ready to playback. Or you can go to the

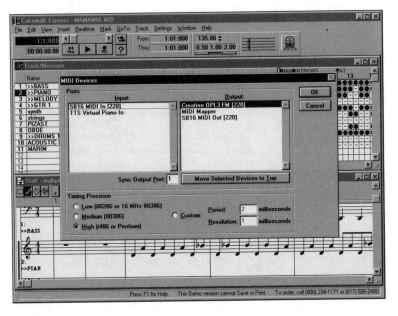

Figure 9.12

Move the selected device (in this case, your internal sound card) to the top of the list.

Incredible Sound Resource CD-ROM, and load the SMF **exam1.mid**. In any case, go to the File pull-down menu to load a MIDI file.

4. If you followed the directions and you have no strange conflicts within your system, you now have a MIDI file loaded into Cakewalk Express. Press play (or the space bar) and you should now have music.

If, at this point, there's no sound, what do you do? First check your speaker connection and make sure your speakers are turned on. The next question: Did you actually load a sequence (see Figure 9.13)? If all else fails, repeat steps 2 through 4. If you end up back here again, the only suggestion I can make is to call Bill Gates.

Using Vision 2.0 as an example, we'll now take a quick look at a few of the advanced features that appear in this sequencing software. The List (or event) Window is a numerical list of all MIDI data appearing on a track (Figure 9.21). Using this window, precise editing of all MIDI parameters may done on a track by track basis. You may also edit in the Notation or piano roll windows.

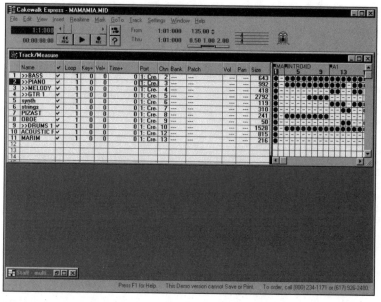

Figure 9.13

With a MIDI file loaded into Cakewalk Express, your main screen should look something like this.

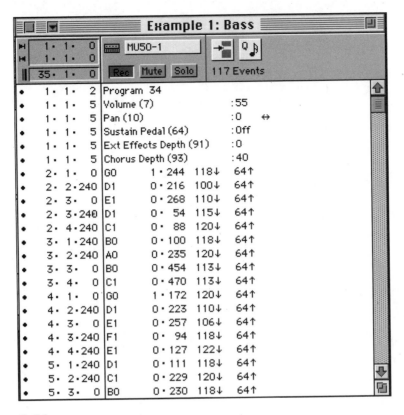

Figure 9.21

Notice the MIDI setup information at the front of the track.

You should now have enough basic knowledge to load, play back, and do a little editing in a MIDI file. If you've been bitten by the bug and want to learn more, *Keyboard* magazine is an excellent place to start. Regardless of whether you're a beginner or a professional musician, the articles, editorials, and reviews in *Keyboard* offer a wealth of information.

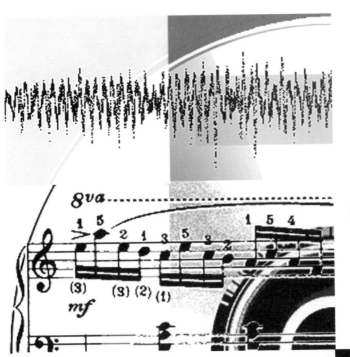

The Process—

Recording,

Mixing,

and Mixing

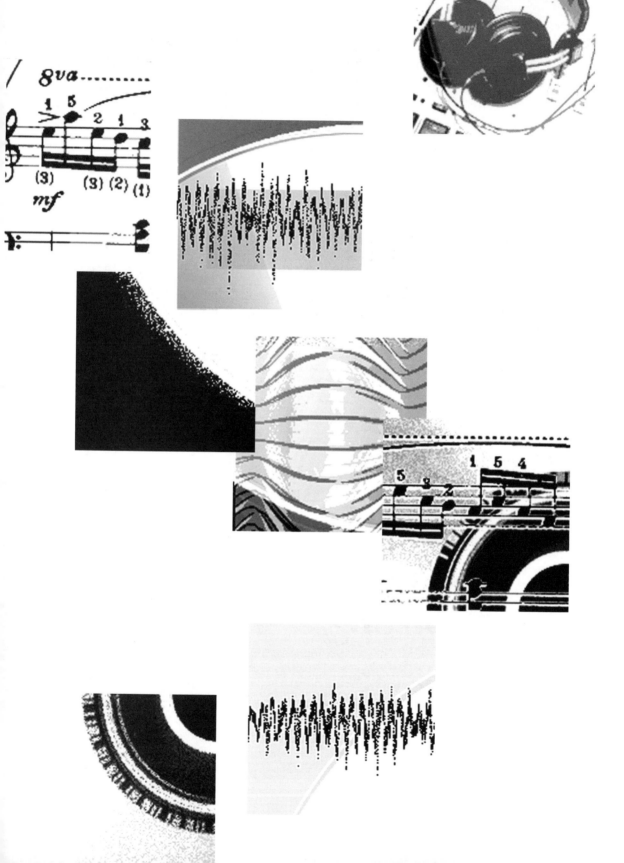

Chapter 10

Ron Simpson

Key Topics:

- **Find out how to convert CD audio to digital audio**

- **Convert to different sound file formats**

- **Learn how to use SoundEdit and Sound Forge**

Hard Disk Recording And Editing

The main purpose in this chapter is to introduce you to working with sound in a virtual environment. Rather than get into the detailed and sometimes confusing aspects of recording music, sound effects, and vocal narration from scratch, we'll focus mainly on the manipulation of existing sound files. We will, however, work through a basic tutorial on recording and editing vocal narration. There are many advantages to recording in the digital environment, but pitfalls lurk where you least expect them. Don't worry. We'll make sure you know exactly which moves to make.

The Incredible Sound Resource CD-ROM includes demo versions of SoundEdit 16 (Mac) and Sound Forge 3.0 (PC) hard disk recording programs. Using sound files supplied on the CD-ROM, we'll run through some tutorials to help you become more familiar with the software.

Converting CD Audio

One of the most essential functions in a sound editing software program is the ability to *digitally* capture an audio track directly from a Red Book Audio CD. No muss, no fuss. You retain that 16-bit 44 kHz cleanliness, and you can edit to your heart's delight, never letting the sound file see the analog light of day. With this function, you can bypass the cheap digital-to-analog converters built into most computers, and avoid picking up any unsightly sonic garbage. In our first tutorial, we will be using SoundEdit 16 for the Mac to convert an existing CD audio file. Unfortunately, none of the Windows-based recording and editing programs that we had access to are capable of this task. With any luck, this function will become standard in the near future.

Unfortunately, SoundEdit 16's demo software disables the Save function, and you will not be able to perform the Convert CD Audio function using the demo software. However, I think it's important to walk you through the process, so install SoundEdit 16 and let's get moving.

1. Start SoundEdit 16, and pop a Red Book Audio CD in the CD player of your computer.

2. Click on the CD icon located in the top-left corner of the main toolbar, as shown in Figure 10.1. You can also access the Convert CD Audio function from the Xtras menu.

3. Choose a track from the CD and open it, as shown in Figure 10.2.

4. Click on the Options menu, shown in Figure 10.3, and choose the resolution and length of the track you wish to import, as shown in Figure 10.4. In this case, I captured the first 30 seconds of the track at 44 kHz 16-bit stereo.

5. Click on Save to convert the file, as shown in Figure 10.5.

Remember: to obtain error-free, high-quality playback, you should save the converted file to an A/V drive. In this case, I saved it to a Syquest EZ135 and experienced flawless playback. File size is always a consideration and, as a rule of thumb, a 16-bit 44 kHz stereo file (CD quality) five minutes in length will take up 50 MB of disk space.

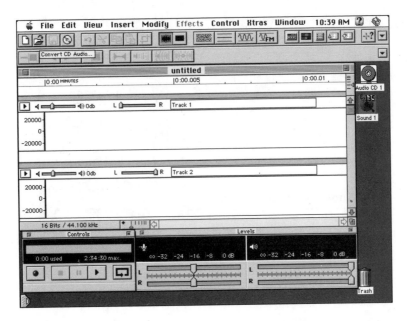

Figure 10.1

Accessing the Convert CD Audio function.

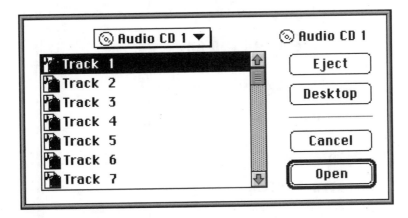

Figure 10.2

Opening a CD track.

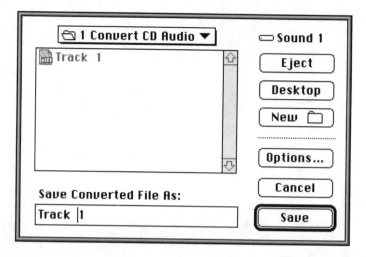

Figure 10.3

The Options menu in SoundEdit 16.

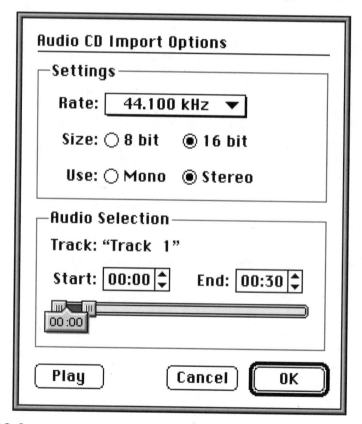

Figure 10.4

Setting track resolution and length with the Options pull-down menu.

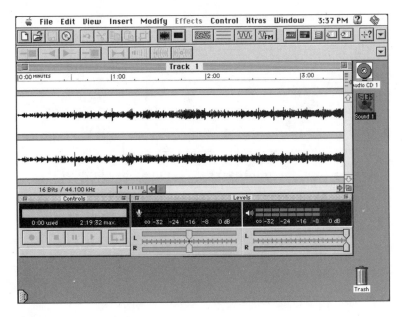

Figure 10.5

A converted CD Audio file in SoundEdit 16.

Working With Different File Formats

Dealing with the many different file formats on various platforms used to be a difficult and confusing process, but no more. In both SoundEdit 16 and Sound Forge 3.0, doing the cross-platform shuffle is as easy as opening or saving a file.

In SoundEdit 16, for example, you can take an AIFF file and save it as a WAV file by simply renaming the file and changing the file format, as shown in Figure 10.6. Even though track2.wav was originally created as a Mac AIFF file, it is now ready to load and playback on any Windows-based machine. SoundEdit 16 is capable of loading and saving 10 different file formats.

In Sound Forge 3.0, the process is similar, although you have access to 16 different file formats. Unfortunately, the QuickTime file format is not yet offered in Sound Forge 3.0...perhaps in a future version.

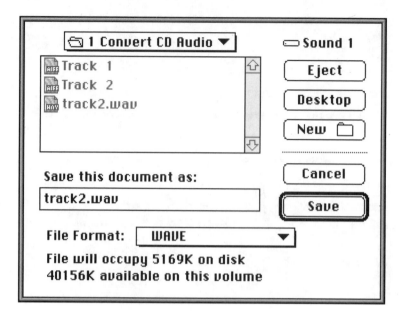

Figure 10.6

Changing file formats for cross-platform work.

Converting Files From 16 Bit To 8 Bit

In a perfect world, we would be able to stream high-quality audio and video through our modems in realtime. Downloading a large audio file would take 10 seconds. Unfortunately, we aren't there yet. So to save time, money, and disk space, we have to take sound that was once CD-quality Red Book Audio, and convert it to a lower resolution. Unfortunately, the lower the resolution, the grungier the sound (and it's not a good grunge). Doing this pains me in ways you can't imagine, but after the first time, it gets easier.

But in interactive development, everyone knows that compromise is the name of the game. For example, you can convert a 30-second, 16-bit 44 kHz stereo WAV file to 16-bit 22 kHz stereo, reducing the file size from 5 MB to 2.5 MB. Of course the file won't sound as good, but saving almost 2.5 MB is pretty significant when every MB counts.

Another lesson in compromise comes with voice narration. Quite often, voice narration is converted down to 8-bit 11 kHz mono files. Of course, these files take up a minuscule amount of disk space which looks great on paper, but the sound can be less than gratifying. Luckily, you have a solution if your initial recording is high quality. When voice narration is recorded through a high-quality professional microphone, mic preamp, and mixing console, it will have considerably more presence and body (not to mention less noise) when converted down to an 8-bit mono file than if it was recorded through low or medium quality equipment. We'll explore a few commonly used methods to counter the problems found in low resolution sound files in this section.

Several other problems become immediately apparent when you convert your sound files down to a lower resolution. We'll use voice narration as our example. The first thing you'll notice when sampling down from 16 bit to 8 bit is the appearance of background noise. One solution to reducing the noise involves using a *noise gate*. Both SoundEdit 16 and Sound Forge 3.0 have a noise gate in their arsenal of editing tools. Essentially, you set this gate to open during the narration and close in the silent spots, eliminating much of the unsightly background crackle and hiss.

Another problem I encountered in converting voice narration files to 8-bit resolution was a major loss of presence and clarity in most female voices. A baritone male voice tends to sound pretty full even at 8 bit, 11 kHz. The only solution I was able to come up with? I converted the female voice no lower than 8 bit, 22 kHz.

Through trial and error on a number of projects, I came up with this very simple process to convert a high-resolution 16-bit sound file down to an 8-bit 11 kHz with the best possible results. *It is important to do these steps in this order*. These general steps work with both SoundEdit 16 and Sound Forge 3.0. We'll provide a detailed tutorial of these steps for each program later in the chapter.

1. Select the Noise Gate feature from the Effects menu and gate the voice narration file to remove extraneous background noise.

2. Select the Compressor function from the Effects menu to compress the file.

This step smoothes out the levels. Look at the file before and after you compress it and you will notice how it levels out the peaks and valleys.

3. Normalize the file. Depending on the level of the original recording, you may not need to Normalize your sound file. The Normalize function raises the level of the file to the maximum value it can achieve without clipping or distorting.

4. Sample the file down (with dither) to 8-bit resolution.

SoundEdit 16: Tutorials

In this section, I have put together three basic tutorials for editing and recording with SoundEdit 16. I'm assuming that you have little to no experience with recording and editing sound, so if you're familiar with the process, you can skip this section (or read it with an open mind). I encourage you to use these tutorials like a basic template and experiment for unique results of your own.

PREPARING AND CONVERTING A VOICE FILE FROM 16 BIT TO 8 BIT

This first tutorial using SoundEdit 16 is a detailed version of the general conversion process we just covered.

1. If necessary, start SoundEdit 16 and load demovoc1.wav from the Incredible Sound Resource CD-ROM tutorial section, as shown in Figure 10.7. Even though this is a PC WAVE file, SoundEdit 16 has no problem loading it. Don't you just love cross-platform compatability?

2. Double click on the sound file and then select Noise Gate from the Effects menu, as shown in Figure 10.8. Because the tutorial voice

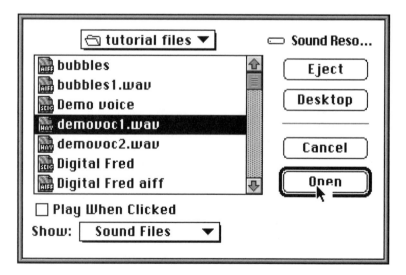

Figure 10.7

Loading a WAVE file into SoundEdit 16.

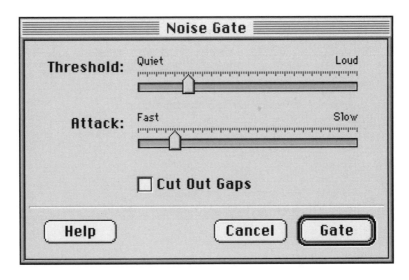

Figure 10.8

Applying the Noise Gate feature to a voice narration file.

file was recorded in a controlled studio environment, you can set the Threshhold more towards quiet, as there is little to no background noise. If the noise in the silent sections has not disappeared, you may need to raise the Threshhold level until it does. You want to set the Attack fairly fast to make sure you don't clip off the front of any words. Experiment with the Threshhold and Attack features until you are satisfied with the results.

3. Compress the file. Because SoundEdit 16 does not come with a compressor, you must use a plug-in compressor, such as CyberSound FX, as shown in Figure 10.9. To compress the file, I used the Increase presence setting.

This next step is optional. Normalizing a file can achieve a positive result, but it can also make the signal a little too hot.

4. Select Normalize from the Effects menu, as shown in Figure 10.10. Experiment with the setting to find what works best for your situation, and always do an A/B comparison. Try a setting of 80 percent to start with. Depending on the type of sound file, its quality, and its resolution, you may want to avoid this process altogether. You make the call.

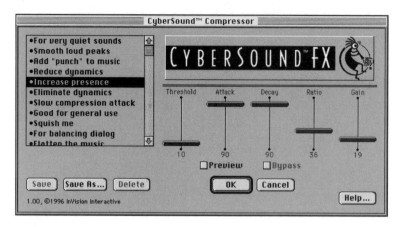

Figure 10.9

Compressing a voice narration file with CyberSound FX.

5. Select Sound Format from the Modify menu to display the Sound Format dialog box.

6. Select a sample rate of 22.050 kHz, a sample size of 8 bits, and *no* compression, as shown in Figure 10.11. Because there will be a loss of high end and presence when we sample down to 8 bits 22 kHz, compensate by selecting the Boost Highs and Use Dither boxes.

7. Click on OK.

The first thing you will notice: The voice narration has picked up some noise, but because you used the noise gate earlier, there is little or no noise in the silent spots between the narration. This 8-bit 22 kHz sound

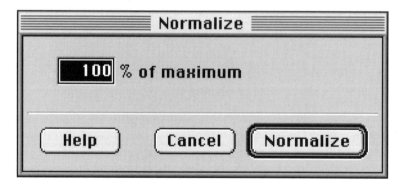

Figure 10.10

100 percent of the maximum will amplify the sound to its peak volume without distortion or clipping.

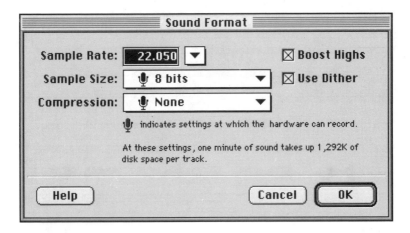

Figure 10.11

Specifying sound format options.

file is about one quarter the file size of the original 16-bit 44 kHz file. There's that nasty compromise again — disk space for quality. I wish they would hurry up with DVD and the super fast modems!

MIXING TRACKS IN SOUNDEDIT 16

Mixing tracks is an easy and necessary task in basic sound editing. In SoundEdit 16, you can record up to two tracks in a file at one time. Fortunately, you can import previously recorded files into an existing file as an additional track. This feature is helpful when you want to mix a stereo music file and a mono voice file together, and save it as a single stereo file. The following steps give you the basics of taking two separate sound files and combining them. So without any further fuss, lets jump in the pool.

1. If necessary, start SoundEdit 16 and load music1.wav from the Incredible Sound Resource CD-ROM tutorial section.

2. Select Import from the File menu and choose the file demovoc1.wav to import. You will now have a stereo track of music and a mono track of voice narration open in SoundEdit 16, as shown in Figure 10.12.

3. Click at the beginning of the narration track, select Silence from the Insert menu, and insert 3 seconds of silence, as shown in Figure 10.13. We're going to add a little musical ambiance before the narration starts.

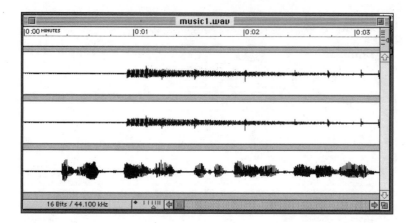

Figure 10.12

Music and narration tracks.

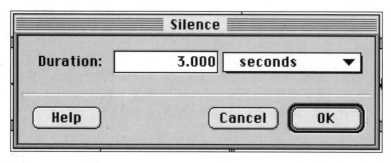

Figure 10.13

Inserting silence into a track.

4. Use the Command All feature to highlight all three tracks, and then select Mix from the Effects menu to display the the Mix dialog box.

5. In the Mode section of the dialog box, select Stereo.

6. In the Mix section, you can select either Simple Mixer or Deluxe Mixer. The Deluxe Mixer allows you to adjust the pan and level on each track and then preview the results, as shown in Figure 10.14. Using the Deluxe Mixer, you can lower the level of the music during the narration and bring it back up afterwards. You are also able to control the gain level of the overall file.

The potential for sound manipulation in SoundEdit 16 is mind boggling. Add the CyberSound FX plug-ins and you have a really powerful, yet

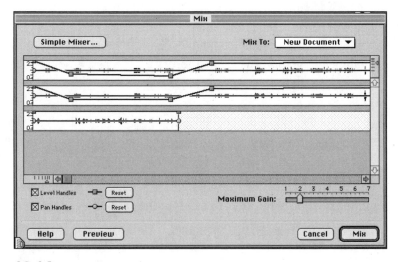

Figure 10.14

The Deluxe Mixer allows you to adjust volume and pan prior to mixing.

inexpensive, sound-editing tool. I recently did a demo of some of the functions of SoundEdit 16 with the CyberSound FX plug-ins for a client. Even though Pro Tools is his bread and butter, he was impressed with the price/performance ratio of this package, and decided to purchase it for his studio. Granted, in comparison to Pro Tools 3.0, SoundEdit 16 is small potatoes, but for many interactive developers, it will get the job done at a fraction of the price.

RECORDING VOICE NARRATION

If you just have to try things on your own, I've included a tutorial on recording voice narration. For this little experiment in home recording, I used an Audio Technica ATM63HE microphone, a Mackie 1202 VLZ Micro Mixer, and a pair of Bose Mediamate speakers as my reference monitors.

For connection, I used a standard XLR microphone cable and a second audio cable with a stereo RCA plug on one side and two quarter-inch phone connectors on the other side. (Depending on your computer, you may need or want to use a stereo miniplug in place of the RCA.) The RCA plug was then connected to the audio input of the computer and the main stereo outputs of the Mackie 1202. I highly recommend using a microphone stand.

At this point, I was ready to set the levels on the mixer. Remember, every recording situation is going to be different and can be affected by a number of factors. The setup information discussed here worked great, but you should only use it as a guideline.

After making all the proper connections (microphone in channel 1), I muted channels 2 through 12. Using channel one as the record channel, I set the trim and auxiliary 1 and 2 to the far left (off) positions. I then went to the EQ and Pan sections and set them to the 12 o'clock (straight up) position. Finally, I set the gain to the far left (off) position. Figure 10.15 shows these settings.

The following combination of settings worked best for voice narration: On channel 1 the trim and gain were set at about 11 o'clock. The master gain was set at 12 o'clock, and a slight boost was added to the bass in the EQ section. When testing the microphone level on the

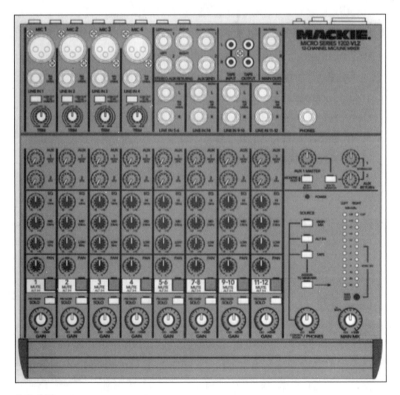

Figure 10.15

Front view of the Mackie 1202 VLZ.

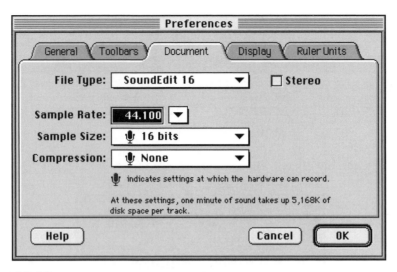

Figure 10.16

Setting document preferences.

mixer (using the INPUT CH METERING), there was a peak level of slightly over 0 dB.

Note: If you have the microphone in the same room as your speakers, *turn off your speakers when recording*. Use headphones to monitor when you're recording because the microphone can (and will) pick up sound from the speaker, creating a feedback loop.

1. If necessary, start SoundEdit 16 and select Preference from the File menu to display the Preferences dialog box.

2. In the Document section, set your sample rate to 16-bit 44 kHz mono, as shown in Figure 10.16, and click on OK.

3. Select New from the File menu.

4. Open the Window menu and make sure the Control and Level functions are enabled. Test your microphone level in regards to SoundEdit 16, as shown in Figure 10.17. Make sure your maximum input level is no higher than 0 dB and is not peaking in the red. Increase or decrease your input level controls to achieve the proper level. In the control panels, make sure your sound input is set to external. You are now ready to record.

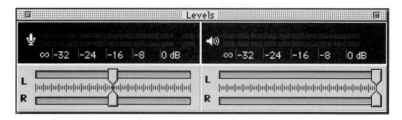

Figure 10.17

The Levels window allows you to adjust recording and playback levels.

Figure 10.18

The record and playback controls for SoundEdit 16.

5. Press the record button (see controls) to begin and the stop button (or spacebar) when you are finished recording, as shown in Figure 10.18. Now press play to see if you've achieved the desired results.

When you are happy with the recording, use the noise gate and compressor on your voice file as described in *Preparing and Converting a Voice File from 16 Bit to 8 Bit*. A number of other features in the Effects menu allow you to alter the sound file once it is recorded. Try them all out and most of all enjoy yourself.

Sound Forge 3.0: Tutorials

In this section, I've put together three basic tutorials for editing and recording with Sound Forge 3.0. I'm assuming that you have little to no experience with recording and editing sound, so for those of you in "the biz," bear with me. I encourage you to use these tutorials as a basic template and experiment for unique results of your own.

PREPARING AND CONVERTING A VOICE FILE FROM 16 BIT TO 8 BIT

This first tutorial using Sound Forge 3.0 is a detailed version of the general conversion process we covered earlier in the chapter.

1. If necessary, start Sound Forge 3.0 and load the demovoc1.wav file from the Incredible Sound Resource CD-ROM tutorial section, as shown in Figure 10.19.

2. Select Noise Gate from the Effects menu to display the Noise Gate dialog.

3. Select Noise Gate 1, as shown in Figure 10.20, then press Preview. If you like what you hear, click on OK and proceed with step 4. If the noise in the silent sections has not disappeared, you may need to raise the Threshhold level until it does.

4. Select Dynamics from the Effects menu to display the Dynamics dialog box shown in Figure 10.21.

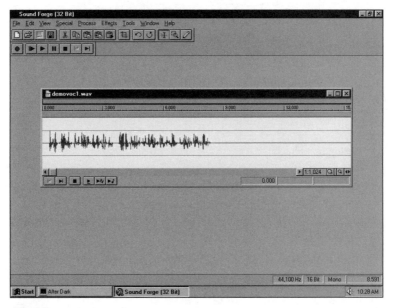

Figure 10.19

Loading a WAVE file in Sound Forge 3.0.

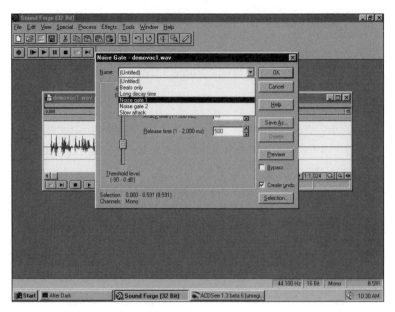

Figure 10.20

Adjusting settings for the noise gate.

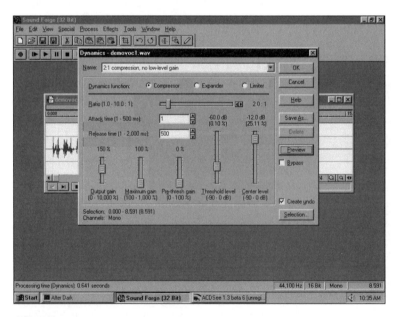

Figure 10.21

Compressing a sound file in Sound Forge 3.0.

    5. Select the "2:1 compression with no low level gain" option, and then preview the result.

6. Click on OK to compress the file.

This next step is optional (Figure 10.22). Normalizing a file can achieve a positive result, but it can also make the signal a little too hot.

7. Select Normalize from the Process menu. Experiment with the setting to find what works best. Always do an A/B comparison. Normalizing a poorly recorded sound file may cause less than pleasant results.

8. Select Dither to 8 bit from the Process menu, as shown in Figure 10.24. Using the preview as a reference, set the Dither Depth. I used 1.0. (Do an A/B comparison on the difference in sound between 8 and 16 bit.) At this point, your file has been converted from a 16-bit 44 kHz mono file into an 8-bit 44 kHz file.

The final step of this process is to resample the file to a lower resolution (Figure 10.22).

9. Select Resample from the Process menu to display the Resample dialog box, as shown in Figure 10.25. Select 22.050 kHz. I also chose

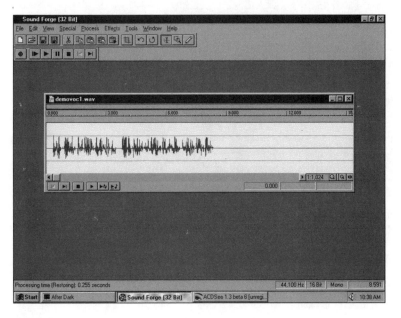

Figure 10.22

Before normalizing the file...

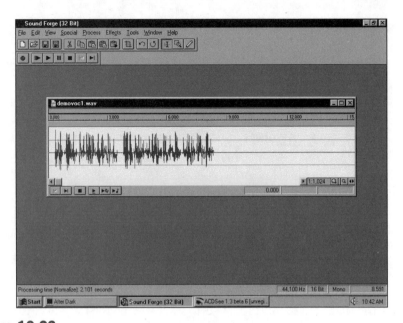

Figure 10.23

After normalizing the file.

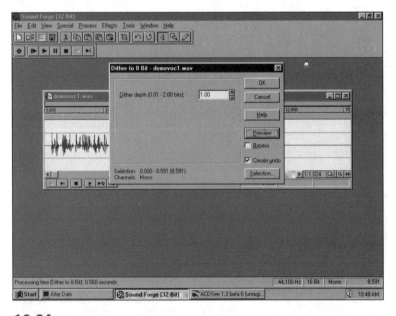

Figure 10.24

Dithering the voice narration file.

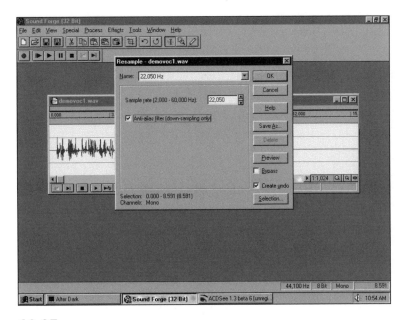

Figure 10.25

Selecting resample options.

to use the anti alias filter, which can help prevent high frequencies from becoming low-level distortion when sampling down to a lower frequency.

There are enough variables in this process alone to devote to a whole chapter. I recommend that you experiment frequently and discover what works best for you. You will be amazed at the many changes you can inflict on a sound file with the effects that are available to you in Sound Forge. Discovery can be a good thing, so try adding Reverb, EQ, or change the pitch of a file (reverse is my favorite).

MIXING TRACKS IN SOUND FORGE 3.0

This is both easy to accomplish and a necessary function. In Sound Forge 3.0, you can have a maximum of two tracks in a file. Normally, this would be one stereo pair. But what if you want to mix a stereo music file and a mono voice file together? The following steps give you the basics of taking two separate sound files and combining them.

1. If necessary, start Sound Forge 3.0 and load the demovoc1.wav and music1.wav files from the Incredible Sound Resource CD-ROM tutorial section. You will now have two separate files open.

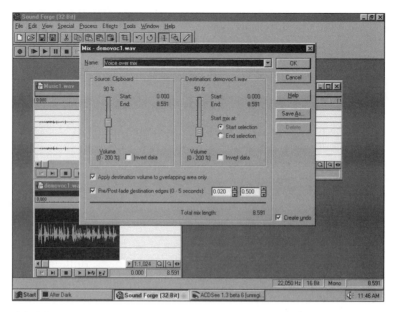

Figure 10.26

Setting the mixing options.

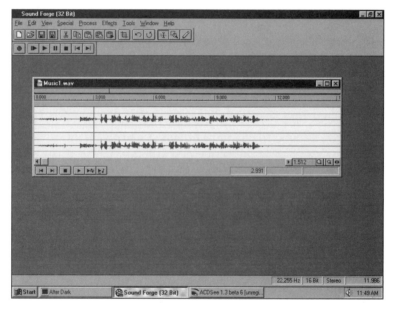

Figure 10.27

The mixed file shown in playback.

2. Copy the contents of demovoc1.wav to the Clipboard.

3. Listen to the music.wav file, and then use the cursor to select the starting location for the demovoc1.wav file.

4. Select Mix from the Edit menu to display the Mix dialog box, as shown in Figure 10.26, and select the voiceover mix option.

5. Click on OK and playback the mixed file, as shown in Figure 10.27.

Obviously, there are a number of variables, and for this tutorial, we've kept it simple. I suggest you experiment with different settings, and then create one that sounds best to you. Remember: Before attempting to mix two files together, be sure they are of the same resolution.

RECORDING VOICE NARRATION

For a brief review on the basic setup I used for voice narration, refer back to *Recording Voice Narration* in the *SoundEdit 16 Tutorials* section of this chapter. Because the setup is the same, instead of duplicating the information here, I will simply insert the steps that are specific to Sound Forge 3.0.

1. If necessary, start Sound Forge 3.0, then select New from the File menu, as shown in Figure 10.28.

2. Set the sample rate to 16-bit 44 kHz mono, as shown in Figure 10.29.

3. For the next step, push the record button. In the Record dialog box, √ the monitor input (Figure 10.30). Test the microphone at the maximum level you will be speaking, and make sure your peak level stays below 90 percent. If your level is going into the red, slowly back the gain off the record channel of your mixer.

4. Press record to begin recording and stop when you are finished. Press play to hear the results (Figure 10.31).

When you are happy with the recording, use the noise gate and compressor on your voice file as described in *Preparing and Converting a Voice File from 16 Bit to 8 Bit*. I recommend that you experiment with the other features in the Effects menu to alter the sound file once it is recorded.

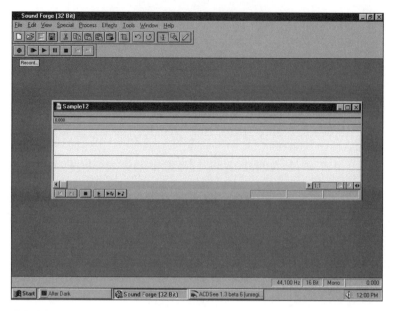

Figure 10.28

Opening a new file in Sound Forge 3.0.

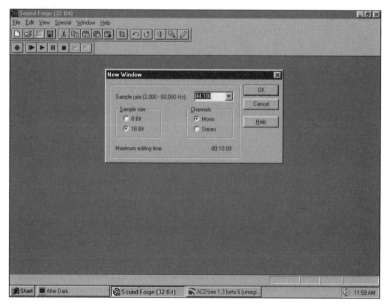

Figure 10.29

Setting the sampling rate.

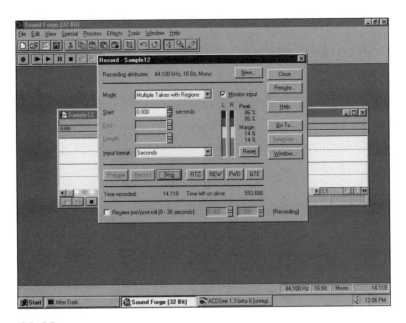

Figure 10.30

Turning on the Monitor input.

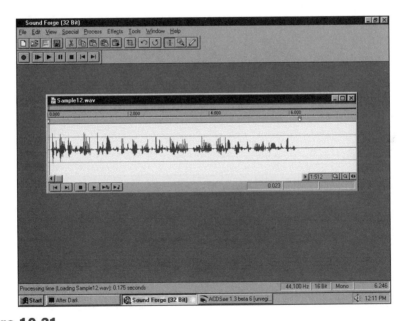

Figure 10.31

The recorded vocal narration should look something like this.

Screw Art, Let's Dance!

I have to admit, next to playing music, working with sound is the most fun I can possibly have (in a working environment anyway). This chapter is merely the tip of the proverbial iceberg when it comes to recording and editing sound. One of the main tasks we hope to accomplish with this book is to open your eyes and your mind to the potential uses of sound and music on the Web (and this goes for Multimedia developers too). If you use music and sound as an integral part of your project from the early planning stages (don't forget to allot a budget for it), you will be pleased with the synchronicity you achieve as everything comes together.

Chapter **11**

Ron Simpson

Contracting Talent

Whether you develop CD-ROMs, Web sites, or corporate multimedia presentations, chances are you contract outside talent. While working with graphic artists, photographers and 3D animators is the norm for Web designers, music and sound design is at best a gray area for most. After reading this chapter, you should have enough information to hire knowledgeable, competent professionals without getting burned in the bidding process.

Cross Training

An effective composer and sound designer in this new field of Web development has to be competent in a number of related areas. A wonderful record producer might not have a clue about how to deal with the technologies involved in music and sound design for the interactive developer. "What's a WAVE file, dude? I'm a musician not a surfer," is not what you need to hear.

So what criteria do you use in hiring an individual or business to handle your sound? Number one, remember that professionals call this the music *business*! Just because your girlfriend's brother is a really talented guitar player and has really cleaned up his act since returning from the Betty Ford clinic, doesn't mean you should hire him.

Ideally, you want a MIDI and computer literate musician who is also a recording engineer. And an individual who has scored corporate videos, documentaries, and films is going to have a better feel for creating music for multimedia and the Web than a rock guitarist. The musician who is at home both in the studio and in live performance will more than likely have a more well-rounded approach to your project as well.

So what should you avoid when searching for Web sound development contractors? Steer clear of the "sensitive" artist who puts the importance of his or her music above the overall Web project itself. On most projects of this type, the music is there to enhance the visual aspect, and is for all practical purposes, in the background. The last thing you need is some tweaked out self-important idiot slowing down production because he is unhappy with the way you're using (or abusing) his art. When you're paying, *you* make the call.

If at all possible, also avoid the semi-professional composer/musician. He could be an insurance salesman who took piano lessons as a kid and now has a computer-based MIDI setup, and has announced to the world that he is also a composer. By using a slick line describing his equipment and so-called qualifications, this individual can BS his way past the uninitiated, and in one fell swoop, lay waste to your entire sound and music budget. On more than one occasion, I've been underbid by these pretenders.

For instance, a charitable individual decided to give one seemingly talented new guy a break (and save $500 in the process). More often than not, the final product is substandard, and in these situations, I often get hired to do the repair work. The client usually ends up paying the original costs in addition to eating the expense of subsidizing the new guy. While everybody needs a break, always remember that you get what you pay for.

Your sound developer will also need to understand and work with the many different audio files and formats used in computer-based, digital sound recording and editing. Sound engineers who aren't used to working in this environment will have no clue how to prepare an AIFF or WAVE file for sampling down to a lower resolution. Without a knowledge of the best hardware/software combinations and a few simple procedures, even an experienced engineer will end up with low quality results.

The individual or company you hire will, in essence, be the producer or project manager of all aspects of sound for your project. So, in addition to possessing the right combination of musical and technical skills, your contracter must understand the managerial side of Web development. Your contractor will probably be responsible for hiring the proper voice talent and recording facility. When all aspects of sound and music are being handled by a competent professional, you'll be able to concentrate on the part of your project you do best.

The Screening Process

So, how do you develop a screening process to ensure that you hire the right individual or company to handle your sound and music needs? One way is request a proposal from all bidders. As the client, you obviously have specific tasks for the contractor to accomplish and a budget in mind. After having gone through this process a number of times, I've developed a streamlined procedure that makes it easier for both parties. I request a potential client to provide me with a precise budget and a list of project parameters. With this information in hand, I can then write a detailed proposal that includes a breakdown of all expenses and potential cost overruns.

The advantage of this approach should be obvious. Let's say that three potential contractors are in the running for the same project. In addition to evaluating their past work, you can take a detailed look at where your money is going. If someone is fluffing out a budget or trying to cut corners, this should become apparent when you make a side by side comparison of all three proposals. Because there is an artistic factor involved as well, it's just as important to keep your ears open. Not only does the proposal have to look good on paper, but the result has to *sound* good as well.

Contracts

So you've already hired someone to take care of all the sound and music needs for your project. Now what? How do you make sure the work will be done on time and to your satisfaction? A contract and sign-off sheet can provide the answer. In the corporate world, it is a common practice for a contractor to draw up a work order, take a down payment, and invoice the client for the balance when the project is completed. But due to the unique nature of intellectual property, Web development sometimes requires a contract to be negotiated a little differently.

For projects between the interactive developer and the musician/sound designer, the contract does not need to be complicated. Quite often, my contract is not that different from an invoice, and simply includes a detailed description of project parameters, as well as who has final ownership of the sound and music. One very effective clause in my standard contract states that all sound and music is my copyrighted property until all payments have been received. Revocation of the right to use copyrighted material can be a powerful motivation to pay on time.

A sign-off sheet is used for the protection of both parties. While not necessary on a small job, it is essential for medium to large projects. You can tailor-make this document as an extension of your contract. Here's an example of how I use a sign-off sheet.

I was hired once to do sound design and original music for a corporate multimedia presentation. After looking at the project parameters, I agreed to a price. Although I was looking at only about three days worth of work, the project itself was expected to take six months to complete. My work was to be delivered in three different stages, and I was to be paid upon completion and *acceptance* of my work.

Acceptance is the key word here.

When my work was accepted, the client would sign-off (using the sign-off sheet, of course) and I would be paid. If, at a later date, there were changes (to already accepted work), I, the contractor, would not get stuck with the bill. On the other hand, if the work was not up to par or was inappropriate, the client would have the right of refusal for that segment, and henceforth, would not have to sign off (or pay) until satisfied. By keeping the sign-off sheet short and simple with payments specified to be made when each phase of work is acceptable, the client is not obligated to pay until acceptance. At the same time, once work has been accepted, the contractor does not have to eat the cost of a change in work that the client has signed off on and accepted. This is a good way for both parties to cover their assets.

Session Management: The Project

The best way to describe the production process is to use one of my past projects as an example. While there's neither the time nor space to describe in detail the entire six- to seven-month production schedule, a brief review will give you a good idea of the situations and problems you will run into. Armed with this knowledge, you should be able to anticipate and avoid most problems with sound and music. So, here we go....

I had been hired to do all the sound and music for a CD-ROM on the Grand Canyon (called, appropriately enough, *Explore the Grand Canyon*). Some of the movies, stories, and other elements that did not make it on the CD would later be included on a Coriolis Group Web site. After I received my budget and the parameters of the project, I did an initial breakdown of costs and expenses. After assuring the client that everything could be done within the budget and on time, we signed a contract and I went into production. Some costs were easily fixed, while with others, there was a gray area that made it next to impossible to accurately estimate the expenses. On this particular project, I had three main areas of responsibility: the narration, the music, and the sound effects.

1. Voice Narration

For this project, my budget allocation included payment to the voice artists, recording studio time, and doing the final edits using a hard disk recording and editing system.

The costs of narration were (and still are) extremely difficult to estimate. If there is a final script for the narration before you start production, costs are a little easier to approximate. Currently, the hourly rate for a voice artist can run anywhere from $200 to $800.

When I started working on *Explore the Grand Canyon*, there was no finished voiceover script. So, not only was I unfamiliar with the material, but I had no clue about its final length. A word of advice, here: You can't overestimate the costs of producing, recording, and editing a voiceover script. (Trust me on this one.) On a large project, these costs will always be more than you have allocated. While we would eventually edit all the narration down to around three hours, our initial scripts ran closer to eight hours in duration. The uncut sessions were between 16 to 20 hours in length, and one of my responsibilities was to pull all the weeds. My back still aches from that one.

In trimming the narration down to its final size, I had to become overly familiar with all aspects of the material. Many of the scripts were excerpts from the diaries of historical figures, so the voiceover artists had to be character actors as well. This part was fun. The early explorers of the Grand Canyon were pretty colorful, to say the least, and as the narrators got involved in the stories, they became one with the characters.

One problem with the voiceover artists was their inability to digest unfamiliar content. Most voiceover pros can read commercial copy and narration for corporate video at the speed of light. Get them into geological or historical material, and it's a different ball game. More often than not, learning the terminology and dialect was slow going for the voiceover artists. One of the first lessons I learned here: It's a good idea for the client (or executive producer) to be present at the voiceover sessions. If there are any problems with articulation or concept, the client can identify it immediately and save you the expense of another session. It's also a good idea for the producer to know the material inside and out. There will be strange or unfamiliar words in your script and it's important to comprehend the context and correct pronunciation before the session.

Here's another hint in controlling the cost of a voiceover session. Convince the voiceover artist to agree to a flat fee. Supply the script in advance and come to an agreement that works for both parties. If the session runs slower than anticipated, your only cost overrun is for the studio time.

In the editing of narration, we ran into a completely unforeseen event. As you may know, when sampling a file down to an 8-bit resolution, insignificant background noise at a higher resolution begins to jump out at you. One of the most natural events in a narration is for the reader to take an occasional deep breath. In an 8-bit low resolution file, the sound of that breath is not unlike the sound of a percussionist using your multimedia speakers to play the drum solo from *In-A-Gadda-Da-Vida*. This can be more than a little distracting when trying to listen to the reader. Needless to say, part of the editing process included removal all of the breath noise from three hours of narration—a time-consuming process.

I can't stress this one factor enough: When you hire someone to oversee your sound production, be sure he or she is experienced in the medium in which you operate. This is not the record or video business. There's a new set of multimedia rules that we all are learning to play by.

2. The Music

The music on this project was divided into two sections. WAVE files were used in the areas where music was of primary importance, while MIDI files were used for the secondary locations. I had been allotted approximately 10 minutes of disk space for the musical WAVE files at a resolution of 16-bit, 22 kHz stereo. Due to the nature of this project, the length of the musical (WAVE files) cues were going to run between 15 seconds and one minute. Since many of these cues were going to be repeated, I tried to make them loopable and theme oriented.

Being the composer and principal musician on this project, I was able to accurately estimate my expenses on this part of the project. It's important to remember to use the highest-quality recording facility available. I'll discuss some of the options you have for recording a little later in this chapter.

Other than the main theme, the music on a project such as this is composed to fit the corresponding segments as they are completed. This is akin to putting together an interactive jigsaw puzzle. As the CD-ROM would reach different stages of completion, the producer and I would decide where music placement was critical and what would work stylistically. This same principle is important in Web development, because different presentations will be part of different Web pages and will encompass dozens or more files.

Because of the sonic inconsistency between the different types of sound cards, we used WAVE files in the priority areas. The original plan had been to stay away from music using the MIDI sound cards for playback. We found that using a GS or XG sound card for playback improved the quality of the MIDI-based music considerably. What I have done in retrospect is to optimize the General MIDI files for playback on a number of different sound cards and to make these files available for downloading.

MIDI music was a necessity for playback in the 3D model. As WAVE files were interrupted during screen redraws when moving through the Canyon in 3D, we looked to the sound card for our solution. Fortunately, playback of MIDI files is not memory intensive and we encountered no further problems. The original MIDI files for this section were composed using the General MIDI section of a Roland JV-1080 and sounded incredible. When we played the same files back through a Soundblaster 16, the results bordered on annoying. I had to compromise my artistic integrity (remember my caution about using a "sensitive" artist), and did a simplified version of these files that sounded passable on the old Soundblaster16.

My initial budget had enough flexibility to allow a number of musicians to participate in addition to myself. I had originally planned to spend between one to two days in the studio using soprano saxophone and fretless electric bass in addition to myself on keyboards. As the musical needs of the project began to define themselves, the addition of the other instruments became less critical. Extreme cost overruns in my narration expenses had forced me to trim a little from the music budget. While the addition of the extra musicians would have been a nice touch, I was able to do the job without compromising quality.

3. The Sound Effects

To effectively estimate costs in this area, I needed a list of primary and secondary sound effects. On this project, a variety of water sounds were required. Fortunately for me, they were quite easily obtained. Birds and various animals indigenous to the Canyon were next on the list. As we soon discovered, specialty animal and bird sounds can easily run as high as $200 apiece, so the 39 birds on the original list were cut down to around 10 of the most important.

A number of companies sell sound effects libraries (see Chapter 13), and these definitely helped in locating some of the more generic sounds. Another available option was to take a portable DAT deck and several specialty microphones into the Canyon to capture the sounds of nature myself. The original production schedule didn't allow this option to become reality because many of the birds were vacationing somewhere in Mexico and were not taking my calls.

Whether you are the client or the contractor on a project such as this, you have to be extremely flexible in some areas. The rest of the world is still not very hip to the difference between a video production and the development of an interactive project such as a CD or Web site. Here's a good example. In trying to obtain the bird calls, I called (no pun intended) the Cornell Library of Ornithology and spoke with a clerk. I explained what the project was and the role that the sound of the different bird species played on this CD-ROM. Because this product was going to be sold and licensed commercially, the cost to me for recordings of the 39 different birds on my list came to $7,800 (plus tape time). This was way out of my budget, especially considering that the birds were about 1/10th of 1 percent of the total material we were covering. Now, if this had been a CD-ROM on birds, $7,800 might not have been such an unreasonable amount, but for a CD about the Grand Canyon, this was way too much. Even after I explained this point, the clerk remained inflexibile about the price and just did not seem to comprehend the big picture.

This is typical of the problems you will run into as an interactive developer. The reality is that multi-million dollar budgets are not going to exist for the development of most CD titles or Web site projects. Hopefully, we can educate the sources who sell information, and get them to adjust their prices to accommodate these new media.

Here's a little jump into the potential abuse of copyright law. And copyright infringement on the Web is just as serious as infringement on a CD. There was a commercially available audio Compact Disc (about $40) that contained about 90 percent of all the bird sounds I needed. This was the answer to all my budget problems, right?

Wrong.

When you buy a CD, you have purchased the right to listen but not to broadcast, duplicate, or resell any of the sound or music. While it's doubtful anyone was able to get a signed release form from the birds involved on this particular CD, the recording itself was a copyrighted performance. Unless you are given written permission, you may not legally duplicate a copyrighted performance. I know more than one person who would have done it anyway and just feigned ignorance if caught. For more information on this subject, read Chapter 12 to make sure you cover yourself.

At least for the time being, producing sound and music for your Web clients will not be as time consuming or expensive as putting together these components for a CD-ROM project. Anyway, the lessons and techniques we all are learning in all areas of interactive development can be passed onto each other so that we can improve upon our work as technology advances.

Finding The Right Recording Studio

How do you find the right studio to fit your budget and needs while still maintaining a high level of quality? Read on as I attempt to demystify the process for you. Don't ever forget you are the executive producer (in other words, it's your money and reputation on the line). The more you know about the recording process in general, the more effective you can be in the search for sonic perfection.

There are times when your presence at a recording session is greatly appreciated. If there's a question about the context of the music or any aspect of a performance, you can provide an immediate answer. As with most musicians, I have a particular facility that I do the bulk of my work in. The advantage is that familiarity with the equipment and staff leads to a smoother running session.

The Project Studio

One of the best kept secrets in the music business is the project studio. Located anywhere from a remodeled garage to a commercial space, the recording and sound equipment in most project studios is as good as or better than what you might find in many of the more expensive commercial recording facilities. One of the obvious advantages of these owner-operated facilities is the low overhead. Granted you won't find leather couches or a cappucino machine in the reception area (if there even is a reception area), but with a savings of somewhere between $35 and $50 per hour, who cares?

While the project studio is usually small and out of the way, the music and sound for many major motion pictures, as well as CDs, have been recorded all, or in part, in the project studio environment. As sound on the Web unfolds and increases, project studio owners rapidly have been modernizing their facilities to meet the needs of the interactive developer.

An example of a good project studio is Anthem Recording, located in Phoenix, Arizona (Figure 11.1). Studio owner Billy Spoon spent over six months transforming his 600 square foot, three-car garage into one of the finest midsized recording facilities in the Phoenix metro area. According to Spoon, the client base of his studio is a diverse one. "We have expanded our services to meet the needs of music and sound design for the interactive developer, as

Figure 11.1

Anthem Recording—Phoenix, Arizona.

well as tracking for national recording artists," says Spoon. In addition to its 24 tracks of ADAT and a 24 track, 2 inch Otari MX-80, Anthem also has Pro Tools for digital audio editing and an extensive MIDI rack. One of the strengths of Anthem Recording is the Otari Concept I automated recording console and the relaxed environment of the facility. In its first year of operation at the current location, Anthem was featured by *Mix* magazine in its "Class of 94" issue.

Originally, the project studio was conceived to record demo tapes, jingles, and commercial music scores. Over time, it has mutated into a form of life that has threatened the existence of many successful commercial recording facilities. With the emergence of quality sound for multimedia and now the Web, studio owners with a little foresight are going to be modernizing their facilities to meet the needs of the interactive developer. We hope this chapter has helped you in the quest for the right sound and music for your projects.

Chapter 12

Ron Simpson

Licenses

You've designed an innovative and some even feel ground breaking Web site for one of your major clients. The integration of sound, music, graphics, and animation is unparalleled in Web design. Word of your work spreads like wildfire and your client takes over 10,000 hits in the first week alone. Your phone (or email connection) is ringing off the hook and you are an overnight success.

Unfortunately, you didn't read this chapter and now both you and your client are being sued for $10 million (plus punitive damages) for illegal use of music and sound clips. If the complaintant can prove you acted willfully in your violations of U.S. copyright law, the amount can jump to as much as $100,000 per violation. In a nutshell, you are screwed, and any funds you obtain through the year 2045 are subject to forfeiture — not to mention that your former client and his battery of attorneys will get anything that might be left after that (even the coin collection that you've had since you were five). Depressed, you move into your parents' basement and fill your days and nights watching reruns of Star Trek.

Okay, so this *is* a worst case scenario, but there is a point to be made: *Read this chapter!* You won't find all your legal answers here, nor can they currently be found at any one place. While U.S. copyright law is pretty straightforward, the process of licensing music for this new medium is still in a state of development and experimentation. Everyone you talk to will have an entirely different opinion or set of rules on how they deal with licensing music and sound for the Web. In this chapter, I'll give you a look at the many different types of licenses, the performing rights organizations you need to be familiar with, and some low-cost, safe alternative ways to play sound and music from your Web page.

Performance Rights Organizations

Let's start with an overview of the music performance rights organizations. Most composers and publishers belong to either ASCAP (American Society of Composers, Authors and Publishers), BMI (Broadcast Music Incorporated), or SESAC. BMI's Web logo is shown in Figure 12.1, while ASCAP's logo is shown in Figure 12.2.

These groups license any business that plays music from their particular repertory. This includes the department store that plays background music, the office that has music piped through the PA system, or a radio station playing when the phone system puts you on hold — even your favorite restaurant that has a live performer

Figure 12.1
Welcome to bmi.com.

Figure 12.2

ASCAP's home page logo.

or a juke box. Using a formula that varies somewhat between each organization, these licensers require an annual fee, for which a business is granted a blanket license. Radio and television stations also pay a fee to these organizations. There are, however, certain restrictions that you must obey. I'll try to give you some easy-to-understand examples as I discuss each particular license.

AFTRA (The American Federation of Television and Radio Artists) is yet another performance rights organization. Its main function is to make sure the performers (musicians and vocalists, in our case) get paid a royalty for broadcast performances. Let's say that I (assuming I'm a dues paying member of AFTRA) played piano on the theme for a popular television show that was seen nationwide on a weekly basis. AFTRA would make sure that I received (quarterly) payments for my performance. This organization also covers actors and voiceover artists. While no one is sure at this point how the Web is going to effect AFTRA, you can bet it will. I made some phone calls to AFTRA's Los Angeles office and was told that the development of policy for performance on the Web in regards to their members was under consideration.

Let's not forget the SAG (The Screen Actors Guild) while we're discussing professional organizations. At the time we went to press, there was no SAG policy about playback of motion picture and television performances through the Internet. You can bet that with the speed achieved by cable modems, SAG will formulate some sort of policy in the near future.

The Interactive Service

Before covering the actual different types of licenses, I need to make sure you understand the legal definition of an interactive service. According to the Digital Performance Rights and Sound Recordings Act of 1995, an interactive service is an on-demand service that enables a member to receive on request a particular sound recording chosen on or on behalf of the recipient. An Internet radio station playing music through the Web would not be considered an interactive service. If one were able to go to a Web site and choose from a menu of songs to download or listen to through streamed audio, this would be considered an interactive service.

The Blanket License

With this license, you pay an annual fee to each of the performing rights organizations, which then give you permission to play music from their repertoires. This would apply to restaurants, bars, or any place of business that plays background music or has live performances. Many of these businesses buy into cable and satellite-based music subscription services where the license fees are included in the monthly payment.

Radio and Television stations are also covered under the blanket license. The rate paid in the annual fee is determined by the size of the listening or viewing audience. A station in New York City will pay more than one in, say, Flagstaff, Arizona.

So, how would the fee be calculated for an Internet radio station playing back music from the Web? The logical approach would be to tie the fee to the amount of hits for each individual site. At this point, it's too early to tell whether logic will actually prevail.

ASCAP has an experimental license agreement for computer online services, electronic bulletin boards, Internet sites, and similar operations. As of the first quarter of 1996, ASCAP has four separate rate schedules (A through D). To find out which schedule (if any of them) applies to your business, it is best to contact ASCAP. BMI also has an experimental license for online services, although at the time of our deadline, the information had yet to arrive.

SESAC is in the process of developing its own licensing policy with performance on the Web, so we expect to see something from them quite soon. Check out our Web page for current updates about policy changes regarding music on the Web from each of these organizations.

With any luck, a standard that makes sense to everyone will soon be adopted by all of the performance rights organizations. As policy is currently at the experimental stage and may change literally overnight, it is best to contact each of the performing rights organizations listed at the end of this chapter.

So, does a blanket license cover performance on an interactive site? The answer is "Yes." But even though the performance is covered, you may have to obtain a *synchronization license* and pay mechanical royalties as well. Read on and I'll explain what these licenses are and how they apply to sound on the Web.

The Synchronization License

Any music used in conjunction with a film or video requires a synchronization license. Be aware this can include computer animations and QuickTime movies as well. Even if the use is an in-house corporate multimedia or video presentation never to be seen by the public, you still need this license from the owner of the music *and* the performance. Is that confusing or what? The music in this case is the actual song itself, whereas the performance would be the sound recording of the song. If your Web page has even simple motion (from an animation for instance), and music is part of the process, this requires a synchronization license.

Here's where you luck out. On the Incredible Sound Resource CD-ROM, all of the original music is pre-approved for playback on the Web or for multimedia presentations. Permission to synchronize for these two particular media is already there. While there are some restrictions, they are spelled out clearly in the license. You should have no problem understanding them after finishing this chapter.

Karaoke is another form of musical expression (if you can call a bunch of drunks howling loudly out of key in a public place musical expression) that requires a synchronization license. With the video background and the lyrics flashing across the screen, karaoke does fall into this category. Karaoke has become a wonderful new source of revenue for publishers. An important note: After a piece of music has been published, anyone may record and distribute it as a sound recording (audio CD, record, or tape), as long as they follow the guidelines set by United States copyright law. Synchronization, however, is a different story. The copyright owner may refuse to let his or her music be synchronized, and there is nothing you can do about it (except to offer a substantial amount of cash) if the owner chooses not to issue you a license. Rumor is that George Harrison refuses to license any of his songs for Karaoke. I always liked George.

The Mechanical License

Feeling inundated with a barrage of seemingly endless information? All you wanted to do was play back a few tunes on your Web page, and we keep slamming you with more and more possibly irrelevant stuff. The mechanical license may not be applicable to your specific situation, but you need to be aware of it just in case. The mechanical license grants CD, record, and tape manufacturers the right to reproduce and sell recordings of copyrighted songs in the form of CDs, phonograph records (do stores still sell vinyl?), and pre-recorded tapes.

There is a statutory mechanical royalty rate set by the Copyright Royalty Tribunal in the United States. As of January 1996, that rate was 6.25 cents for a recorded song with an average length of five minutes. Like everything else in the world, this rate is subject to change. Songs and music appearing on videocassettes, laser discs, and the soon to be released DVD format are also covered in the realm of the mechanical license. If you are an interactive site providing downloadable audio on demand, you need a mechanical license for each sound recording you make available.

Remember: Any music showing up on film, videotape, behind an animation, or anywhere where there is motion also requires a synchronization license. So where do you go to get clearance to synchronize a musical work? This brings us to The Harry Fox Agency (Figure 12.3).

The Harry Fox Agency is without a doubt the most prevalent of the mechanical rights licensing organizations. Fox represents over 7,000 publishers and has reciprocal agreements with mechanical rights licensing societies in most countries. Chances are, if you want to synchronize a piece of music, the Fox Agency represents the publisher involved. Of course, there is another option. In recent years, a number of small businesses have popped up that specialize in clearance of not just music, but sound clips and other forms of copyrighted material. The advantage of a small company like this? You won't get lost in the shuffle quite as easily.

One of the really great features on ASCAP and BMI's Web pages is access to their entire repertory of songs. Between these two organizations, you are able to search their databases to find the composer and publisher of just about any tune ever written.

The Original Music And Sound License

This is not unlike a software license. Essentially, as the owner of a piece of music *and* the sound recording, I can license the use of this music with any restrictions I see fit. To give you a practical example of an original music license, I'll use the license I have written for the original production music that is included on the Incredible Sound Resource CD-ROM. Please note that additional software and sound effects on this CD-ROM is covered by their own individual copyright and licensing restrictions. Here's the copyright notice:

The Incredible Sound Resource CD-ROM is ©1996 by Coriolis Group Books, Scottsdale, Arizona. The original music and performance is ©1996 by Ron Simpson, Jr. (Southwest Digital Music). All rights including broadcast performance are reserved.

License Agreement

Here's the licensing agreement: Any original music and sound from the Incredible Sound Resource CD-ROM may be used royalty free in playback for multimedia and Web presentations. By purchasing this book, you are also granted the right to synchronize the music in these two specific mediums. Use for Film, Broadcast Radio, Television, or Video is prohibited without obtaining written permission. Repackaging and sale of these music and sound clips in any collection of music and sound is also prohibited.

Use for information kiosks or computer games is allowed with one restriction. An additional license and fee is required in the installation of this music and (or) sound in more than 25 kiosks, or in a computer game with sales in excess of 500 units.

Requests or questions about licensing the music and sound on the Incredible Sound Resource CD-ROM may be sent to Southwest Digital Music, PO Box 12231, Scottsdale, AZ 85267 or emailed to swdigtlmuz@aol.com.

In addition, purchasers of this book and the Incredible Sound Resource CD-ROM are granted a waiver from any royalty fee to ASCAP or BMI for multimedia and Web playback of the musical contents.

Thanks to us, you now won't have to pay a fee to ASCAP or BMI for performance of this music from your Web page. That alone leaves you enough cash left over to go to a concert, have a late dinner, and possibly even pay for the limo as well. How many books can offer these benefits?

Seriously, the beauty of this type of license is that it can be tailored to the specific needs of this emerging medium of sound and music on the Web. Even though I am an ASCAP member, I have the right to grant the purchaser a waiver of fees from this organization. While some rules are set in stone, it is nice to be able to write your own once and a while.

The Buyout

Another often affordable option is the "buyout," where you commission a musician to compose and record a piece of music. This is generally considered a work-for-hire situation. The end result is that you own the copyright to the music and the performance. While this can be an initially more expensive route, it is more often than not to your advantage to own the work outright. An example of work for hire is a commercial jingle.

So, you've finally chosen a piece of music and your client is willing to pay the freight for the rights to use it in your presentation. The next step is to obtain clearance. Both ASCAP and BMI have a clearance department. Or you can go straight to the Harry Fox Agency. Let's assume you have obtained written permission to use a piece of music from the copyright owner. Just in case you haven't noticed, the copyright owner of a musical work is not always the recording artist, and that's true in this case. So now you need permission from the owner of the sound recording, as well. Depending on circumstances, this could be the actual artist or a record company. Quite often, the Harry Fox Agency represents both the owner of the song and the sound recording, so you can obtain all the permissions you need with one-stop shopping.

One way to avoid paying the original artist an exorbitant amount for the use of the sound recording, is to contract a musician to record a custom version of the song for you. (We will cover this process in Chapter 11.) While you still have to obtain written permission and the proper licenses from the copyright owner of the music, in this situation you become the owner of the sound recording itself. In many cases, this can be a better deal financially than using the original artist. Rumor has it that Microsoft paid in the neighborhood of $11 million to use the Rolling Stones recording of "Start Me Up" for the launch of the Windows 95 advertising campaign. It makes you wonder if we are all in the wrong business.

Library Music

So what is Library Music? It is a collection or library of sound recordings in a variety of musical styles, usually on CD or CD-ROM. These collections are quite often reasonably priced and have few restrictions. Some are available as a buyout, while with others, you lease the library on an annual basis. With some libraries, you also pay what's known as a *needle drop fee* for each musical cue that is used. These companies have traditionally targeted video and radio production as their main market.

In the past year or so, a number of small companies have come out with some good, (and occasionally really bad) reasonably priced libraries of royalty-free music and sound effects for the interactive developer. These companies specialize in music and sound effects geared to specifically fit the needs of this emerging market. As an example, we have included music and sound effects geared towards this new market on the Incredible Sound Resource CD-ROM. Because file size is still an issue, we have included some short sound files that are easily loopable.

One company that comes to mind in the genre of music for the multimedia and Web developer is Jawai Interactive in Austin, Texas. Providing the ability to cut and paste a multitude of sound files, "Java Beat" is tailor made to meet the needs of interactive developers. With music clips in WAVE, AIFF, MIDI, and QuickTime formats (as well as Red Book Audio), Jawai Interactive is one of the first companies to offer these options in a music and sound library. Expect to see the marketplace inundated with CD ROMs of interactive production music.

Because of file size problems, many developers of music and sound for this interactive market are shipping their music files in a lower resolution and, needless to say, the sound quality is suffering. The final decision should be left up to the end user regarding the desired resolution and how grungy a sound file should be. Poorly recorded music, while sounding fine at 16-bit 44 kHz, picks up all sorts of background grunge and loses presence when converted into, say an 8-bit 22 kHz mono WAVE file. Whenever possible, purchase music that has been recorded in a high-quality professional recording studio. While the packaging might look great, the content might not. So, look for reviews if they are available and possibly download sample files from the Web.

Public Domain Music And Sound

We're all looking for the most modern and technically savvy sounds, so the music rumbling around in the realm of public domain probably seems like it would never be of interest for serious use on the Web, but you'd be surprised.

Any piece of music copyrighted before 1929 is now in the public domain. Lots of great (but not politically correct) tunes were written around the time of the Civil War, and its' easy to imagine that you would want to re-create some of these little gems to be heard from your Web page. How about a series of pre-1900 songs for a Karaoke machine! While you might find a song that is public domain and it is copyrighted, it is the particular arrangement and (or) sound recording that is actually copyrighted, not the song itself.

Enforcement Of Copyright Laws

While you would think it is the job of the performing rights organizations to handle enforcement of copyright infringement from their repertoires, this task falls upon the judicial system. Under current United States copyright laws, the courts are allowed to levy a fine of between $500, up to a maximum amount of $20,000, per infringement. If the infringer is found to have acted willfully, the court can increase the damage award to $100,000 per infringement. Even if you claim ignorance of the law and throw yourself on the mercy of the court, 100 or so hits a day on your Web page at $500 a pop could add up if the court doesn't have a lot of mercy on you (and they probably won't).

Perhaps you're sitting there thinking, "It's my personal Web page, no money is changing hands, so I'm gonna do it anyway." Chances are Michael Jackson isn't going to send any of his brothers over to your house to collect a royalty payment. At the same time, it wouldn't be all that fun if someone decided to use you as an example. I can promise you that if someone were to use my music without permission and I found out about it, I would take them to court and win. Ignorance of the law is no excuse, and pretending you won't get caught doesn't do any good when you do. Take our advice and get the proper license and clearance before you play any music back from your Web page.

When In Doubt, Make The Call

We are listing the contacts for all of the major performing rights organizations for a very good reason. At press time, many of the licensing policies were still under development or experimental. These contacts are the only sure way to receive up-to-date information on current policy regarding musical performance on the Internet and the Web. You might especially be interested in reviewing the experimental ASCAP license that appears at the back of this book.

ASCAP-New York
One Lincoln Plaza
New York, NY 10023
(212) 621-6000
Fax: (212) 724-9064
Contact: Bennett Lincoff
Email: info@ascap.com
Web address: http://www.ascap.com

BMI
320 West 57th St.
New York, NY 10019
(212) 586-2000
Email: licensing@bmi.com
Web: http://bmi.com/

SESAC-Nashville
55 Music Square East
Nashville, TN 37203
(615) 320-0055
Contact: Dan Meyer

NMPA (National Music Publishers Association)
The Harry Fox Agency
711 3rd Avenue, 8th floor
New York, NY 10017
(212) 370-5330
Web: http://www.nmpa.org

Chapter **13**

Ron Simpson
Anthony Helmstetter

3D Sound

What is 3D Sound? That's like asking, "What is a car?" We use it with sound design regularly, and we know what it is, but how do we describe it in everyday terms that make sense? Well, if you don't knowingly use or abuse the many types of 3D sound, we're gonna give it a shot. In this section, we're going to cover several of the different 3D sound technologies, as well as take a brief look at what the Godfather of Enhanced Sound — Dolby Audio Laboratories — has on the plate. For the most part, we will stick to the multimedia and Web playback applications.

The rush to develop a better sonic mousetrap has caused many hardware and software manufacturers to license technology at an incredible rate. Due to the many under-employed law school graduates our institutes of higher learning are churning out, there are a number of lawsuits involving many of these companies and their technologies. Lucky for you, we will steer clear of who is right and who is evil, patent-infringing pond scum. Although the impact of 3D and enhanced sound has yet to be seen, we will guarantee you it will play a major role in every area of society where sound is reproduced.

Here's a good example of how 3D sound technology can amaze, amuse, and, in some cases, annoy you in everyday life. You are watching a movie in the comforts of your own home, and your stereo TV just happens to be equipped with a sound-enhancing device of some sort (let's say SRS). The doorbell rings, your dog barks, and you get up and answer the door to see who's there. Thanks to 3D sound, your aural perception (and the dog's) has been sonically tricked. You scratch your head, laugh, and then kick yourself in the butt for being fooled. We're aware of this phenomena, and it still catches us on occasion. So how does it work?

For the most part, the technology used by all of the 3D sound companies is similar in nature. One way to get the effect to you, the consumer, is by encoding the sound recording during the studio process. A delay can be inserted in the encoding process in the left or right track, simulating the time it takes for sound waves on one side to reach the other ear. So, instead of hearing a sound either left- or right-forward, your brain has been tricked into being surrounded as if you were in the middle of it.

Here's the best real-world A/V test we can think of. Find a CD of a solo pianist (any style will do) playing acoustically. If it's an excellent recording, and the pianist is one of the great ones, it may border on being a religious experience. Now rush out to the nearest concert hall and listen to an unamplified live performance of a solo pianist. Instead of the sound coming out of a couple of speakers, you will be surrounded, and possibly even engulfed in sound.

A stereo recording (even a great one) is still just a reproduction, while in real life, the music resonating off the sound board of the piano encircles you, and can even rattle the bones in your body. The 3D sound process tricks your brain into thinking you're right there in the middle of it.

The Different Technologies

In the preparation of this book, we looked at a number of different companies and their products. There are a few major players out there with some really cool stuff and this is where we talk about it.

The Q Files: QSound

What is QSound, and what does it do? Like all 3D sound, the technology is a bit of a mystery to the layman. But since you were smart enough to purchase this book, comprehension should be a snap. QSound Virtual Audio creates an illusion that allows you to hear sound as though you are in over your head and completely covered with it. Amazingly enough, it works. But how?

Well . . . Q1, the core process of QSound, takes a number of mono inputs and produces a stereo signal with QSound enhancements. This is like having a stereo mixing board with four (or eight with the QSystem II) mono inputs and a stereo pair of outputs. Each input has a 3D pan control that allows you to place that particular mono signal anywhere across a 180-degree arc of space. You could place a helicopter on top of someone's head and create the illusion of it circling around his head. You can imagine a number of applications in which this could be useful and fun.

QSound allows you the luxury of either encoding the 3D effect during the recording (studio) process or placing the sounds interactively at run time. The QSound effect can be added to any redbook audio or stereo WAVE (or AIFF) file, and it actually becomes part of the signal. The pre-processed sound file is then ready to playback through the stereo speakers of your personal computer in panoramic, multi-dimensional 3D sound. An environment well-suited for pre-processing would be music or a background ambiance, such as the sound of the ocean. Think of the possibilities of audio playback from a Web site using this technology.

For game developers, the runtime interactivity of QSound is the ticket. The ability to have all components (including sound) react to unpredictable user input is a must in today's game and multimedia CD-ROMs. Using a variation of the Q1 process called IFP (Image File Panning), interactive sound is possible on platforms lacking programmable DSP capability. For each interactive element, the playback platform must be capable of controlling the volume and stereo pan positions of two audio files running simultaneously. You are essentially playing back the original sound file and a second image file that creates the interactive movement. Both the pre-processed and runtime QSound effects are compatible with each other in playback.

The Tools

Plug-ins for Sound Forge, Sound Designer II, and Pro Tools III are the most cost-effective way to access the QSound process. These pre-processing software tools are available for both Mac and PC. Interactive QSound tools are available to developers for use on the PC, as well as on the Sega Saturn and Sony Playstation. If you've got money burning a hole in your pocket, then you need to take a look at the QSystem II. This whopping piece of hardware is an 8 channel, real-time Q1 processor intended for the professional recording studio. Features include a remote joystick and AES/EBU digital audio I/O.

For a list of current and future QSound products, see the QSound Web site at:

http://www.qsound.com

SRS (Sound Retrieval System)

What is SRS? I've often wondered, since it does happen to be one of the features on my trusty Sony Trinitron. With SRS engaged on my television, the sound always seems to be a little more realistic. Unlike the encoding method used by QSound, the SRS effect works by amplifying the frequencies the brain uses to locate sounds. Hence the illusion that a sound is in (and in some cases on) your face. Here ís the lowdown: When you record sound, it becomes two dimensional. SRS provides a wider stereo image, and restores the sense of direction that gets lost during the recording process. Granted, the effect is a bit more subtle than Spatializer or QSound technology, but it still does work.

NuReality has licensed SRS technology for a number of its multimedia products, including the Vivid 3D Proex. You simply place this device in your audio chain between the computer and speakers, and adjust the effect to suit your personal taste. One of the distinguishing features of this technology is that it is compatible with other surround sound technologies. With many other audio enhancing devices and technologies, your location in a "sweet spot" directly between the two stereo speakers is a must. This is not the case with SRS technology. Its full effect is found anywhere in the room.

The Spatializer

With a technology similar to that of Qsound, Spatializer Audio Laboratories has burst onto the market with a number of Home and Pro audio solutions. It's only appropriate that this technology would begin to show up in multimedia as well. Spatializer technology is based on the science of "psychoacoustics," the study of how the ear and the brain work to perceive sound. To keep it short and simple, you are tricked into hearing a second pair of rear speakers in the room, when in fact, there is just one stereo pair.

There are currently two ways to use this technology. The first is an encoding process that needs no additional hardware for playback, and the second is a stand-alone processor. For more information on current and existing Spatializer-based products, check out its Web site at:

http://www.spatializer.com

She Blinded Me with Logic (Dolby Pro-Logic)

The big questions are: what is it, and how does it work? Dolby Pro-Logic is a four-channel system that sends dialog, effects, and music through a five-speaker system. In addition to the normal stereo pair (of speakers), there is a center and two rear speakers. Unlike other enhanced sound technologies, to get the surround sound effect from Dolby Pro-Logic, the material must be pre-encoded and then played back through an audio (or computer) system equipped with a Dolby decoder. The Dolby system works by laying down the additional channels out of phase with the main stereo signal, and then routing the out-of-phase signal to the other speakers. It sounds pretty simple, but the effect can be pretty awe-inspiring. Although Dolby technology is not at this time especially prevalent in computer systems, you can bet it will be in the near future.

The Final Word on 3D Sound

So what should I do? Which technology is going to work best for me? Which kind of car should I buy? It's a tough call no matter what. Our personal favorite has got to be the QSound plug-ins. They cover the needs of the interactive developer, and their software-based products were geared towards the multimedia market from the start. Sound-enhancing technology is just going to get better and less expensive. In most cases, a software plug-in that works within your existing setup will be the winner in price and performance. No matter what people tell you, the best judge will always be your own ears.

Sound Effects

No film, television program, or interactive CD-ROM would be complete without the addition of sound effects. Imagine a Stallone movie in which you had to rely only on the dialog. I think you get the picture. As technology marches forward, you will soon need sound effects to sonically spruce up your Web page. So now you're thinking, "I need them, I want them, so where do I find them?"

There are a number of companies that specialize in sound design for major motion pictures. One such company is Soundelux Studios, which has created an extensive commercially available collection, *The Hollywood Edge Sound Effects Library.* Soundelux recently won an Academy Award for sound editing in the film "Braveheart," and has over 300 films to its credit. As a rule of thumb, if it's good enough for Mel, it will probably work just fine for you.

The high-quality recordings in this collection have the distinction of being the only sound effects library originally created for film. That's a pretty good indication of the overall quality. Variety isn't a problem either, as there are a number of different volumes geared to match your every need. As you know, talk is cheap, so on the *Incredible Sound Resource CD-ROM,* we have included a sampling of sound effects from the *Hollywood Edge* for your use.

VRML And 3D Sound

Virtual reality! Just say those buzz words to your friends and neighbors and watch excitement fill their faces. Well, *some* friends. The media has done a lot to hype our expectation of this fledgling technology. Hollywood has released a number of movies centered around the fictitious VRML experience that may someday be a reality. For now, actual VRML capabilities are very limited, but the idea has sex appeal.

VRML (Virtual Reality Modeling Language) is a way to generate a 3D environment instead of a flat HTML Web page. Rather than relying on text links within a page to navigate, VRML allows you to *move* from room to room, and ultimately interact with objects within the environment. The space exists in three dimensions, so moving *into* a Web room or down a corridor is possible.

The technology, tools, and the time table are beyond the scope of this book. However, as these developments race along at break-neck speeds, sound integration into the virtual environment will be very important. A good place to investigate current VRML capabilities would be the VRML FAQ at:

http://www.oki.com/vrml/VRML_FAQ.html

The objective in creating a virtual anything is to create the *successful illusion* of reality. The more realistic the experience, the better the virtual report card. Just as sound effects or audio of any kind will enhance any experience, this is never more true than in a virtual experience. Today's current release specifications of VRML 1.0 does not allow for audio integration. VRML 1.1 was envisioned as a quick addition to VRML 1.0, adding a few features to do sound and simple animations, but not enough to start multi-user development. It has quickly become clear that what is needed is to push forward to VRML 2.0.

Knowledge and understanding of successful audio design, recording, processing, and integration will be a fundamental requirement to these new virtual worlds. And keep in mind that virtual people will have to populate these new virtual worlds. People talk, which means a lot more audio recording. Remember what we said back in Chapter 2: "Most of us *hear* many times more data in one busy hour than we will *read* in an entire day." The same holds true for virtual worlds as well.

Multiplayer Games On The Web

There is no disputing the fact that the Web has become a major new source for entertainment. An entire new industry has emerged to provide content material solely for the purposes of entertaining people on-line. (Okay, maybe a secondary purpose is to make a profit.) Entertainment can be interpreted in many different ways, but one that everyone will agree on is games!

We've already talked about the merits and contributions made by computer games and the gaming industry. Good news — they're still occurring! The Web has opened up a whole new forum (literally) for on-line, interactive, multi-player games. Visit the Happy Puppy Web page (Figure 13.1) as a starting point to see what's developing in Web games. Within the site, *Mark Shander* has a weekly radio show dedicated to the topic. The current week and show archives are RealAudio-encoded so you can quickly catch up on the latest developments.

Here's the direction things are going: Game developers want to provide awesome, elaborate graphics, realtime interactivity, and audio and multiplayer settings for their games. The better they do, the more money they make. The Web, however, is still relatively bandwidth-constricted. Instant response to a laser blast won't happen if graphics take 30 seconds to download.

The nature of Web gaming allows for initial download or installation of some parts of the game scenario, and real-time interactive downloads are reserved smaller, more efficient gaming elements. For example, the entire room of a castle dungeon may be downloaded to your system as part of a session setup, but the wizard's voice may be streamed in real-time based on your interaction. This non-continuous data stream can actually consume much less bandwidth than rapid browsing of today's graphics-heavy static pages.

New 3D rendering engines (like in Doom) can render rapidly changing graphic scenes much faster than downloading large bit mapped images. So while game developers employ new techniques to deliver their games over a new medium,

Figure 13.1

The Happy Puppy Web site is dedicated to multiplayer games and related developments. http://www/happypuppy.com.

we benefit from technological innovations, as well as greater bandwidth availability.

By early 1997, look for both significant new technical innovations and really captivating gaming features. For example, in a multiplayer environment, player identification becomes a challenge and an opportunity. Many soon-to-be-released games will allow you to select from a bank of pre-created characters, or take scanned images of you and your friends, and map them onto existing character models. Prior to combat, ugly monsters can be replaced with three dimensional image maps of real people. (I suggest politicians, which adds a new meaning to "political correctness.")

Once you and your friends are running or flying around in a virtual battlefield, wouldn't it be nice to talk to each other? Well, your wish will come true. Initially, look for the ability to pre-record "taunts" and brief messages to be activated by hot keys on your keyboard. So, as a squadron of enemy Tie-fighters close in on your X-wing, you can really *call* for help. The next generation of games will replace the pre-recorded messages with open, realtime, Web-telephony capabilities, allowing you direct communication to the other players in the gaming environment.

All of this will take place with the inclusion of audible laser blasts, explosions, gunfire, shrieks, groans, and music. *That's* what games are made of. And the Web will deliver. These games will not likely be played through your existing browser, but rather through proprietary, dedicated Internet player-software combining the game control panel with a TCP/IP connection. Look for games that will support 50 to 60 participants in a session. And when you have to take a break to eat dinner, you will have options for player control to "hide" or "sleep," or continue playing under an established "artificial intelligence" mode based on your personal patterns of interactions.

These games will quickly move from the obscure to mainstream. Look at how many corporate computers have a networked version of Doom up and running. Entertainment is about to take on a new, expanded definition. It's 3D action, multi-player, audio-visual interactivity over the Web, and we're gonna find a way to get paid to play them.

Glossary Of Technical Terms

ADC (analog to digital converter)

An ADC converts a signal from analog to digital form so it can be read or processed by a digital machine.

AES/EBU digital standard

This digital audio standard was developed jointly by the AES (Audio Engineering Society) and the EBU (European Broadcast Union). This standard describes one of the formats for transmitting two channels of digital audio along a serial cable.

Bandwidth

The capacity for data throughput over a given delivery system. Throughput is always constrained by the smallest bandwidth connection in the pipeline. Currently, standard phone lines and slow modems (14,400 and 28,800) are very limited in bandwidth, making the delivery of high-quality audio and video impossible.

Baud rate

The speed at which digital information is transmitted, in bits per second. It is named after Jean Maurice Emile Baudot, the inventor of the first teletype code.

Chorus

An electronic musical effect that uses a series of short varying delays to produce slight pitch shifts and to add thickness to a sound. This effect creates the feeling of more than one instrument (or voice) operating in unison.

Compressor

This is an audio device that reduces the dynamic range of a signal. In the real world, it means that the loud parts stay softer, and the soft parts get louder. In the case of recording voice narration, a compressor can be adjusted to prevent distortion from signal overload (or clipping), bring the quiet sections up in volume, and smooth out the overall signal.

DAC (digital to analog converter)

A DAC converts a digital (binary) signal into an analog (wave form) signal.

DAT (Digital Audio Tape)

This is a (stereo) digital tape recording format using a small cassette. Most, if not all, recording studios use DAT for final mixdown, safety copies, and storage. DAT has a sampling rate of 32, 44.1, or 48 kHz, and is currently the most cost-effective way to make and archive high-quality digital stereo recordings in a portable and re-recordable format.

DAW (Digital Audio Workstation)

This one is a no-brainer. If you have set up your computer to record and edit digital audio, you already have your very own DAW. There are a number of DAWs that are dedicated pieces of hardware. These can range in cost and features from very affordable to "if you have to ask the price don't even bother."

dB or decibel

This is a unit of measurement named after Alexander Graham Bell. The bel is a power ratio of 10, and the decibel is one-tenth of a bel. This is used to measure change in signal levels.

dither

Dithering a sound file reduces the audible effects of quantization noise found in an 8-bit sound file. This effect is used when converting a sound file from 16 bit to 8 bit.

DSP

Digital signal processing.

DSP TrueSpeech

See TrueSpeech.

Effects

These are specialized devices used in recording studios and live performances to create a special effect. Reverbs, digital delays, and harmonizers are a few examples.

Effects return

An input from the mixing board that receives the signal from an effects device.

Effects send

An output from the mixing board that is connected to the input of an effects unit.

Encoder

Generic term for a software tool used to modify, compress, and/or convert a file into a (generally) proprietary format. After a file has been encoded, a *decoder* or player is usually required to process (play or view) the file.

EQ (equalization)

In simple terms, EQ is used to adjust sound frequency. An equalizer can boost or attenuate a certain frequency, although equalize means to boost. The treble and bass controls on your computer speakers are good examples.

Gain

The amount of increase in the power of an audio signal.

Gate

A gate is a device used to open or close an audio signal path. It can be set to different user-defined levels, and is good for silencing noisy equipment when recording.

Graphic equalizer

This is a multi-band variable equalizer used to shape sound. A parallel series of sliders is used to boost or cut the signal. This is what you might call a complex and more versatile variation of bass and treble controls.

Ground loop

An occurrence in which several ground pathways exist between two units. The result is a nasty hum that will tend to drive all but the hearing impaired (and maybe a few drummers who will think it's sort of cool) crazy.

Headphones

This is another no-brainer. If it needs to be explained, you are probably better off not knowing.

I/O

Input/Output

ISDN Line

Higher bandwidth phone line connections allowing significantly faster data throughput than conventional phone lines. It is more expensive than conventional phone lines, and may not be available in many residential areas.

kHz

Kilohertz. Audio frequency is measured in cycles per second, or Hertz (Hz). One thousand Hertz is a kilohertz (kHz).

Java, Java applets

A programming environment and object-oriented language produced by Sun Microsystems. Java applications (applets) are architecture-neutral byte codes that can be executed over any computer, making them ideal for Web delivery. A Java-capable browser, like HotJava, is required to browse a Java applet.

Limiter

The limiter prevents a signal from exceeding a preset level no matter how high the input level might be. This device is used to prevent distortion and is similar to a compressor.

Microphone

Although we're sure this is another no-brainer, here we go. The microphone is an electroacoustic device used to transmit or record sound by changing sound waves into variations of an electric current.

MIDI

Musical Instrument Device Interface is a standardized way for musical equipment to communicate. MIDI is used to send control timing and data information between devices for triggering noises, synchronization, and sample dumps. A MIDI sample will not sound the same on all sound cards due to the way different cards process a MIDI instrument.

MIME, MIME Types

Multipurpose Internet Mail Extensions, originally defined as encoded Internet mail formats, has evolved into a method of communicating all file formats. The "standard" set of MIME types are defined by the IANA (Internet Assigned Numbers Authority), and MIME types that are not officially recognized must be indicated with a leading "x-" like this: audio/x-noise.

Mini plug/jack

This is a 1/8-inch connector used commonly in computers for audio input and output.

MPC computer

Multimedia Personal Computer (MPC level-1 and MPC level-2) are a set of industry standards for minimum processor speed, RAM, pixel depth, audio, and video capabilities.

MPEG

Motion Picture Experts Group, which is a committee chartered for the creation of standards for compressed video and audio. Using MPEG compression allows excellent audio quality with impressive file size reduction.

Near field monitor

This is usually a small studio monitor used for mixing sound at a close distance. This greatly reduces error in a room that is acoustically bad.

Normalize

When using a disk-based recording system (such as Sound Edit 16 or Pro Tools), this operation raises the level of the highest peak to 0 dB. It then raises the level of the other samples to that same level.

Panning

Panning gives you the ability to place a sound anywhere from extreme left to extreme right in the stereo field.

Phantom power

This is a sort of a battery eliminator for a condenser microphone. Phantom power sends DC (between 9 and 52 volts) through the same microphone cable that carries the audio signal.

Phone plug (or connector)

This is commonly referred to as an RCA connector and is found mainly on home audio and video equipment.

Pot (potentiometer)

This is a variable resistor usually controlled by a rotary knob and is used to adjust tone or volume.

RA

RealAudio compressed file format. See RealAudio.

RCA connector

See phone plug.

RealAudio

Streamed audio technology developed by Progressive Labs. RealAudio is one of the best quality streamed audio formats available over a 28.8 modem. Browsers require a plug-in to process (play) the audio file. Server setup requires a license and proprietary software.

Red Book Audio

The set of standards that defines the compact disc format.

Resolution

The sample size or bit depth of an audio sample. The resolution refers to the number of bits used to represent a single sample. Typically, 16-bit samples are used because greater quality can be achieved with more sample data. While 8-bit samples take up less hard disk space, they are inherently lower quality than 16-bit samples.

Reverb (reverberation)

The sound that remains in a room after its source has stopped. A good example of natural reverb is the tile bathroom, in which your normally so-so singing voice is propelled to new heights by the natural reverb of that enclosure.

SCMS

SCMS is an acronym for Serial Copy Management System. This system is being used on both consumer and some pro DAT decks to prevent the general public from making an unending series of digital copies. The original reasoning behind this was to prevent copying of compact discs.

Shocked, Shockwave

MacroMedia's Web-delivery method for compressed interactive capabilities, as created in Director or Authorware. Its compression utility (Afterburner) compresses and prepares the program for cross-platform Web delivery. Web browsers require a Shockwave plug-in to process (view) the shocked content.

Signal to noise ratio

This is the ratio of signal power at a certain reference point in a circuit to the level of electrical noise at the same point.

SMPTE time code

The Society of Motion Picture and Television Engineers began using SMPTE time code in 1972 as a way to locate exact frames in film and video. This time code system is also used to synchronize tape decks and computers for the recording process. The code is recorded into hours, minutes, seconds, and frames using a 24-hour clock.

Solo

This is a feature on a mixing board that, when selected, routes the signal to the headphone and monitor outputs without interfering with the main mix. This is often used to isolate a specific instrument, sound effect, or voice to adjust the EQ or effects.

S/PDIF

S/PDIF (Sony/Phillips Digital Interface) is a consumer digital interface that uses coaxial or fiber optic connections.

StreamWorks

Audio MPEG compression technology developed by Xing Technology Corporation. It provides excellent compression and quality results. Players are free, but network servers must be purchased.

T1, T3 Line

Highest bandwidth phone line connections allowing significantly faster data throughput than conventional or ISDN phone lines. They are expensive and may not be available in many areas.

TCP protocol

An Internet communications protocol can send data without packet loss, but at a slower pace than a UDP protocol. TCP is more reliable, but only at the cost of occasional substantial delays when the protocol "retransmits" information from the server to the client, and waits for its receipt to be acknowledged.

ToolVox

A speech-only audio compression developed by Voxware. It is easy to use, free, and provides excellent compression, but with a noticeable loss in audio quality.

TRS

This is an abbreviation for Tip/Ring/Sleeve. This is a type of connector where the tip and ring carry the audio signal, and the sleeve is the ground.

TrueSpeech

A speech and music audio compression developed by DSP Group. Free encoder, player, and automatic access through Windows 95 make it an easy-to-implement streamed audio solution.

UDP protocol

An Internet communications protocol without guaranteed reliability. UDP does not guarantee packet delivery. Instead, it provides a stream of data packets without significant delay at the cost of occasional lost packets.

VOX

ToolVox-compressed file format. See ToolVox.

Wave or waveform

Common audio file format deriving its name from the visual representation of a sound file. When the amplitude of air pressure (sound) is graphed over time, pressure variations generally form a smooth waveform. The PC Windows audio standard is the .WAV file.

XLR

A multi-pin connector used for audio equipment. The three-pin XLR connectors and jacks are used for microphones.

Software And Hardware Vendors

We've put together this handy reference to help make it easy for you to contact vendors whose software and hardware is featured in this book. For each vendor, we've listed as much contact information as we could find—phone numbers and addresses, email addresses, Web sites, and so on. Also, be sure to check out our Web page at http://www.monsoon.org/sound_advice for updates and additional information as it becomes available to us.

Computers

Again, we were able to obtain little to no information from the companies selling Windows-based computers, but hopefully that problem will be resolved in the future.

Apple

In recording and editing the music and sound for this book, we found the Power Macintosh 8500 to be an invaluable tool. With superior quality audio and video outputs as standard features on the 8500, you can record and edit high quality audio right out of the box. Whether you are a developer or just curious, you can get more information about Apple hardware and software by accessing Apple's Web address at http://www.apple.com.

Apple Computer Inc.
1 Infinite Loop
Cupertino, CA 95014-2804
(408) 996-1010

Apple's QuickTime home page address:
http://quicktime.apple.com

Apple's Developer home page address:
http://dev.info.apple.com

Apple's Developer Hotline phone number:
(408) 974-4897

Power Computing

This young upstart clone company currently has the fastest Mac-compatible computer on the planet. While I'm sure that will change eventually, it's still not a bad feather in their cap. For more information, check out their Web Site at http://powercc.com.

Power Computing
2555 North IH 35
Round Rock, TX 78664-2015

(512) 388-6868
Fax: (512) 388-6799

Internet email: info@powercc.com

Order direct at 1-800-410-7693

Data Storage And Modems

Seagate

Like we've said in the book, "Seagate sets the standard." After you've used the Barracuda A/V drives, you'll find it hard to imagine using anything else. Regardless of what a salesperson may tell you, if you want consistent high quality in sound (and video), don't cut corners: Get an A/V drive. Any questions about Seagate's product line? Go to http://www.seagate.com.

Seagate Technologies
920 Disc Drive
Scotts Valley, CA 95066

1-800-SEAGATE
1-408-438-8111

Web http://www.seagate.com
CompuServe: GO SEAGATE
Fax on demand: 408-438-2620
SeaBOARD: 408-438-8771

Syquest

With the removable drive wars heating to a fever pitch in the summer of 96, we are anxiously awaiting the release of the SyJet. Because of its cost/ performance ratio, and the fact that it has a fast enough seek time to operate like a hard drive, the EZ 135 is already a winner in our eyes. The EZ 135 was one of the invaluable tools we used in putting together the music and sound for The Incredible Sound Resource CD-ROM. That says it all. Here's a quick little update, though: Syquest has just released the EZflyer 230. This drive has the same seek time as a EZ135, and also reads the 135 cartridge. The retail price is $299 and the 230 MB cartridge should run around $30.

Syquest Technologies Inc.
47071 Bayside Parkway
Fremont, CA 94538-6517

510-226-4000
Fax: 510-226-4102

http://www.syquest.com

Iomega

With the Jaz and Zip drives selling faster than the company can make them, Iomega has made their mark. For more information, contact:

Iomega Corporation
1821 West Iomega Way
Roy, UT 84067

800-my-stuff
801-778-1000

Micropolis

Micropolis
21211 Nordhoff St.
Chatsworth, CA 91311

818-709-3300

Quantum

Quantum
500 McCarthy
Milpitas, CA 95035

408-894-4000

Diamond Communications Division (Supra brand modems)

We used a couple of different modems to cruise the Web while writing this book, and the Supra Sonic 288V+ was among them. To keep a long story short, it performed flawlessly.

Supra Communication Division
312 SE Stonemill Drive Suite 150
Vancouver, WA 98684

360-604-1400
Fax: 360-604-1401

America Online (Keyword: DIAMOND; Email: SUPRACORP2)

CompuServe: Communications: (GO SUPRA)

Europe: (GO SPEA)

The Microsoft Network: Find DIAMOND

FTP sites: ftp.diamondmm.com; or Supra: ftp.supra.com

Internet Web Site, Communications: http://www.supra.com; or

Europe (Germany): http://www.spea.com

US Robotics

There are probaly two names you think of when it comes to Modems, and US Robotics is one of them. The Courier is a screamer, but wait till you see what they've got planned for the future. For more information:

Corporate Headquarters

US Robotics

8100 N. McCormick Blvd.

Skokie, IL 60076-2999

Main number: 847-982-5010

Where to buy Courier: 1-800-USR-CORP

Where to buy Courier fax: 847-933-5800

Where to buy Sportster: 1-800-DIAL-USR

Where to buy Sportster fax: 847-676-7320

World Wide Web: http://www.usr.com

US Robotics BBS: 847-982-5092

Email: support@usr.com, ftp.usr.com

Fax-On-Demand 1-800-762-6163

Courier modem products toll-free tech support: 1-800-550-7800

Sportster modem products tech support: 847-982-5151

Customer support fax: 847-982-0823

Live tech support hours: 8 a.m. to 6 p.m. M-F

Online tech support: CompuServe forum GO USROBOTICS

Hard Disk Recording And Editing Hardware And Software

Digidesign

This company should need no introduction. With their Pro Tools line of digital audio workstations, Digidesign has set the standard for the rest of the industry. While the top of the line Pro Tools III is now available for the PCI (as well as NuBus) based Power Macintosh, Pro Tools IV should be released sometime in the latter part of 1996. A recording engineer we greatly respect told us there were three things we really needed to know: Pro Tools, Pro Tools, and Pro Tools. Any questions?

Digidesign
3401-A Hillview Ave.
Palo Alto, CA 94303

1-800-333-2137

Sonic Foundry

With Sound Forge 3.0, Sonic Foundry has become one of the major players in the quest for sonic perfection on Windows-based machines. It's powerful, easy to use, and affordable. What more do you need to know? How about that a new improved version, Sound Forge 4.0, will be released in the summer of 1996? As new products are made available, we will let you know via our Web page (http://www.monsoon.org/sound_advice). On the PC side of things, Sound Forge was our first choice.

Sonic Foundry
South Baldwin Suite 204
Madison, WI 53703

Phone: 800-577-6642 (U.S.)
Fax: 608-256-7300
BBS: 608-256-6689
Internet: http://www.sfoundry.com
Email: sales@sfoundry.com
FTP site: ftp://sfoundry.com/sonic
CompuServe: Go Sonic
Microsoft Network: Go Sonic

Macromedia

With Director and Authorware setting the standard in the industry, Macromedia is a name that goes hand in hand with interactive development. SoundEdit16 and Deck 2.5 are two of the tools we highly recommend for anyone developing sound for the web (or multimedia). SoundEdit 16 was one of the more important tools we used for file conversion, and editing the music and sound for The Incredible Resource CD-ROM. To get a good overview on all of Macromedia's products, call 415-252-2295 for the latest version of the Showcase CD-ROM.

Macromedia
600 Townsend Suite 310W
San Francisco, CA 94103

Web site: http://www.macromedia.com/
America Online: KEYWORD MACROMEDIA
CompuServe: GO MACROMEDIA
Microsoft Network: GO MACROMEDIA

Customer Service: 800-/288-4797
Sales: 800-288-8108
Technical Support: 415-252-9080
Made With Macromedia: 800-499-3329
Macrofacts: 415-863-4409
Showcase CD: 415-252-2295

MIDI Hardware And Software

InVision Interactive

With the Cybersound VS software-based General MIDI synthesizer and the Cybersound FX plug-ins for Deck 2 and SoundEdit16, InVision Interactive has got a couple of winners on their hands. For more information and a demo CD, call 1-800-468-5530.

Invision Interactive
2445 Faber Place Suite 102
Palo Alto, CA 94303

Web site: http://www.cybersound.com
Phone: 800-468-5530 or 415-812-7380
Fax: 415-812-7386

Cakewalk Music Software

With sequencing software like Cakewalk Express and Cakewalk Pro Audio, it's hard to go wrong.

Cakewalk Music Software
PO Box 760
Watertown, MA 02272

1-800-234-1171
24 hour fax-back service: 1-800-370-6912

Web site: http://www.cakewalk.com

Opcode

This is probably unfair, but I've been a satisfied user of Opcode hardware and software for a long time. They have set the standard for both Mac and PC MIDI interfaces, and their music software (and hardware) is what I use on all of my projects. We have included demo software from a number of Opcode products on The Incredible Sound Resource CD-ROM, and by the time you see this book, Vision 2.5 for the PC should be available.

Opcode Systems, Inc.
3950 Fabian Way Suite 100
Palo Alto, CA 94303

415-856-3333
Fax: 415-856-0777
Fax-back system: 415-812-3207

Web site: http://www.opcode.com
email: info@opcode.com

Roland

Roland is a major player in synthesizers and sound cards. Their extended GM format GS has paved the way for higher-quality MIDI-based music through the PC.

Roland Corp.
7200 Dominion Circle
Los Angeles, CA 90040

800-868-3737

Yamaha

Yamaha has been breaking new ground ever since the release of the DX-7 in 1983. In addition to the XG line of Synthesizers, Yamaha has just released a Netscape MIDI plug-in. This software-based synthesizer for both the Mac and PC is just another tool available for sound on the Web.

Yamaha
6600 Orangethorpe
Buena Park, CA 90620

714-522-9011

For XG developers, call: 714-522-9330

Sound Equipment

Audio-Technica

For more information about Audio-Technica's product line of microphones and sound equipment, contact:

Audio-Technica U.S. Inc.
1221 Commerce Drive
Stow, OH 44224

216-686-2600
Fax: 216-686-0719

Bose

The only negative thing we can think of to say about the Bose Acoustimass and Mediamate Multimedia Speaker Systems is how bad they make the competition sound. We used them extensively in the preparation and mixing of the sound for The Incredible Sound Resource CD-ROM. That says it all. For sales information, contact:

Bose
The Mountain
Framingham, MA 01701

1-800-444-2673

The Bose Web Site is currently under construction.

Mackie Designs

If you're serious about sound and are working on a budget, then buy a Mackie. In addition to the 1202 VLZ that we featured in the book, there is a wide variety of Mackie mixers that can fit any and all recording and sound needs.

Mackie Designs
16220 Wood-Red Road NE

Woodinville, WA 98072

800-898-3211
206-487-4333

email: sales@mackie.com

Yamaha

With their ground-breaking digital mixing consoles, Yamaha has made it possible to produce high-quality digital audio for a fraction of what it cost only a few years ago. For information on the 02R, call 1-800-937-7171 ext. 580.

Yamaha
6600 Orangethorpe
Buena Park, CA 90620

714-522-9011

Sound Effects

The Hollywood Edge

With the largest collection of sound effects on the planet (they told me to say that), the Hollywood Edge probably has any and every sound you could ever use. For more information and the latest demo CD, contact Scott Whitney at 1-800-292-3755.

The Hollywood Edge
7060 Hollywood Blvd #1120
Hollywood, CA 90028

800-292-3755
In California, call: 213-466-6723

email: edgesw@aol.com

Music Sources

Jawai Interactive

This was one of the first production music CD-ROMs that we've seen with music geared toward the interactive developer. For more information, visit their Web site at http://www.jawai.com.

Jawai Interactive Inc.
501 East Fourth St. #511
Austin, TX 78701

1-800-600-6706
512-469-0502

Southwest Digital Music

Since we're authors, we get to plug our own company, right? In July of 96 we plan on releasing our first (in a series of eight) production music CD-ROM geared specifically towards Multimedia and Web developers. In addition to the music, there will be sound effects, button sounds, and short, high-quality music clips that will be made specifically for looping. We will also include MIDI files optimized to play back through a number of different General MIDI sources — including GS, XG, Cybersound VS, QTMA, and even the SoundBlaster 16. All music and sound will be Red Book Audio quality (16 bit, 44 kHz stereo). While the list price has yet to be determined, it will be less than that of the competition. For more information, visit our Web site at http://www.monsoon.org/sound_advice.

Southwest Digital Music
PO Box 12231
Scottsdale, AZ 85267-2231

602-788-5532

email: swdigtlmuz@aol.com

3D Sound

NuReality

NuReality has a number of 3D hardware products including the Vivid 3D Pro*ex.* For more information, visit their Web site at http://nureality.com.

Nu Reality (Vivid 3D Plus)
2907 Daimler St.
Santa Ana, CA 92705-5810

714-442-1080
Fax: 714-852-1089

QSound

After researching and subsequently using a number of the QSound plug-ins, we were more than impressed. Knocked over might be a better word. For more information, visit their Web site @ www.qsound.ca.

QSound Labs Inc.
2748 37th Ave N.E.
Calgary, Alberta
Canada T1Y-5L3

403-291-2492
Fax: 403-250-1521

Spatializer

Spatializer Audio Laboratories
20700 Ventura Blvd., Suite 134
Woodland Hills, CA 91364-2357

818-227-3370
Fax: 818-227-9750

The Incredible Sound Resource CD-ROM

Well it's obvious you're intuitive, intelligent, and have deep insight, because you've elected to purchase not only this book, but the companion Incredible Sound Resource CD-ROM. I do hope you obtained it through purchasing the book and not from some illicit source on the back streets of Beijing or Moscow. (With any luck, I may have just created my first international incident!)

This CD-ROM is not unlike a Supreme Pizza loaded with a little something from each of the four food groups. You have high-resolution music files, sound effects, demo software, and a few shareware utilities—all in one easy-to-swallow package. It is also fat free, low in cholesterol, and high in fiber. The music clips on this CD-ROM are easily worth the price of the book, so pat yourself on the back for making a smart purchase. Now I'll give you a basic overview of what is in each of the sections on the CD-ROM. The rest is up to you!

We've partitioned the CD-ROM into two obvious main sections—Mac and PC. With the exception of the demo software and shareware, the files and sections are duplicated exactly. If you have a PC, you'll only be able to read the PC partition. If you have a Mac, you'll only be able to read the Mac partition unless you have SoftWindows or some other hardware/software setup that allows you to read PC files from a CD.

Music

These files are both Mac and PC (the aif is just for reference) and were recorded at 16 bit, 44 kHz. There is a wide variety (relatively speaking, anyway) of music styles and lengths. Using the lessons you learned in the tutorials on sound editing as a guide, you can sample down and trim the length of any of these music clips to fit your needs.

music1.aif (wav)= Synth 1

music2.aif (wav)= Synth 2

music3.aif (wav)= Synth 3

music4.aif (wav)= Synth 4

music5.aif (wav)= Alto Sax

music6.aif (wav)= Soprano Sax

music7.aif (wav)= The Groove

music8.aif (wav)= Nylon Space

music9.aif (wav)= The Do

music10.aif (wav)= Blues guitar

music11.aif (wav)= Surf Zorro

music12.aif (wav)= Surf Guitar

music13.aif (wav)= More Surf Guitar

music14.aif (wav)= Synth Sax and Guitar

The Ambient Sounds

These sound files fall somewhere between music and sound effects in nature. These can be used as a background ambiance for your recordings. Several of them are trimmed to loop seamlessly (I hope). I created them using the Roland JD-990 and JV-1080 synthesizer modules.

amb1.aif (wav)= computer sounds

amb2.aif (wav)= space

amb3.aif (wav)= space

amb4.aif (wav)= forbidden planet

amb5.aif (wav)= more space

amb6.aif (wav)= reverse hit

amb7.aif (wav)= sample and hold (loop this one)

amb8.aif (wav)= terminate

amb9.aif (wav)= loop me

amb10.aif (wav)= loop me too

MIDI Files

The dreaded MIDI files—so pleasant to listen to on a good sound card (or synth) and yet quite painful when played back on one of those low-level, FM-based dinosaurs. All of the Standard MIDI Files (SMF) in this section are General MIDI (GM) compatible. SMF 1 through 9 have been tweaked so they sound best through a Roland GS compatible sound card or synthesizer while smf1 through 9xg are optimized for Yamaha's XG hardware. Because of slight variations in the sounds and sample quality of each particular sound card, results will vary. I hope to have a set of MIDI files optimized for the Soundblaster 16 and ready to download from our Web site (http://www.monsoon.org/sound_advice) by the time this book is released.

1. smf1.mid	10. smf1xg.mid
2. smf2.mid	11. smf2xg.mid
3. smf3.mid	12. smf3xg.mid
4. smf4.mid	13. smf4xg.mid
5. smf5.mid	14. smf5xg.mid
6. smf6.mid	15. smf6xg.mid
7. smf7.mid	16. smf7xg.mid
8. smf8.mid	17. smf8xg.mid
9. smf9.mid	18. smf9xg.mid

Hollywood Edge SFX List

What can I say? You've got a nice cross sampling of sound effects from the Hollywood Edge free—that's right *free*—to use on your productions. The only restrictions are that these sounds may not be repackaged and sold as sound effects. That's pretty simple, right? To save disk space, we picked files that were short. To get a really good idea of the overall quality of these effects, listen to the file **edge1.** I think you will be impressed.

1. **edge1.aif (wav)** (Hollywood Edge Intro) (25 MEG)

2. **edge2.aif (wav)** (Hawk Screech)

3. **edge3.aif (wav)** (Rooster Crow)

4. **edge4.aif (wav)** (Frog Ribbit)

5. **edge5.aif (wav)** (Sheep Baas)

6. **edge6.aif (wav)** (.357 Magnum)

7. **edge7.aif (wav)** (Ricochet)

8. **edge8.aif (wav)** (12 gauge shotgun)

9. **edge9.aif (wav)** (M-60 Automatic Fire)

10. **edge10.aif (wav)** (Claymore Antipersonnel mine)

11. **edge11 aif (wav)** (Explosion)

12. **edge12.aif (wav)** (Black Powder Musket)

13. **edge13.aif (wav)** (Helicopter)

14. **edge14.aif (wav)** (Cobra start, idle)

15. **edge15.aif (wav)** (Cobra by, fast)

16. **edge16.aif (wav)** (Zip Bys, Autos)

17. **edge17.aif (wav)** (Firetruck Siren W/horn)

18. **edge18.aif (wav)** (Bottle Rocket)

19. **edge19.aif (wav)** (Sword Shing)

20. **edge20.aif (wav)** (Drop ice, pour soda)

21. **edge21.aif (wav)** (Wood Door)

22. **edge22.aif (wav)** (Applause)

23. **edge23.aif (wav)** (Record Scratches)

24. **edge24.aif (wav)** (Elevator)

25. **edge25.aif (wav)** (Bubbles)

Tutorial Files

While the file content is the same for both PCs and Macs, some of the extensions have been changed to protect the innocent. Probably my favorite MIDI file out of the bunch is **exam1.mid** (or **exam1xg.mid**). To get the proper effect, remember to play this one back through a GS or XG compatible GM sound card. Every file you need to work with the tutorials in the book is available among the tutorial files on the CD.

Macintosh

1. Buttons.DCR
2. demovoc1.wav
3. exam1.mid
4. exam1xg.mid
5. baxter.wav
6. music1.wav
7. sample.aif
8. sample.au
9. sample42.aif
10. sample51.aif
11. baxter.vox

PC

1. Buttons.DCR
2. demovoc1.wav
3. exam1.mid
4. exam1xg.mid
5. baxter.wav
6. music1.wav
7. sample.wav
8. sample.au
9. sample42.wav
10. sample51.wav
11. baxter.vox

Demo Software

The title says it all ....

Macintosh

For hard disk recording and editing, we have included demo versions of Deck II (2.5) and SoundEdit 16 (Version 2), both from Macromedia. These are both fully functional with the exception of being save disabled.

For MIDI sequencing, we have included save-disabled versions of Musicshop (entry level) and Vision 2.0 (advanced) from Opcode. As an added bonus, we've also included a demo version of Overture (a MIDI based notation program) and OMS 2.1 (also from Opcode).

Windows

For hard disk recording and editing, we have included a demo version of Sound Forge 3.0 from Sonic Foundry. Of course, it is save disabled (what do you want for free?).

For MIDI sequencing, we have included save-disabled versions of Cakewalk Express and Cakewalk Pro Audio.

Shareware Utilities

As if you didn't have enough free stuff already ....

Macintosh

SoundAPP 1.5.1: This easy to use utility converts audio file formats between AIFF, IFF, MOD, DVI, SND, and System 7 sounds.

SoundMaster 1.8.1: This is an all-in-one sound organizer and player. It also allows assignment of sounds to system functions, such as startup.

Windows

Cool Edit 1.33: This waveform editor supports WAV, VOC, AU, and SMP file formats. Special effects processing includes flange, echo, and reverse manipulations.

Galt Audio Sampler: This is a waveform player and organizer.

VuePrint 4.1: Single Viewer/Player supports graphic and audio formats— including GIF, BMP, PCX, JPG, and TIF. Audio formats include MID, WAV, and MCI, as well as video animation files in AVI, MPG, MOV, MMM, FFI, and FLC formats.

A Sample License Agreement

The following pages contain the content, printed verbatim, of a sound and music licensing agreement drafted by the American Society of Composers, Authors, and Publishers (ASCAP). This experimental license includes the licensing terms (definitions) as well as licensing fee structures (Rate Schedules A through D). The license must be completed by the proprietors of any online service (CompuServe, America Online, the Web, a BBS, and so on) that uses ASCAP-protected music. If you plan on putting music on your Web site, you would be well served to read this agreement so that you know your legal obligations *ahead of time.*

Rate Schedule A is a statement of revenue for the online computer service itself. If you charge a fee for access to your Web site or sell products and services on the Web site, this schedule applies to you.

Rate Schedule B is a statement of revenue for online service areas (such as certain Web pages) that contain ASCAP-protected music. If you have ASCAP music on your Web site and you charge special entry fees for use of music-related pages, this schedule applies to you. Revenue is based on the actual number of hits (accesses) to the music service area.

Rate Schedule C is a statement of revenue for music online that is actually played or downloaded. Revenue is based upon the number of hits (accesses) to the music itself.

Rate Schedule D is a budget report for non-profit organizations that run an online computer service that contains ASCAP-protected music.

Notice that the License agreement is labeled "experimental." This does not mean that the agreement is optional, only that it is an evolving document. If you have suggestions on how to improve this document, contact ASCAP. See the end of Chapter 12 for ASCAP's address and contact information.

1.   Parties: This is an agreement between the American Society of Composers, Authors and Publishers ("We," "Us" or "ASCAP"), located at One Lincoln Plaza, New York, New York 10023 and

("You" or "Licensee"), located at

2.   Experimental Agreement: This is an experimental agreement which applies for its term only and is entered into without prejudice to any position you or we may take for any period subsequent to its termination.

3.   Computer Service Defined: Your "Computer Service" is a computer online service, electronic bulletin board, Internet site or similar operation,

known as	
with the Internet Protocol (IP) address of	
the Universal Resource Locator (URL) of	
the primary telephone dial-up (modem) number of	
or which may otherwise be accessed by the public as follows:	

4.   Computer Service Users Defined: "Computer Service Users" are all persons, firms or corporations who access your Computer Service.

5.   Repertory Defined: Our "Repertory" consists of all copyrighted musical compositions written or published by our members or by the members of affiliated foreign performing rights societies, including compositions written or published during the term of this agreement, and of which we have the right to license non-dramatic public performances.

6.   Grant of License: We grant you a license to publicly perform, or cause to be publicly performed, by means of transmissions on your Computer Service, non-dramatic renditions of the separate musical compositions in our Repertory.

7.   Term of License: The license granted by this agreement commences on _____ , 19 _____ (the "Effective Date"), and ends on December 31 of the same calendar year, and continues after that for additional terms of one year each unless you or we terminate it by giving the other party notice at least thirty days prior to the end of a calender year.

8. **Limitations on License:**

(a) This license extends only to you and your Computer Service and is limited to performances presented by means of transmissions on your Computer Service, and by no other means, to Computer Service Users.

(b) This license may not be assigned without our written consent.

(c) This license is limited to the United States, its territories and possessions, and the Commonwealth of Puerto Rico.

(d) Nothing in this agreement grants you, or authorizes you to grant to any Computer Service User, or to anyone else, any right to reproduce, copy or distribute by any means, method or process whatsoever, any of the musical compositions licensed by this agreement, including, but not limited to, transferring or copying any such musical composition to a computer hard drive, or otherwise downloading the composition onto any other storage medium.

(e) Nothing in this agreement grants, or authorizes you to grant, to any Computer Service User, or to anyone else, any right to perform by any means, method or process whatsoever, any of the musical compositions licensed under this agreement.

(f) This license is limited to non-dramatic performances, and does not authorize any dramatic performances. For purposes of this agreement, a dramatic performance shall include, but not be limited to, the following:

(i) performance of a "dramatico-musical work" in its entirety;

(ii) performance of one or more musical compositions from a "dramatico-musical work" accompanied by dialogue, pantomime, dance, stage action, or visual representation of the work from which the music is taken;

(iii) performance of one or more musical compositions as part of a story or plot, whether accompanied or unaccompanied by dialogue, pantomime, dance, stage action, or visual representation; and

(iv) performance of a concert version of a "dramatico-musical work."

The term "dramatico-musical work" includes, but is not limited to, a musical comedy, opera, play with music, revue, or ballet.

9. **License Fees:** For each year during the term of this agreement you agree to pay us the license fee applicable to your "Amount Subject to Fee" as defined in the Rate Schedule applicable for that year.

10. Rate Schedules: There are four alternative Rate Schedules attached to and made a part of this agreement. Rate Schedule "A" contains rates based on your Computer Service's gross revenue; Rate Schedule "B" contains rates based on your Computer Service's total music revenue; Rate Schedule "C" contains rates based on your Computer Service's total ASCAP music revenue; and Rate Schedule "D," which only applies to non-profit corporations, contains rates based on the total budget for your Computer Service. Each Rate Schedule includes a specific definition of "Amount Subject to Fee" applicable to that Rate Schedule and a Statement of Account for providing required reports. Rate Schedules "B" or "C" may only be used if (a) you maintain your books and records in a manner which enables you to furnish the required information, (b) your Annual License Fee Report is submitted when due, and (c) you are current in payment of license fees. In all other instances, the rates contained in Rate Schedule "A" apply.

2

11. **Reports and Payments:** You agree to furnish license fee reports and payments to us as follows:

(a) Annual License Fee Reports. You will submit an Annual License Fee Report for each year of this agreement, by the first day of April of the following year, by fully completing the Statement of Account form on the applicable Rate Schedule.

(b) Initial License Fee Report. Within thirty days after you and we execute this agreement, you will submit an Initial License Fee Report based on a good faith estimate of your Computer Service's "Amount Subject to Fee" for the first full year of operation from the Effective Date of this agreement.

(c) Quarterly License Fee Payments. You will submit license fee payments quarterly on or before the first day of January, April, July and October of each year. The payments due by April 1, July 1 and October 1 of each year, and by January 1 of the following year, are each equal to one-fourth of the license fee for the preceding calendar year (annualized for any reported period less than a year).

(d) Late Report Payments. If we do not receive your Annual License Fee Report when due, you will submit quarterly license fee payments that are 24% higher than the quarterly payments due for the preceding year, and payments will continue at that increased rate until we receive the late report.

(e) Annual Adjustment. With each annual report you will submit payment of any license fees due over and above all amounts that you paid for that year. If the fee is less than the amount that you paid, we will apply the excess to the next quarterly payment due under this agreement. If the excess is greater than one quarterly payment, we will refund it to you at your written request.

(f) Late Payment Charge. You will pay a finance charge of 1-1/2% per month, from the date due, on any required payment that is not made within thirty days of its due date.

12. **Report Verification:**

(a) We have the right to examine your books and records in order to verify any required report. We may exercise this right by giving you thirty days notice of our intention to conduct an examination. We will consider all data and information derived from our examination as completely confidential. You agree to furnish all pertinent books and records, including electronic records, to our authorized representatives, during customary business hours.

(b) If our examination shows that you underpaid license fees, you agree to pay a finance charge of 1-1/2% per month on the license fees due from the date we bill you for that amount or, if the underpayment is 5% or more, from the date or dates that the license fees should have been paid.

(c) You may dispute all or part of our claim for additional fees. You may do so by advising us in writing within thirty days from the date we bill the additional fees to you of the basis for your dispute, and by paying the undisputed portion of our claim with the applicable finance charges. If there is a good faith dispute between us concerning all or part of our claim, we will defer finance charges on the disputed amount until sixty days after we have responded to you, and will pro-rate finance charges based on our resolution of the dispute.

13. Breach or Default: If you fail to perform any of the terms or conditions required of you by this agreement, we may terminate your license by giving you thirty days notice to cure your breach or default. If you do not do so within that thirty day period, your license will automatically terminate at the end of that period without any further notice from us.

14. Interference With ASCAP's Operations: We have the right to terminate this license effective immediately, if there is any major interference with, or substantial increase in the cost of, our operation as a result of any law in the state, territory, dependency, possession or political subdivision in which you or your Computer Service is located which is applicable to the licensing of performing rights.

15. Indemnification: We will indemnify you from any claim made against you with respect to the non-dramatic performance under this agreement of any composition(s) in our Repertory, and will have full charge of the defense against the claim. You agree to notify us immediately of any such claim, furnish us with all the papers pertaining to it, and cooperate fully with us in its defense. If you wish, you may engage your own counsel, at your expense, who may participate in the defense. Our liability under this paragraph is strictly limited to the amount of license fees that you actually paid us under this agreement for the calendar year(s) in which the performance(s) which are the subject of the claim occurred.

16. Notices: We or you may give any notice required by this agreement by (a) sending the notice to the other party's last known address by United States Mail or by generally recognized same-day or overnight delivery service, or (b) transmitting the notice electronically to the other party's last known facsimile number or e-mail (or similar electronic transmission) address. We each agree to inform the other in writing of any change of address.

IN WITNESS WHEREOF, this Agreement has been duly executed by ASCAP and Licensee this _____ day of _____, 19_____.

AMERICAN SOCIETY OF COMPOSERS, AUTHORS AND PUBLISHERS	
	Licensee Name
By _____	By _____
	Signature
_____	
Title	Print Your Name
	Title
	(Fill in capacity in which signed: (a) If corporation, state corporate office held; (b) If partnership, write word "partner" under printed name of signing partner; (c) If individual owner, write "individual owner" under printed name.)

PART I.   ACCOUNT INFORMATION   REPORT PERIOD: ▨▨▨▨ THRU ▨▨▨▨

LICENSEE:

ADDRESS:

COMPUTER SERVICE NAME:

FACSIMILE NUMBER: ▨▨▨▨▨▨   PHONE NUMBER: ▨▨▨▨▨▨

PART II.   DEFINITIONS

NOTE: Definitions of Licensee's "Computer Service" and "Computer Service Users" are contained in paragraphs 3 and 4 of the license agreement. All "Revenue" definitions include all specified payments whether made directly to Licensee, any entity under the same or substantially the same ownership, management or control as Licensee, or to any other person, firm or corporation as directed or authorized by Licensee or any of Licensee's agents or employees.

1. "COMPUTER SERVICE USER REVENUE" means all payments made by or on behalf of Computer Service Users for the Computer Service including, but not limited to, subscriber fees and connect time charges.

2. "SPONSOR REVENUE" means all payments made by or on behalf of sponsors, advertisers, program suppliers, content providers, or others for the use of the facilities of the Computer Service including, but not limited to, payments made for "hotlinks."

3. "ADJUSTMENTS TO SPONSOR REVENUE" means: (a) advertising agency commissions not to exceed 15% actually allowed to an advertising agency that has no direct or indirect ownership or managerial connection with Licensee or the Computer Service; and (b) bad debts actually written off and discounts allowed or rebates paid.

4. "NET SPONSOR REVENUE" means all Sponsor Revenue less Adjustments to Sponsor Revenue.

5. "PROMOTIONAL REVENUE" is the reasonable value of the facilities of the Computer Service for promotion of any product(s) or service(s), other than the Computer Service, offered by Licensee or any entity under the same or substantially the same ownership, management or control as Licensee.

6. "AMOUNT SUBJECT TO FEE" is the total of Computer Service User Revenue, Net Sponsor Revenue and Promotional Revenue.

PART III. AMOUNT SUBJECT TO FEE COMPUTATION

1. Computer Service User Revenue .... $_____
2. Net Sponsor Revenue (from Part IV, line 9).. $_____
3. Promotional Revenue... $_____
4. Amount Subject to Fee (add lines 1, 2 and 3)... $_____

PART IV. NET SPONSOR REVENUE CALCULATION

5. Sponsor Revenue.. $_____
6. Advertising Commissions.............................$_____
7. Bad Debts..$_____
8. Total Adjustments to Sponsor Revenue (add lines 6 and 7)............................. $_____
9. Net Sponsor Revenue (line 5 minus line 8)... $_____

PART V. LICENSE FEE

10. The annual license fee under this Rate Schedule "A" is the applicable fee based on Amount Subject to Fee (from Part III, line 4), as shown in the Table below (pro-rated for partial year).................... $_____

Amount Subject to Fee	Annual License Fee
Less than $ 31,000.00	$ 500.00
$ 31,000 to $ 39,999.99	$ 575.00
$ 40,000 to $ 49,999.99	$ 725.00
$ 50,000 to $ 59,999.99	$ 890.00
$ 60,000 to $ 69,999.99	$ 1,050.00
$ 70,000 to $ 79,999.99	$ 1,210.00
$ 80,000 to $ 89,999.99	$ 1,370.00
$ 90,000 to $ 99,999.99	$ 1,535.00
$ 100,000 to $ 119,999.99	$ 1,777.00
$ 120,000 to $ 139,999.99	$ 2,100.00
$ 140,000 to $ 159,999.99	$ 2,423.00
$ 160,000 to $ 179,999.99	$ 2,745.00
$ 180,000 to $ 199,999.99	$ 3,068.00
$ 200,000 to $ 224,999.99	$ 3,432.00
$ 225,000 or More	$3,432.00 plus 1.615% of the Amount Subject to Fee in excess of $225,000

PART VI. CERTIFICATION

We certify that all books and records necessary to verify this report are now and will continue to be available for your examination in accordance with the terms of the license agreement.

_____   _____
Signature   Date

_____
Print Name and Title

A - 2

PART I. ACCOUNT INFORMATION

REPORT PERIOD: ▨▨▨▨ THRU ▨▨▨▨

LICENSEE:

ADDRESS:

COMPUTER SERVICE NAME:

FACSIMILE NUMBER: ▨▨▨▨▨ PHONE NUMBER: ▨▨▨▨▨

PART II. DEFINITIONS

NOTE: Definitions of Licensee's "Computer Service" and "Computer Service Users" are contained in paragraphs 3 and 4 of the license agreement. All "Revenue" definitions include all specified payments whether made directly to Licensee, any entity under the same or substantially the same ownership, management or control as Licensee, or to any other person, firm or corporation as directed or authorized by Licensee or any of Licensee's agents or employees.

1.   "COMPUTER SERVICE USES" means the total number of "hits" or "accesses" of the Computer Service by Computer Service Users.

2.   "MUSIC SERVICE(S)" means any area(s) offered by Licensee, or otherwise available to Computer Service Users as part of the Computer Service, which contain(s) music.

3.   "MUSIC SERVICE USERS" means all Computer Service Users who access any Music Service(s).

4.   "MUSIC SERVICE USES" means the total number of "hits" or "accesses" of the Music Service(s) by Music Service Users.

5.   "COMPUTER SERVICE USER REVENUE" means all payments made by or on behalf of Computer Service Users for the Computer Service including, but not limited to, subscriber fees and connect time charges.

6.   "MUSIC SERVICE CONNECTION REVENUE" means all payments made by or on behalf of Music Service Users for access to the Music Service(s).

7.   "NON-MUSIC COMPUTER SERVICE USER REVENUE" means all Computer Service User Revenue that is not Music Service Connection Revenue.

8. **"SPONSOR REVENUE"** means all payments made by or on behalf of sponsors, advertisers, program suppliers, content providers, or others for the use of the facilities of the Computer Service including, but not limited to, payments made for "hotlinks."

9. **"TARGETED SPONSOR REVENUE"** means all Sponsor Revenue that is targeted for specific area(s) offered by Licensee, or otherwise available to Computer Service Users as part of the Computer Service, and that are only available to Computer Service Users who access those area(s).

10. **"TARGETED MUSIC SERVICE SPONSOR REVENUE"** means all Targeted Sponsor Revenue for the Music Service(s).

11. **"NON-TARGETED SPONSOR REVENUE"** means all Sponsor Revenue that is not Targeted Sponsor Revenue.

12. **"PROMOTIONAL REVENUE"** is the reasonable value of the facilities of the Computer Service for promotion of any product(s) or service(s), other than the Computer Service, offered by Licensee or any entity under the same or substantially the same ownership, management or control as Licensee.

13. **"TARGETED PROMOTIONAL REVENUE"** means all Promotional Revenue that is targeted for specific area(s) offered by Licensee, or otherwise available to Computer Service Users as part of the Computer Service, and that are only available to Computer Service Users who access those area(s).

14. **"TARGETED MUSIC SERVICE PROMOTIONAL REVENUE"** means all Targeted Promotional Revenue for the Music Service(s).

15. **"NON-TARGETED PROMOTIONAL REVENUE"** means all Promotional Revenue that is not Targeted Promotional Revenue.

16. **"ATTRIBUTABLE REVENUE"** is that portion of the total of (a) Non-Music Computer Service User Revenue, (b) Non-Targeted Sponsor Revenue, and (c) Non-Targeted Promotional Revenue which bears the same ratio to that total as the total number of Music Service Uses bears to the total number of Computer Service Uses.

17. **"MUSIC REVENUE/AMOUNT SUBJECT TO FEE"** is the total of Music Service Connection Revenue, Targeted Music Service Sponsor Revenue, Targeted Music Service Promotional Revenue and Attributable Revenue.

PART III. AMOUNT SUBJECT TO FEE COMPUTATION

1. Music Service Connection Revenue .... $_____
2. Targeted Music Service Sponsor Revenue .... $_____
3. Targeted Music Service Promotional Revenue .... $_____
4. Attributable Revenue (from Part IV, line 13) .... $_____
5. Amount Subject to Fee (add lines 1, 2, 3 and 4) .... $_____

PART IV. ATTRIBUTABLE REVENUE CALCULATION

6. Non-Music Computer Service User Revenue.................................... $_____
7. Non-Targeted Sponsor Revenue... $_____
8. Non-Targeted Promotional Revenue.. $_____
9. Total (add lines 6, 7 and 8).. $_____
10. Total Music Service Uses...................................... _____
11. Total Computer Service Uses................................ _____
12. Ratio (divide line 10 by line 11)(to 3 decimals)............................. _____
13. Attributable Revenue (multiply line 9 by line 12)........................... $_____

B - 2

PART V.   LICENSE FEE

14.   The annual license fee under this Rate Schedule "B" is the applicable fee based on Amount Subject to Fee (from Part III, line 5), as shown in the Table below (pro-rated for partial year) .... $_____

Amount Subject to Fee	Annual License Fee
Less than $ 20,650	$ 500.00
$ 20,650 to $ 25,999.99	$ 565.00
$ 26,000 to $ 31,999.99	$ 702.00
$ 32,000 to $ 39,999.99	$ 871.00
$ 40,000 to $ 49,999.99	$ 1,089.00
$ 50,000 to $ 62,999.99	$ 1,367.00
$ 63,000 to $ 78,999.99	$ 1,718.00
$ 79,000 to $ 99,999.99	$ 2,166.00
$ 100,000 to $ 125,999.99	$ 2,735.00
$ 126,000 to $ 159,999.99	$ 3,461.00
$ 160,000 to $ 199,999.99	$ 4,356.00
$ 200,000 to $ 249,999.99	$ 5,445.00
$ 250,000 to $ 299,999.99	$ 6,655.00
$ 300,000 or More	$ 6,655.00 plus 2.42% of the Amount Subject to Fee in excess of $300,000

PART VI.   CERTIFICATION

We attach to this report a written statement of the method used to identify and track Computer Service Uses, Music Service Uses, and that portion of the revenue of the Computer Service that is derived from, or in connection with, or is attributable to, performances of music on the Computer Service. We certify that all books and records necessary to verify this report are now and will continue to be available for your examination in accordance with the terms of the license agreement.

_____   _____

Signature   Date

_____

Print Name and Title

```
╔══════════════════════════════════════════════════════╗
║     RATE SCHEDULE "C" – STATEMENT OF ACCOUNT          ║
║          ASCAP MUSIC REVENUE REPORT                   ║
║     ASCAP EXPERIMENTAL LICENSE AGREEMENT FOR          ║
║   COMPUTER ONLINE SERVICES, ELECTRONIC BULLETIN BOARDS,║
║        INTERNET SITES AND SIMILAR OPERATIONS          ║
╚══════════════════════════════════════════════════════╝
```

PART I.   ACCOUNT INFORMATION   REPORT PERIOD: [   ] THRU [   ]

LICENSEE:

ADDRESS:

COMPUTER SERVICE NAME:

FACSIMILE NUMBER: [   ]   PHONE NUMBER: [   ]

PART II.   DEFINITIONS

NOTE: Definitions of Licensee's "Computer Service" and "Computer Service Users" are contained in paragraphs 3 and 4 of the license agreement. All "Revenue" definitions include all specified payments whether made directly to Licensee, any entity under the same or substantially the same ownership, management or control as Licensee, or to any other person, firm or corporation as directed or authorized by Licensee or any of Licensee's agents or employees.

1.   "COMPUTER SERVICE USES" means the total number of "hits" or "accesses" of the Computer Service by Computer Service Users.

2.   "MUSIC SERVICE(S)" means any area(s) offered by Licensee, or otherwise available to Computer Service Users as part of Licensee's Computer Service, which contain(s) music.

3.   "MUSIC SERVICE USERS" means all Computer Service Users who access any Music Service(s).

4.   "MUSIC SERVICE USES" means the total number of "hits" or "accesses" of the Music Service(s) by Music Service Users.

5.   "MUSIC USES" means the total number of "hits," "accesses," "downloads," "plays" or other transmissions on the Computer Service of musical works.

6.   "ASCAP MUSIC USES" means the total number of "hits," "accesses," "downloads," "plays" or other transmissions on the Computer Service of works in the ASCAP repertory.

7.   "ASCAP MUSIC USE CONNECTION REVENUE" means all payments made by or on behalf of Music Service Users for ASCAP Music Uses.

8.   "COMPUTER SERVICE USER REVENUE" means all payments made by or on behalf of Computer Service Users for Licensee's Computer Service including, but not limited to, subscriber fees and connect time charges.

9.   "MUSIC SERVICE CONNECTION REVENUE" means all payments made by or on behalf of Music Service Users for access to the Music Service(s).

10.   "NON-MUSIC COMPUTER SERVICE USER REVENUE" means all Computer Service User Revenue that is not Music Service Connection Revenue.

11. **"SPONSOR REVENUE"** means all payments made by or on behalf of sponsors, advertisers, program suppliers, content providers, or others for the use of the facilities of the Computer Service including, but not limited to, payments made for "hotlinks."

12. **"TARGETED SPONSOR REVENUE"** means all Sponsor Revenue that is targeted for specific area(s) offered by Licensee, or otherwise available to Computer Service Users as part of Licensee's Computer Service, and that are only available to Computer Service Users who access those area(s).

13. **"TARGETED MUSIC SERVICE SPONSOR REVENUE"** means all Targeted Sponsor Revenue for the Music Service(s).

14. **"NON-TARGETED SPONSOR REVENUE"** means all Sponsor Revenue that is not Targeted Sponsor Revenue.

15. **"PROMOTIONAL REVENUE"** is the reasonable value of the facilities of the Computer Service for promotion of any product(s) or service(s), other than the Computer Service, offered by Licensee or any entity under the same or substantially the same ownership, management or control as Licensee.

16. **"TARGETED PROMOTIONAL REVENUE"** means all Promotional Revenue that is targeted for specific area(s) offered by Licensee, or otherwise available to Computer Service Users as part of the Computer Service, and that are only available to Computer Service Users who access those area(s).

17. **"TARGETED MUSIC SERVICE PROMOTIONAL REVENUE"** means all Targeted Promotional Revenue for the Music Service(s).

18. **"NON-TARGETED PROMOTIONAL REVENUE"** means all Promotional Revenue that is not Targeted Promotional Revenue.

19. **"ATTRIBUTABLE REVENUE"** is that portion of the total of (a) Non-Music Computer Service User Revenue, (b) Targeted Music Service Sponsor Revenue, (c) Non-Targeted Sponsor Revenue, (d) Targeted Music Service Promotional Revenue, and (e) Non-Targeted Promotional Revenue which bears the same ratio to that total as the total number of Music Service Uses bears to the total number of all Computer Service Uses.

20. **"ATTRIBUTABLE ASCAP MUSIC REVENUE"** is that portion of Attributable Revenue that bears the same ratio to that amount as the total number of ASCAP Music Uses bears to the total of all Music Uses.

21. **"ASCAP MUSIC REVENUE/AMOUNT SUBJECT TO FEE"** is the total of ASCAP Music Use Connection Revenue and Attributable ASCAP Music Revenue.

PART III. AMOUNT SUBJECT TO FEE COMPUTATION

1. ASCAP Music Use Connection Revenue .... $_____
2. Attributable ASCAP Music Revenue (from Part V, line 18)............................ $_____
3. Amount Subject to Fee (add lines 1 and 2)... $_____

PART IV. ATTRIBUTABLE REVENUE CALCULATION

4. Non-Music Computer Service User Revenue... $_____
5. Targeted Music Service Sponsor Revenue... $_____
6. Non-Targeted Sponsor Revenue.. $_____
7. Targeted Music Service Promotional Revenue.. $_____
8. Non-Targeted Promotional Revenue.. $_____
9. Total (add lines 4, 5, 6, 7, and 8).. $_____
10. Total Music Service Uses.................................... _____
11. Total Computer Service Uses.............................. _____
12. Ratio (divide line 10 by line 11)(to 3 decimals)................................. _____
13. Attributable Revenue (multiply line 9 by line 12) .... $_____

C - 2

PART V. ATTRIBUTABLE ASCAP MUSIC REVENUE CALCULATION

14. Attributable Revenue (from Part IV, line 13)... $_____
15. Total ASCAP Music Uses.................................. _____
16. Total Music Uses... _____
17. Ratio (divide line 15 by line 16)(to 3 decimals).. _____
18. Attributable ASCAP Music Revenue (multiply line 14 by line 17)..................... $_____

PART VI. LICENSE FEE

19. The annual license fee under this Rate Schedule "C" is the applicable fee based on Amount Subject to Fee (from Part III, line 3), as shown in the Table below (pro-rated for partial year)..................... $_____

Amount Subject to Fee	Annual License Fee
Less than $ 11,200	$ 500.00
$ 11,200 to $ 14,999.99	$ 584.00
$ 15,000 to $ 19,999.99	$ 780.00
$ 20,000 to $ 26,999.99	$ 1,048.00
$ 27,000 to $ 35,999.99	$ 1,405.00
$ 36,000 to $ 47,999.99	$ 1,873.00
$ 48,000 to $ 63,999.99	$ 2,498.00
$ 64,000 to $ 84,999.99	$ 3,323.00
$ 85,000 to $ 112,999.99	$ 4,415.00
$ 113,000 to $ 149,999.99	$ 5,865.00
$ 150,000 to $ 199,999.99	$ 7,805.00
$ 200,000 to $ 264,999.99	$ 10,392.00
$ 265,000 to $ 349,999.99	$ 13,714.00
$ 350,000 or More	$ 13,714.00 plus 4.46% of the Amount Subject to Fee in excess of $350,000

PART VII. CERTIFICATION

We attach to this report a written statement of the method used to identify and track Computer Service Uses, Music Service Uses, Music Uses, ASCAP Music Uses, and that portion of the revenue of the Computer Service that is derived from, or in connection with, or is attributable to, performances on the Computer Service of music in the ASCAP Repertory. We certify that all books and records necessary to verify this report are now and will continue to be available for your examination in accordance with the terms of the license agreement.

_____   _____
Signature   Date

_____
Print Name and Title

C - 3

NOTE: This Rate Schedule "D" applies only if: (a) the Computer Service is owned or operated by a not-for-profit entity recognized under Title 26, United States Code, § 501(c)(3); and (b) "Computer Service Budget," as defined below, is greater than the Amount Subject to Fee which would otherwise apply under Rate Schedules "A," "B" and "C."

PART I.   ACCOUNT INFORMATION

LICENSEE:

ADDRESS:

COMPUTER SERVICE NAME:

FACSIMILE NUMBER: PHONE NUMBER:

NOTE: If you identify and track "Computer Service Uses" and "Music Service Uses," each as defined below, you may complete either Parts III and IV or Parts V and VI. Otherwise, you must complete Parts III and IV, and omit Parts V and VI.

PART II.   DEFINITIONS

NOTE: Definitions of Licensee's "Computer Service" and "Computer Service Users" are contained in paragraphs 3 and 4 of the license agreement.

1.   "COMPUTER SERVICE BUDGET" means the total operating budget of the Computer Service.

2.   "COMPUTER SERVICE USES" means the total number of "hits" or "accesses" of the Computer Service by Computer Service Users.

3.   "MUSIC SERVICE(S)" means any area(s) offered by Licensee, or otherwise available to Computer Service Users as part of Licensee's Computer Service, which contain(s) music.

4.   "MUSIC SERVICE USES" means the total number of "hits" or "accesses" of any Music Service(s) by Computer Service Users.

5.   "AMOUNT SUBJECT TO FEE" under Part III below is your Computer Service Budget, and "Amount Subject to Fee" under Part V below is that portion of your Computer Service Budget which bears the same ratio to that amount as the total number of Music Service Uses bears to all Computer Service Uses.

PART III. AMOUNT SUBJECT TO FEE

1. Computer Service Budget/Amount Subject to Fee.. $_____

PART IV. LICENSE FEE

2. The annual license fee is the applicable fee based on Amount Subject to Fee (from Part III, line 1), as shown in Table I below (pro-rated for partial year)... $_____

TABLE I

Amount Subject to Fee	Annual License Fee
Less than $ 31,000	$ 500.00
$ 31,000 to $ 39,999.99	$ 575.00
$ 40,000 to $ 49,999.99	$ 725.00
$ 50,000 to $ 59,999.99	$ 890.00
$ 60,000 to $ 69,999.99	$ 1,050.00
$ 70,000 to $ 79,999.99	$ 1,210.00
$ 80,000 to $ 89,999.99	$ 1,370.00
$ 90,000 to $ 99,999.99	$ 1,535.00
$ 100,000 to $ 119,999.99	$ 1,777.00
$ 120,000 to $ 139,999.99	$ 2,100.00
$ 140,000 to $ 159,999.99	$ 2,423.00
$ 160,000 to $ 179,999.99	$ 2,745.00
$ 180,000 to $ 199,999.99	$ 3,068.00
$ 200,000 to $ 224,999.99	$ 3,432.00
$ 225,000 or More	$3,432.00 plus 1.615% of the Amount Subject to Fee in excess of $225,000

D - 2

PART V. AMOUNT SUBJECT TO FEE COMPUTATION

1. Computer Service Budget.. $_____
2. Total Music Service Uses... _____
3. Total Computer Service Uses... _____
4. Ratio (divide line 2 by line 3) (to 3 decimals).. _____
5. Amount Subject to Fee (multiply line 1 by line 4) .... $_____

PART VI. LICENSE FEE

6. The annual license fee is the applicable fee based on Amount Subject to Fee (from Part V, line 5), as shown in Table II below (pro-rated for partial year)... $_____

TABLE II

Amount Subject to Fee	Annual License Fee
Less than $ 20,650	$ 500.00
$ 20,650 to $ 25,999.99	$ 565.00
$ 26,000 to $ 31,999.99	$ 702.00
$ 32,000 to $ 39,999.99	$ 871.00
$ 40,000 to $ 49,999.99	$ 1,089.00
$ 50,000 to $ 62,999.99	$ 1,367.00
$ 63,000 to $ 78,999.99	$ 1,718.00
$ 79,000 to $ 99,999.99	$ 2,166.00
$ 100,000 to $ 125,999.99	$ 2,735.00
$ 126,000 to $ 159,999.99	$ 3,461.00
$ 160,000 to $ 199,999.99	$ 4,356.00
$ 200,000 to $ 249,999.99	$ 5,445.00
$ 250,000 to $ 299,999.99	$ 6,655.00
$ 300,000 or More	$6,655.00 plus 2.42% of the Amount Subject to Fee in excess of $300,000

PART VII. CERTIFICATION

If our annual license fee is based on the Amount Subject to Fee from Part V, line 5, we attach to this report a written statement of the method used to identify and track Computer Service Uses and Music Service Uses. In all instances, we certify that all books and records necessary to verify this report are now and will continue to be available for your examination in accordance with the terms of the license agreement.

_____   _____

Signature   Date

_____

Print Name and Title

D - 3

Sound And Music Web Sites And Newsgroups

There are literally hundreds, maybe even thousands, of sites on the Web that deal with sound and music. However, many of these deal with small niche areas in the field of sound and music, such as the Cuban Music site or the National Press Club Luncheon Broadcasts. In the next several pages, we describe several Web sites that offer general information on sound or music—especially sites that provide clips that you can use or that provide tools or information on recording and editing sound and music. Of course, we would like your first visit to be to our own Web site, at www.monsoon.org/sound_advice/tutorial.

The Underworld Music Archive

www.nd.edu/StudentLinks/jkeating/links/sound.html

This site includes links to several archives, where you'll find sound clips from animals to TV shows. The site also includes links to more specialized sound and music archives, as well as to voice repositories (for speeches, radio shows, and other voice clips). Especially check out the "They Might Be Giants" link, which contains numerous demos and unreleased songs by wannabe music stars.

The Sound Page

www.ucsalf.ac.uk/pa/soundp/sphome.htm

The Sound Page contains one of the largest collections of sound and music links on the Web. The opening page is somewhat deceptive, because it appears to contain only about a dozen links. But several of the links take you to indexes of different sound categories, and some indexes link you to even more

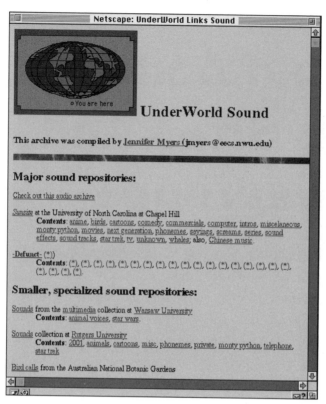

The Underworld Music Archive.

specialized indexes. It's easy to get lost here, but it's also a fun site to explore.

Be sure to check out the "Other music sites" link, which takes you to a major index of several sound and music categories, including MIDI, Synthesizers, Acoustics, Digital Audio, Music Newsgroups, Record Labels, and more. When you click on one of these links, you'll be taken to another index of links for that category. The top level index at this site also includes a link to an interesting paper on the history and technology of remixing.

Multi-Media Music

www.wavenet.com/~axgrindr/quimby.html
The Multi-Media Music site claims to be targeted for "anyone interested in high quality audio for their computer presentations and multimedia projects." And they really do seem to deliver on this promise.

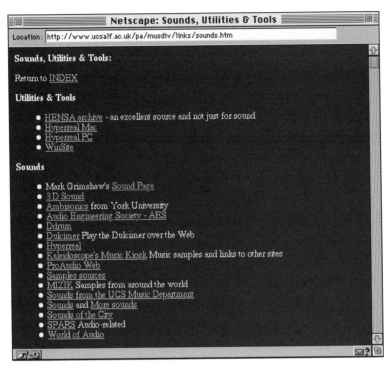

The Sound Page Web site.

Links are grouped into three categories:

- Sound effects

- Sound utilities

- Music loops and logo stings

You'll need to scroll past a few pages of self-promotional material before you see these categories.

The sound effects category includes not only sound effects but links to just about every MIDI utility available, including (for the Mac) All Midi, CommMidi, Midi Typer, Midi Control, Midi Packen, Midi Scope, Midi Split, and more. For the PC, you'll find links to EZ Improve, Midi Jukebox, Midi Device, Midi Kap, Midi Machine, and dozens more.

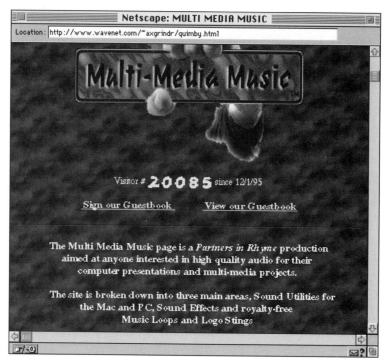

The Multi-Media Music Web site.

Sound utilities for the PC include Cool Edit, Wham, Gold Wave, 2PAT, True Speech Audio, and dozens more. There's a brief review of each utility. Sound utilities for the Mac include Easy AIFF, Sound Hack, Sound Edit, Sound Effects, and Sound Machine.

At this writing, only seven music loops are available. However, you can download and freely use all of them in your Web site or multimedia production.

Music Previews Network

www.mpmusic.com/

The Music Previews Network contains an archive of music clips by hundreds of artists in 10 major categories:

- Rock

- Alternative

- Rap/Hip Hop

- R & B

- Country

- Jazz & Blues

- Soundtracks

- New Age

- Classical

- Christian

For instance, the Rock category contains clips from Jimmy Buffett, Gloria Estefan, Metallica, George Michael, and many others. Jazz clips are available for such artists as Tom Scott, Horace Silver, Danilo Perez, and Quincy Jones. The best way to view the complete list of available clips is to click on the "Or for more artists, click here!" link at the end of any list in each category. When you do this, you'll be taken to a full list of all artists and their performances, organized alphabetically.

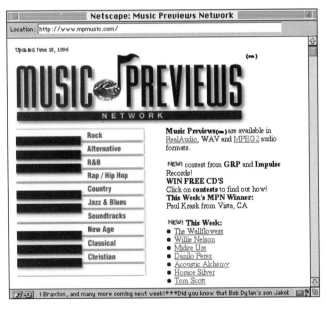

The Music Previews Network.

Do keep in mind that all of the clips here are copyrighted. You'll need to get permission or pay the appropriate licensing fees before you can use any of them legally within your Web pages.

FutureNet - Music

www.futurenet.co.uk/music.html

FutureNet (from England) is largely a collection of *FutureNet* magazine's articles and interviews. You might not have much interest in these unless you're a musician or an audiophile, but you'll probably find the "High Tech" link to be of great interest. Here, you'll find information on high-tech and multimedia recording, as well as reviews of state-of-the-art hardware from Yamaha, Roland, and Korg. You'll also find some great buyer's guides for sound hardware, other gear, and even professional studio recording equipment.

You'll need to register before you can enter FutureNet. But registration is free and only takes a few minutes.

The FutureNet - Music Web site.

Computer Music Journal

ftp://mitpress.mit.edu/pub/Computer-Music-Journal/CMJ.html

Computer Music Journal (CMJ) is a quarterly journal that covers a wide range of topics related to digital audio signal processing and electroacoustic music. It is published (as hard copy) by MIT Press and is now in its 20th year. The topics addressed in *Computer Music Journal* include:

- Software and hardware for digital audio signal processing

- Electroacoustic, electronic, and computer music

- Software for music notation, printing, and archival systems

- Music representation languages and music cognition

- New physical performance interfaces

- Sound localization and 3D sound spatialization

- Sound in computer user interfaces and virtual realities

- Aesthetics of contemporary music, and other areas

We suggest you try the "Sound Files" link. This area contains 30 sound files, only a few of which you'll probably find to be useful. (Most of the files are simply used to demonstrate different sound file formats.) However, be sure to scroll down to the "Music-related Documents" area. Here, you'll find links to the full MIDI specification as well as links to descriptions and specifications of common sound file formats.

The Digital Audio Directory

www.westworld.com/~wizard/dad.html

The Digital Audio Directory is just a list of links—but what a list it is! You'll find links to virtually every hardware and software company involved in producing or supporting digital sound, as well as links to digital audio resources, newsgroups, and organizations.

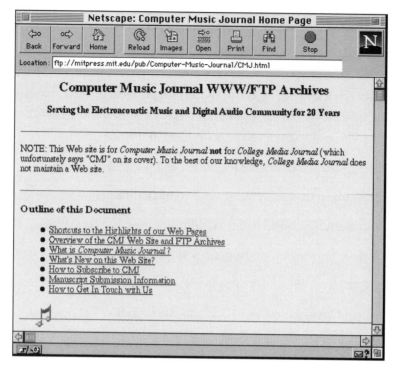

The *Computer Music Journal* Web site.

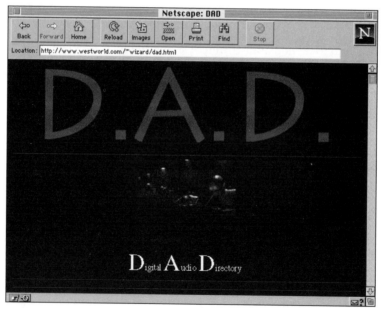

The Digital Audio Directory.

Pro Audio And Recording Arts Page

This is the premier site for information directed at professionals in the recording arts industry. You'll find dozens of useful links to technical information, audio-related companies, people involved in professional audio recording, and much more. General categories of links include:

- Audio education and research
- Other pro audio sites
- Audio equipment
- Professional audio companies
- Professional audio people
- Professional audio recording studios
- Computers and audio
- Technical instruments
- Electronic music and MIDI software
- Musical instruments
- Radio and broadcast newsgroups
- Other net audio indexes
- Search the Web for audio
- Links to audio publications
- Record labels

Harmony Central

www.harmony-central.com/Newp/
Harmony Central is provided by Scott Lehman at MIT, and is probably the best place on the Web to find links to new products related to making music on the Web and other digital audio products.

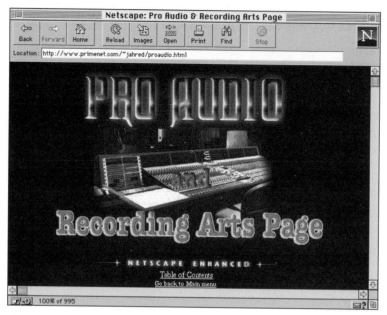

The Pro Audio and Recording Arts Page.

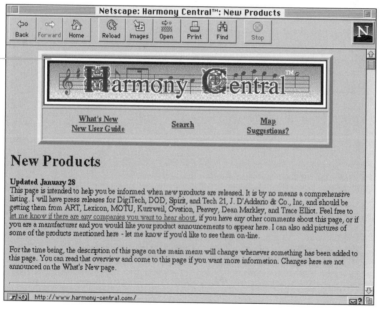

The Harmony Central New Products Web page.

The Classical MIDI Archives

www.prs.net/midi.html#index

The title of this Web site just about says it all. Here, you'll find the world's largest collection of Classical music MIDI sequences, organized alphabetically or searchable by the composer's name. All of the notable composers are represented here, but you'll also find hundreds of MIDI sequences by more obscure composers. (We've never even heard of Giles Farnaby's *Fantasia* or Luca Marenzio's *Madrigal in Five Parts.* Actually, we've never even heard of Giles Farnaby or Luca Marenzio.)

Archivist Pierre Schwob has marked good-to-high-quality sequences with a paragraph symbol, and moderate-to-poor-quality sequences with a plus symbol so you can easily identify the best of the lot.

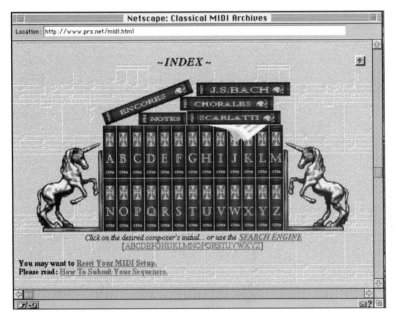

The Classical MIDI Archives Web site.

Doctor Audio Links

www.doctoraudio.com/links.html

This is easily the most comprehensive list of links to MIDI and audio-related hardware and software vendors (78 companies are represented). You'll also find excellent lists of links to Web audio and MIDI sites, music-related online resources, and Web audio and music publications.

MIDI

http://www.eeb.ele.tue.nl/midi/index.html

This Web site is an invaluable resource for anyone working with MIDI. It provides information for everyone from novice to expert. Better yet, it has links to dozens of other audio-oriented sites, including hardware manufacturers, software developers, archives, and audio publications. Even if you aren't exploring MIDI yet, it's worth a visit just to bookmark some of the links that are provided.

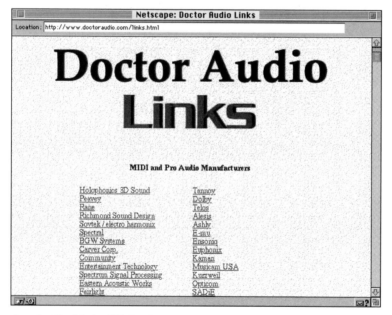

The Doctor Audio Links Web site.

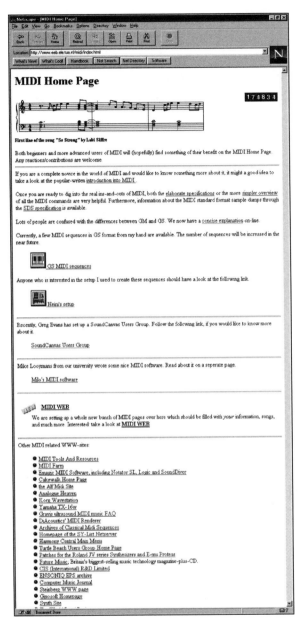

The MIDI Home Page.

Dolby

http://www.dolby.com/

If "Dolby" is just a word you've seen at the end of movie credits all your life, but have no idea what, or who, Dolby is, this will be a worthwhile visit. Ray Dolby founded Dolby Labs and has probably had as much impact on audio as anyone else in the industry. This Web site provides very interesting background and history, as well as current announcements regarding Dolby Surroundsound Multimedia, press releases, newsletter articles, Dolby digital, home theater, and of course, a list of all the movies ever made using Dolby technology.

MPEG

This is an archive collection of information that answers many of the frequently asked questions about the MPEG compression standard. The site covers all aspects of MPEG, with an understandable focus on video MPEG. There is, however, a good explanation of audio MPEG as well as a breakdown of MPEG levels 1,2, 3, and 4.

MPEG-1 Audio

http://www.crs4.it/~luigi/MPEG/mpeg1-a.html

MPEG-2 Audio

http://www.crs4.it/~luigi/MPEG/mpeg2.html#What is MPEG-2 AUDIO

The Dolby Labs Web site.

Software Resources

These audio software Web sites are excellent resources for current product information as well as technical notes, audio FAQs, and downloadable samples.

Sonic Foundry, Developers of Sound Forge

www.sfoundry.com/

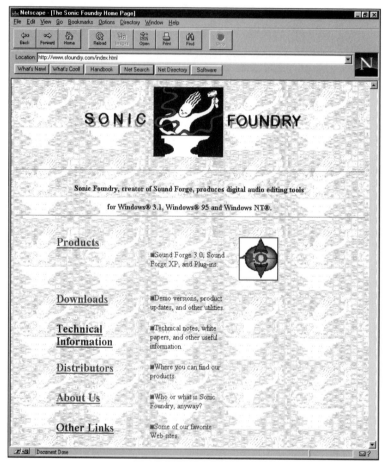

The Sonic Foundry home page.

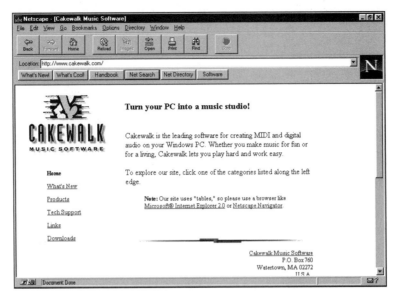

The Cakewalk Web site.

Cakewalk, Developers of Cakewalk Pro Audio

www.cakewalk.com/

Digidesign, Developers of ProTools

http://www.digidesign.com/

Digidesign's Web site.

Usenet Newsgroups

Which are the audio newsgroups? To which audio group should you post? There are several audio-specific and audio-related newsgroups. It is important to post to the right group for a couple of reasons. First, you want to be read by people who are knowledgeable and/or interested in your topic. Second, you want to avoid the ire of people who don't have your perspective or won't tolerate your ignorance. The audio newsgroups are frequented by a wide-ranging group of people, including some outspoken experts who know their stuff and some serious purists who won't consider off-topic postings as acceptable. There is no dedicated Web-audio specific newsgroup, but several have overlapped into areas pertaining to Web audio.

With that said, here's the list of newsgroups and an explanation of their content.

comp.multimedia

comp.music

comp.music.midi

These three newsgroups focus generally on the union of computer capabilities with the audio world. In comp.multimedia, expect to weed through a lot of video and other non-audio postings to get to your topics. But the people who are actually doing things visit here and they're a valuable resource. The comp.music groups cover many topics related to the music industry and digital delivery of music.

rec.audio

The original newsgroup, which is being phased out.

rec.audio.car

This newsgroup supports discussion on different brands and models of car stereos, and also is an open forum for talk about car stereo installation, speaker selection, custom crossovers, and the special noise problems that occur in cars. Unless you want to browse the Web from your car, or your car is the love of your life, you can probably avoid this newsgroup.

rec.audio.high-end

This newsgroup caters to audiophiles and serious music lovers who are interested in discussing the subtle differences between expensive equipment, the nuances involved in selecting the best cables, the love and lore of LPs, and other details of audio that are inaudible to the untrained ear. Currently, rec.audio.high-end is the only group that is available by email. To get this group's messages sent to you, contact:

audio-request@lerc.nasa.gov

This is also the only group that is moderated.

rec.audio.marketplace

Here's the place for selling and buying equipment. This is also a good place to discuss dealers, pricing, product sources, and models with specific features.

rec.audio.misc

If you don't think it fits well in any other newsgroup, post it here.

rec.audio.opinion

Everyone has opinions. Share yours here. Not sure which is better? Ask here. Think you hear a difference? Say it here.

rec.audio.pro

This newsgroup is dedicated to professional audio. It includes discussions on record production, studios, studio equipment, DJ equipment, recording concerts, sound reinforcement, mastering, mixing, special effects, and other topics that might apply to audio professionals. If you are a home audio buff, but like tape recording, you can find good advice here.

rec.audio.tech

Discussion here is about audio theory, home-made audio equipment, specifications, and other technicalities.

Index

3D sound, 124-126, 237-242

A

<A HREF>, 59-60, 62-64
Acquisition, 48-49
AdB International, 159
AFTRA, 227
AIFF file format, 61-63, 65-66, 70-74
Afterburner, 83-84
Ambient sounds, 270-271
Apple, 135-136, 169-170
ASCAP, 226, 229, 233, 236
Attention span, 1-2, 54-55
AVI (Audio/Video Interleave), 8
AU file format, 61-63, 65-66, 70-74
Audio
    acquisition, 48-49
    email, 10
    download times, 41, 52
    downloadable, 37-38, 40, 42, 51-52
    file formats, 20, 23-24, 51, 64-72, 102, 162
    file size, 41, 102, 162
    integration, 45-49
    one-way, 10, 54
    preparation, 49
    streamed, 16, 37-38, 42-45, 53-56, 75-82, 87-113
    test, 19-23
    two-way, 11, 54-55, 88
Audiomedia, 151, 159
Audio Technica 118-120, 128
Authorware, 82-84
AV drives, 130, 133-132

B

Background noise, 79, 270-271
Bandwidth, 16-18, 42, 50, 54, 95, 100, 244
BMI, 226, 233, 236

Bose, 126-128
Browser, 19-20, 22, 54
Buyout, 232-233

C

Cable
    connection, 16
    modem, 17-18
    service providers, 17
Cakewalk, 171-174, 181-183
Cakewalk Web site, 309
CD Audio, 188
CD-ROM, 5, 7, 66, 71, 148, 269-274
Classical MIDI Archives, 303
Commerce, 11-12, 14
Communication, 10
comp. multimedia, 310
comp.music.midi, 310
Compression, 16, 76, 79-80, 83, 87-88, 99-104, 196, 204-205
Compressor function, 193
Computer, 134-137
Computer Music Journal, 299
Contracts, 216-217
Conversion utilities, 66, 71, 88-89, 91, 188, 191
Cool information, 20
Copyrights, 216, 221, 226-231, 234-235
Cost control, 217-224
Creative Labs, 143-144

D

Deck 2, 150-152
Demo software, 273-274
Diamond Multimedia, 139
Digidesign, 138, 148, 151, 153, 159
Digidesign Web site, 309
Digital Audio Directory, 299-300
Digital Audio Interface, 158-159
Digital Audio Workstation, 160
Digital mixer, 122-124

313

S

T

U

US Robotics, 18, 140
Utilities, 22, 66, 71, 274

V

Video, 8, 16-17, 88, 93
Virtual reality, 242-243
Voice e-mail, 11
Voiceover, 118-119, 199, 209-211, 217-219
VOX files, 75-82
Voxware (see ToolVox)
VRML, 242-243

W

WAV file format, 58-60, 61-63, 65-66, 70-74
Windows, 134
Web phone, 11-13, 88
Web radio, 10, 37
Web server, 54-56
Web sites
    91x San Diego, 39
    Asia On-line, 41
    AudioNet, 39
    Cakewalk, 309
    Classical MIDI Archives, 303
    Computer Music Journal, 299-300
    Digidesign, 309
    Digital Audio Directory, 299-300
    Doctor Audio Links, 304
    Dolby, 306
    Earchives, 25
    FutureNet, 298
    Happy Puppy, 245
    Harmony Central, 301-302

Internet Juke Box, 32
Internet Underground Music Archives, 30
Limbaugh, Rush, 90
MIDI, 304-305
MIDI Farm, 31
Mister Rogers' Neighborhood, 38, 53
MPEG, 306
Multi-Media Music, 294-295
Music Now, 34
Music Previews Network, 296-297
Net Radio, 40
Prime Sports Radio, 33
Pro Aduio and Recording Arts Page, 301-302
RealAudio, 43
Simpsons, 26-29
Sonic Foundry, 308
Sound page, 293-294
StreamWorks, 94
Sound Advice, 20
ToolVox, 76
Underworld Music Archive, 293

X

Xing Technology Corporation (see StreamWorks)

Y

Yamaha, 122-124, 128, 142-144, 146, 167

Z

Zip drive, 130-132